LATINA
Mythica II
Troia Capta

by

Bonnie A. Catto

Bolchazy-Carducci Publishers, Inc.
Mundelein, Illinois USA

Editor: Bridget Dean

Contributing Editor: Laurel Draper

Design & Layout: Adam Phillip Velez

Cover Illustration: Farewell of Hector and Andromache; Anton Losenko (1737–1773), Tretyakov Gallery, Moscow (Public Domain)

Latina Mythica II
Troia Capta

Bonnie A. Catto

Bolchazy-Carducci Publishers, Inc.
1570 Baskin Road
Mundelein, Illinois 60060
www.bolchazy.com

Printed in the United States of America
2015
by United Graphics

ISBN 978-0-86516-825-1

Library of Congress Cataloging-in-Publication Data

Catto, Bonnie A., 1951- author.
  Latina mythica II : Troia capta / by Bonnie A. Catto.
    pages cm
  ISBN 978-0-86516-825-1 (pbk.)
  1. Latin language--Readers. 2. Trojan War. I. Title. II. Title: Troia capta.
  PA2095.C33653 2015
  478.6'421--dc23

                                                                      2015033831

Contents

List of Images

Introduction

In 2006, I authored the mythological reader *Latina Mythica*. I designed it for students who had completed one year of high school Latin or one semester of college Latin. The book was intended to improve students' fluidity of reading by providing interesting material in simplified but idiomttic Latin. *Latina Mythica* covered the early periods of Greco-Roman myth and was organized by mythological chronology and mythical cycle. After a chapter naming the basic gods and their attributes, the volume detailed creation stories, the three generations of gods, and their battles for supremacy. These stories described how Prometheus helped Jupiter attain power and how he later alienated Jupiter by helping man. Jupiter punished Prometheus with an agonizing imprisonment and mankind with the gift of Pandora. Man gradually degenerated through four ages from gold to iron, and ultimately Jupiter decided to eradicate sinful mankind with a great flood. Deucalion and Pyrrha, a pious couple, were allowed to survive and to remake the human race by a miracle. The volume then turned to Cretan tales: Theseus's slaying of the Minotaur with the princess Ariadne's help and his subsequent abandonment of her, for which he was punished by his father Aegeus's death. Daedalus and Icarus's ill-fated flight from Crete concluded this section. Then a series of Theban myths was described: the birth of the god Bacchus and his vengeance against the non-believer Pentheus; the complicated tale of Oedipus, the Sphinx, Oedipus's eventual mysterious death in Athens, the war between Oedipus's sons for Thebes, and the noble but tragic figure of his daughter Antigone. Next the birth and labors of Hercules, another Theban hero, were recounted. The myth of Jason and the Argonauts in the generation before the Trojan War was included with particular emphasis on the role of Medea and her vengeance against Jason. Finally, in the last three chapters, the volume began the background to the Trojan War: the births of Helen and Clytemnestra, the wedding of Peleus and Thetis, and the Judgment of Paris that led to Paris's abduction of Helen, and the sacrifice of Iphigenia.

Audience

This second volume is written for students who have completed the study of Latin grammar as included in standard texts (probably one year of college Latin or two to three years of high school Latin). While writing *Latina Mythica* I had intended to write a second volume covering the Trojan War and its aftermath, such as Homer's *Odyssey*, as well as myths involving underworld visits, the metamorphic loves of Jupiter, and some more Roman myths. As work on this second volume proceeded, however, the power and beauty of Homer's *Iliad* bewitched me, and I found that I could not compress and simplify the many scenes from the *Iliad* and still do them justice. Thus this book became, in essence, a Latin version of the Trojan War with particular focus on the *Iliad*. This volume begins with two chapters of mythical material that occurs well before the action of the *Iliad*, which focuses on about a 40-day period in the last year of the ten-year war. Then, after including much of the *Iliad* itself, this volume concludes with two chapters that include scenes beyond the action of the epic to give a more complete sense of the myth of Troy.

I have found that Latin students tend to be less familiar with the plot and characters in the *Iliad*, and thus such a volume will be useful to students who are reading Vergil's *Aeneid*, particularly Books 6–12, the more Iliadic portions. By reading the selections in this volume, students will gain a wider understanding and appreciation of the myths upon which Vergil draws. This book will offer students the opportunity to read episodes of the *Iliad* in Latin epic style.

Of course students don't have to be preparing to read the *Aeneid* to enjoy and benefit from this volume. It can be beneficial for those who would like more practice reading continuous Latin with interesting content based upon ancient myths and authors. Many of the passages are short enough to get a sense of satisfaction from completing a story in a class or two, or as a homework assignment. This works well in intermediate Latin classes where grammar is being reviewed but there is also a desire for considerable reading practice. Also, students who may be reading the *Iliad* in English in their Latin classes might like to try to combine the two efforts by reading some of these chapters in Latin. This volume is designed so that one can skip over passages, since each chapter has an introduction that briefly sums up the preceding material. Finally, many people who are not currently in a school or university setting but who have studied Latin might enjoy using this volume to brush up on their Latin while still reading ancient myths. One can now read Harry Potter in Latin—why not read Homer and other great ancient authors in Latin?

Precedent

There is precedent for translating the *Iliad* into Latin. In about 60–70 CE Baebius Italicus wrote *Ilias Latina* which purports to be a translation of Homer's *Iliad*. The *Iliad* itself totals 15,693 lines of dactylic hexameter in 24 books whereas Baebius compresses his version into 1062 lines plus a brief 8-line coda about his accomplishments as a poet. This abridgement (or epitome) of Homer was used for centuries. The difficulty is that it is very much an interpretation rather than a translation. For instance, Achilles's critical request of Zeus is not specifically attributed to him but put into the mouth of Juno as a complaint made to Zeus. Also, Baebius added very melodramatic touches (e.g. to Hector's funeral at the close of the epic). Any translation does, of course, involve interpretation but it should not add (or subtract) scenes and characterizations. Finally, Baebius's version contained no notes or commentary, although others (Plessis, 1885; Scaffai, 1982, in Italian; Kennedy, 1998) have later provided such assistance to the reader. This volume is not a translation of Homer per se; rather it features and interprets certain key passages throughout the epic that both drive the plot and provide characterization. It also includes pre- and post-Iliadic material to provide both mythical background to the conflict and to conclude the war itself.

The English cleric and philosopher Samuel Clarke published a Latin version of Books 1–12 with facing Greek in 1729. The second half of the epic was published three years after his death in 1732 by his son who edited the work. Clarke's translation, however, was aimed at readers who were relatively fluent in Latin. Although there were some annotations of the Greek text, it contained no notes, vocabulary, or other aids for students. Also it is much longer: the entire epic in Latin—truly a monumental achievement. This volume has a different audience and a much shorter scope and contains a great deal of assistance with grammar, vocabulary, and cultural material.

Content

Homer's *Iliad* is the main source for this book, but it does not begin with the *Iliad* itself, since the epic's action occurs at almost the very end of the war. Most readers are probably familiar with the broad outlines of the *Iliad*, but many of its stories and characters are less familiar, which does not necessarily make them any less important. All readers would benefit from knowing more details about the participants in the first years of the war. Thus I begin this volume in the first two chapters by backtracking somewhat from *Latina Mythica* to explain how Odysseus/Ulysses was tricked by Palamedes into serving and how Ulysses in turn lured the young

Achilles to war. Calchas also delivered a daunting prophecy about the duration of the war. Since it was fated that Philoctetes's bow take Troy, it is important to learn the story of his abandonment en route to Troy and (at the end of this volume) his eventual rescue from a deserted island. When the Greek fleet arrived at Troy Protesilaus was the first to leap from the ships and thus to die. His new wife Laodamia was inconsolable, and her grief led to an amazing though temporary reprieve from death. Finally as prelude I have chosen to recount how Odysseus/Ulysses took vengeance on Palamedes, who tricked him into going to Troy. With these stories as preamble, the *Iliad* proper begins. Obviously it would be impractical to include the entire epic, but I have focused on those episodes that are turning points in the epic and that particularly reveal the characters of some of the participants. Also I have focused on myths that have resonated most in art, literature, and music.

Of course the *Iliad*, to the disappointment of many students, does not end with the fall of Troy but with the death of Hector and the resolution of Achilles's wrath. Thus to give a more complete sense of the myth of Troy I have also chosen to include in the final two chapters a number of significant episodes that occur beyond the action of the *Iliad*: the last conquests of Achilles over the Amazon Queen Penthesilea and Memnon, son of the goddess Aurora; the theft of the Palladium; the death of Achilles and the contention over his arms; the suicide of Ajax; the summoning of Philoctetes to Troy; and the death of Paris. These final two chapers thus include multiple sections rather than the continuous narrative format of the previous chapters. Finally, an Epilogue in English summarizes the aftermath of the Trojan War with the distribution of the Trojan women, now enslaved, and the returns home of the most central heroes.

Motivation and Myth

My motivation for writing this book has been very similar to that for *Latina Mythica*. Many students are fascinated by myth, and it is often their reason for studying Latin. Yet most textbooks do not include much mythical material, nor is the complexity of myth acknowledged. Myth is flexible and ever-changing. There are numerous variants of many of the myths included in this volume. I have tried both in the Latin text itself and in the notes to indicate some of the complexities, but usually I have had to make some choices about which version to retell. Students and teachers can get a broader sense of the variant versions by referring to some of the original sources cited at the beginning of each chapter.

In undertaking the composition of this second volume of *Latina Mythica*, I have thought back on my experiences in prose composition. During my undergraduate years at Mount Holyoke College, Classics majors were required to take a year of composition. Although it was a challenge in both Latin and Greek, I learned a great deal about how the languages actually work and also thoroughly enjoyed the intellectual exercise. I am very grateful to Professor Philippa Goold for her excellent tuition in these courses. As a doctoral student at The University of Pennsylvania I was again required to take composition in both Latin and Greek with Professor Douglas Minyard. At this level poetic composition was also required. One can truly appreciate the complexity and beauty of Catullan poems and Horatian *Odes* when one has tried to create such forms! Also, one gains a fuller appreciation of the difference between poetic and prose vocabularies, since some words simply will not fit certain meters. I decided to write this volume in prose rather than poetry since the volume is aimed at an intermediate reader who will have little experience of the complex word order that poetry often entails and indeed finds desirable.

When I returned to Mount Holyoke as a professor I taught the required Latin composition sequence for a number of years. Students often approached the course with considerable dread, but in the end I think most enjoyed themselves. Many also stated that it was during these courses that they really learned Latin, a comment that greatly pleased me. Also while I was at The University of Pennsylvania, in a class on Greek lyric poetry with Professor Martin Oswald, I learned the importance of the memorization of poetry; the poems thus become alive. I have continued this interest in memorization, and it has helped me to view the ancient languages as living entities. The recent national movement to revive oral Latin has reinforced this feeling. Latin is a language that can and should still be used creatively. Thus during my years teaching at Assumption College I have often created mythological passages for sight translation on exams at the lower levels. It was from these passages that the idea for *Latina Mythica* first arose.

METHODOLOGY

As noted above, this volume is intended for students who have completed basic Latin grammar. Thus all major grammatical constructions are assumed; however, notes are generally given for less common constructions such as the double dative, supines, and gerunds. These notes are provided more frequently in the beginning chapters. As the volume proceeds it is assumed that students have become more familiar with the constructions and less help is given. Often the Grammar and Comprehension Questions give hints about difficult constructions simply by asking questions about them.

To aid students in achieving some fluency in reading I have tried to avoid an intimidating list of vocabulary facing the text. This volume assumes that students are familiar with the Vocabulary to Learn (indicated by asterisks in each chapter's vocabulary and in the "Latin to English Glossary") in *Latin for the New Millennium*, Levels 1 and 2, (*LNM*) by Milena Minkova and Terence Tunberg (Bolchazy-Carducci, 2008, 2009). Since beginning vocabulary is fairly consistent from one textbook to another, this assumption should not prove problematic for students who have learned Latin from other texts. Vocabulary to Learn words from *LNM* are only given in the facing-page vocabulary if they are used in an unusual way. It is not assumed that students know the additional vocabulary words provided in the *LNM* glossary, unless the word is an obvious compound or has a direct English derivative. My English definitions conform to the definitions of the Vocabulary to Learn in *LNM* and, beyond that, primarily to the *Oxford Latin Dictionary*. Once a word has been defined as new vocabulary in a particular chapter, it is generally not given again in that chapter unless the two instances occur quite far apart in a longer chapter. After a word has been given in two chapters, it is usually not given again unless it occurs after a break of many chapters or if it is particularly unusual. If a word occurs with an unusual sense in a particular chapter, the dictionary entry is given again with the specialized meaning. Of course, all vocabulary that occurs more than once in the text is included in the end Vocabulary where students may consult words unfamiliar to them. This inclusion will allow teachers and students to read selected chapters if there is not time to read the entire volume. To help students recognize the components of Latin words, my spelling of compounds generally avoids consonantal assimilation so that the components (the basic roots) are more obvious. For instance, I have chosen *adloquor* rather *alloquor*. Also, since this is a Latin text, as in *Latina Mythica*, I have used the Roman names for gods and heroes, e.g., Ulysses (*Ulixēs*) rather than Odysseus.

I have included macrons (long marks), as I did in *Latina Mythica*. Their inclusion will often help students to differentiate one word from another (e.g., *hīc* v. *hic*). Also, it will prepare students for quantity when they begin to read poetry. The placement of macrons on individual words is not always consistent from one dictionary to another. Scholars disagree! I have chosen to follow the *Chambers-Murray Dictionary*, since its inclusion of macrons is more complete than *The Oxford Latin Dictionary*. For instance, in *Chambers-Murray* all *cons* syllables have a macron, thus *cōns*. This macron does not appear in the *OLD*. *Latin for the New Millennium* conforms more to the *Chambers-Murray* model.

Not all the chapters of this volume are of equal length. Some should be able to be read easily in one class period, but others would take longer. The longer chapters (e.g., Chapter 11 that depicts the deaths of Sarpedon and Patroclus) are generally those whose mythical importance is greater and whose action triggers later events. The final two chapters are much longer and are themselves separated into distinct episodes that could be read separately. Also, in some of the longer passages I sometimes just got carried away with the beauty of Homer! The Homeric chapters in this volume are necessarily a compression of both myth and poetry, particularly in areas such as Homeric similes. I would urge students to learn Greek as well as to read the complete epic in English.

As in *Latina Mythica* I have tried in so far as possible to write in the style of the authors who are our Latin sources for these myths. Each chapter includes a list of these sources with specific references. Of course when treating Homeric source material sometimes there is no Latin model. In these instances, I have tried to write in idiomatic Latin while adhering as closely as I could to Homeric expression in Greek. I also consulted various Latin concordances for phrasing in these passages. I have included some formulaic language, particularly in the Homeric passages that are especially formulaic, but I also varied the vocabulary to suit the exact nuance of a passage as well as to give students a sense of the richness of Latin vocabulary. Throughout the book I have tried to achieve an idiomatic prose Latin, but I must confess I have added more than a few hints of poetic vocabulary. When I found a phrase in Vergil, Lucretius, Catullus, or Ovid that fits well, I have felt free to use it. In my phraseology I have sometimes also drawn on Greek tragedy, though I have used the phraseology of the Roman poets where a Roman source was available.

Chapter Features

Each chapter includes a number of features. In addition to its introduction, list of sources, and facing vocabulary and notes, there are Grammar and Comprehension Questions, Discussion Questions, illustrations, and often a section on Cultural Influences.

The Grammar and Comprehension Questions aim to assist students both in translating the material and in developing a full comprehension of the myth. These questions often single out a particularly difficult construction so that students will pay it sufficient attention. For instance, a question asking what form a noun is should elicit its declension, gender, number, and case. For verbs such questions usually ask students to identify first the conjugation, then the person, number, tense, and voice. Questions about function then refer to the construction in which the word is embedded (e.g., for nouns: is the noun in the accusative a direct object, object of a preposition, or subject of an indirect statement? For verbs, why is a verb in the subjunctive: jussive, conditional clause, purpose or result clause, etc.).

The Discussion Questions are broader in scope and are intended to stir the imagination of students and often to show the relevance of the material to the ancient or our contemporary world.

Each chapter also includes illustrations, mostly at the end of the chapter but sometimes within the chapter itself. Some illustrations are of objects such as a trophy or Nestor's cup; others illustrate cultural practices such as the formal gesture of supplication. Most illustrations are artistic interpretations, both ancient and more recent, of the characters and actions included in this volume. Often these illustrations should provoke discussion about how carefully the artist adhered to the ancient description of the action.

The Cultural Influences sections refer to selected literary, artistic, musical, cinematic, and even cartoon works that have been influenced by myth. It is fascinating to trace the pervasive influence of these myths over many centuries and in many media. In this volume in the Cultural Influences section, however, I have been far less comprehensive than in *Latina Mythica*. Some chapters omit the section entirely, since the same characters in this volume often appear in a number of consecutive chapters. This reduction is also partly because web resources are now so much more readily available. A student (or teacher) can easily use Google or another web resource to come up with reams of material on a character—not all relevant of course. For instance, when I searched for Sarpedon on Google, not only did I find classical and more traditional references, but also a retired American battleship, a beautiful Australian butterfly, and a sci-fi character Lord Sarpedon! This is fascinating and revelatory of the range of influence of just one character. Google Images and Wiki Commons Images also provide wonderful resources, though again sometimes their relevance is quite suspect. It is also interesting to note which characters and myths have had less resonance in modern times. This lack does not mean the myth is any less powerful or important; it simply has appealed less to later artists. As technology continues to develop at an ever-accelerating pace new means to research the nexus between these ancient myths and later artists, writers, and thinkers will surely arise. Perhaps students will be inspired to create their own interpretations in whatever medium appeals to them. Indeed I hope that this book will make some small contribution to keeping mythology thriving in the twenty-first century.

Abbreviations

(1) = first conjugation

abl. = ablative

acc. = accusative

adj. = adjective

adv. = adverb

c. = circa

comp. = comparative

conj. = conjunction

dat. = dative

demon. = demonstrative

f. = feminine

fut. = future

gen. = genitive

imp. = imperative

indecl. = indeclinable

indef. = indefinite

indic. = indicative

inf. = infinitive

interj. = interjection

interrog. = interrogative

m. = masculine

mt. = mount, mountain

n. = neuter

p. = page

pl. = plural

plupft. = pluperfect

prep. = preposition

rel. = relative

s. = singular

subj. = subjunctive

super. = superlative

Chapter One

The Prelude to War; The Reluctant Warriors and a Prophecy

The Trojan Story Thus Far

The final chapters of *Latina Mythica I* described the complicated circumstances that led to the Trojan War. There had been a prophecy that if Jupiter or Neptune slept with a certain but un-named goddess, the union would produce a child greater than the father. Each of these gods therefore feared such a son would overthrow him. There was considerable precedent for this, since Jupiter had overthrown his own father Saturn, who had himself overthrown his father Uranus. When Jupiter discovered that the goddess of the prophecy was the minor sea-goddess Thetis, he arranged for her to marry the mortal Greek king of Phthia, Peleus. The son of this union was in fact the great Achilles, who far exceeded his father but did not overthrow him. All the gods except Eris, the goddess of discord, were invited to the wedding of Peleus and Thetis. During the festivities, however, Eris arrived and threw onto the ground a golden apple engraved with the words "for the fairest." The result was, of course, discord. All the goddesses claimed the apple, but eventually there were three main contenders: Juno, the wife of Jupiter; Minerva, daughter of Jupiter; and Venus, also daughter of Jupiter. The three appealed to Jupiter to make a decision. Very sensibly Jupiter refused to judge among his family members and chose Paris, a very handsome Trojan prince, to decide. The history of Paris is also interesting. When Queen Hecuba, was pregnant with Paris she had a very ominous dream: that she was giving birth to a firebrand that would burn down Ilium, also known as Troy. In fear of this dream Hecuba and her husband King Priam gave Paris to a shepherd to expose on Mt. Ida. The shepherd, however, took pity on the infant and raised him as his own. Eventually, because of his exceptional beauty and talents, Paris was recognized as a royal son and reunited with his family. Later, when Paris was once again on Mt. Ida, the three competing goddesses, accompanied by Mercury, descended to him. Thus began the famous Judgment of Paris. Each of the goddesses offered Paris a bribe to award the golden apple to her. Venus offered him the most beautiful woman in the world, Helen. Paris then awarded Venus the golden apple.

Although his family disapproved of his plan, Paris soon set sail to claim his prize. Helen was the daughter of the mortal Leda who had been seduced by Jupiter in the form of a swan. Before her marriage her beauty had attracted many suitors, and her mortal father Tyndareus, king of Sparta, had worried that one of them would abduct her. Therefore, at the suggestion of Ulysses (Odysseus in Greek), he made all the suitors swear that they would rescue Helen if anyone abducted her. Little did he suspect the abductor might be from a distant land. Ulysses then relinquished his role as suitor and married Helen's cousin Penelope, daughter of King Icarius. Helen chose Menelaus as her husband and he became king of Sparta. When Paris arrived in Sparta, Menelaus, following the ancient principles of guest-friendship, welcomed him into his palace. Soon, however, Menelaus had to leave Sparta to travel to Crete for a funeral. During his absence Paris and Helen left the palace, together with a great deal of Sparta's treasure, and sailed to Troy. The eternal question has been whether Helen left willingly or was abducted. At first Menelaus and Ulysses sailed to Troy to demand the return of Helen and the treasure. When this mission failed, Menelaus invoked the suitors' oaths and demanded their aid in retrieving Helen. Warriors from all over Greece assembled at Aulis on the eastern coast of Greece to sail against Troy, the ancient and wealthy city on the northwestern coast of modern Turkey. Menelaus's older brother Agamemnon, the powerful king of Mycenae, was the leader. The assembled troops could not sail against Troy because the winds were unfavorable. The prophet Calchas reported that the goddess Artemis had been offended by Agamemnon and that, as recompense, she demanded the sacrifice of his eldest daughter, Iphigenia. Agamemnon initially refused to sacrifice his daughter, but eventually he lured Iphigenia to Aulis by saying she was to be married to Achilles. The innocent Iphigenia discovered the plot and begged for her life—to no avail. After her death the fleet set sail to begin 10 years of war.

Latina Mythica I concluded with the marshalling of the Greek troops for the Trojan War and the sacrifice of Iphigenia. Not all the Greek heroes, however, went to war willingly. This first chapter of *Latina Mythica: Troia Capta* begins earlier in the myth to examine how two of the major heroes came to Aulis to join the Greek fleet. In particular, Ulysses (the Greek Odysseus), the king of the small island of Ithaca, was tricked by Palamedes into going to war. Later he cunningly exacted vengeance from Palamedes, as you will see in Chapter 2. Ulysses then used his cunning to bring into war the young Achilles, who had been hidden by his protective mother. Thetis had received a prophecy about her son Achilles, who was mortal. She had heard that if he went to war he would be killed. As the preparations for war began Achilles was still only nine years old. Therefore, Thetis decided to hide him disguised as a girl on the island of Scyros among the daughters of King Lycomedes. As you will read, this disguise resulted in a major surprise. Ultimately both Achilles and Ulysses played extremely important roles

in the war. Achilles is, of course, the hero of Homer's *Iliad* and Ulysses is one
of its major characters. Ulysses is also the hero of the *Odyssey*. Finally, this first
chapter concludes with Calchas's prophecy, as recounted by Ulysses in *Iliad* 2,
of the duration and outcome of the war.

As the story begins, Penelope has just given birth to Ulysses's son and heir
Telemachus.

SOURCES

Homer, *Iliad* 2.299–332 • Apollodorus, *Bibliotheca* 3.6–10; *Epitome* 3.15 •
Ovid, *Metamorphoses* 12.11–23, 13.34–62, 128–172, 295–312 • Hyginus, *Fabulae*
95, 105 • Statius, *Achilleid*

2 **procus, -ī, m.** - *suitor*

3 **linquō, -ere, līquī, lictum** - *to go away from, leave*

Ithaca, -ae, f. - *Ithaca*; island on west coast of Greece; kingdom of Ulysses

pius, -a, -um - *pious, faithful*

Pēnelopa, -ae, f. - *Penelope*; wife of Ulysses and mother of Telemachus

4 **māgnopere** (adv.) - *greatly, exceedingly*

5 **respōnsum, -ī, n.** - *response, answer*

6 **vīcēsimus, -a, -um** - *twentieth*

egēns, -ntis - *needy, in want*

7 **Palamēdēs, -is, m.** - *Palamedes;* king of the Greek island of Euboea; his name means "inventor."

8 **simulō** (1) - *to imitate, pretend, feign*

induō, -uere, -uī, -ūtum - *to put on*

9 **bōs, bovis, m.** - *bull, ox*

arātrum, -ī, n. - *plow*

arō (1) - *to plow*

cōnserō, -ere, -ēvī, -itum - *to sow, plant*

11 **subiciō, -ere, -iēcī, -iectum** (+ acc. + dat.) - *to put under*

sistō, -ere, stitī, statum - *to stop, check, stand still*

simulatiō, -ōnis, f. - *pretense, disguise*

12 **dēpōnō, -ere, -posuī, -positum** - *to put down, lay aside*

ultor, -ōris, m. - *avenger, punisher*

prōmittō, -ere, -mīsī, -missum - *to promise*

13 **invītus, -a, -um** - *unwilling*

ineō, -īre, -īvī, -itum - *to go into, enter*

14 **ob** (prep. + acc.) *on account of, because of*

sapientia, -ae, f. - *wisdom*

aestimō (1) (+ gen. of value) - *to value, consider worth*

GRAMMAR AND COMPREHENSION QUESTIONS

1) What tense and mood is *gererent*? What construction is it in?
2) What form is *eī*? To whom does it refer? (Hint: the nominative is highly irregular (*is*), but the stem is generally *e*-.)
3) What tense and voice is *datum erat*?
4) What verb is *ībis*? What is its stem?
5) What construction is *sociīs perditīs*?
6) What tense and voice is *intellegeret*? Note the construction is introduced by *cum*.
7) What case is *vestēs* and what is its grammatical function?
8) What construction is *eum īnsāniam simulāre*?
9) What tense is *ventūrum esse*? In what construction is it?
10) How should you translate *cum* in the context of *tamen* in the following clause?

Postquam Paris Helenaque Trōiam nāvigāvērunt, Menelāus omnēs
procōs convenīre iūssit ut bellum contrā Trōiam **gererent**. Sed Ulixēs
linquere Ithacam nōlēbat; nam piam coniugem Pēnelopam īnfantemque
Tēlemachum māgnopere amābat.

5   Etiam **eī** respōnsum ōrāculī **datum erat**: "Sī Trōiam **ībis**, domum
redībis, sed redībis post vīcēsimum annum, sōlus, egēns, **sociīs perditīs**."
Itaque **cum** Ulixēs **intellegeret** Menelāum et Palamēdem accēdere,
īnsāniam simulābat. **Vestēs** nōn rēgis sed servī induit; tum postquam
equum cum bove ad arātrum iūnxit arāre et sāle agrum cōnserere coepit.

10   Sed Palamēdēs, sentiēns **eum īnsāniam simulāre**, Tēlemachum arātrō
subiēcit. Statim Ulixēs stitit et filium suum ēripuit. Tum, simulatiōne
īnsāniae dēpositā, Ulixēs sē **ventūrum esse** cum ultōribus prōmīsit.

Ulixēs **cum** bellum invītē inīvisset, fortiter **tamen** in bellō pugnāvit et
omnēs Graecī ob sapientiam cōnsiliumque eum māgnī aestimāvērunt.

DISCUSSION QUESTIONS

1) What does Ulysses do that seems to indicate that he is insane?
2) What other episodes have you heard of in which Ulysses disguised himself?
3) What was odd about Ulysses's method of plowing?

15 **antequam** (conj.) - *before*
16 **calliditās, -ātis, f.** - *cleverness, shrewdness*

dēmōnstrō (1) - *to point out, show, demonstrate*

hērōs, -ōis, m. - *hero*

alliciō, -ere, -lexī, -lectum - *to lure, entice*

18 **oppugnō** (1) - *to fight against, attack, assail*

oppugnāvisset: pluperfect subjunctive because the conditional clause is part of an indirect statement

pereō, -īre, -iī, -itum - *to be destroyed, perish*

19 **iuvenis, -is, m.** - *youth*

novem (indecl. adj.) - *nine*

nōndum (adv.) - *not yet*

barbātus, -a, -um - *bearded*

vātēs, -is, m. - *prophet*

Calchās, -antis, m. - *Calchas*; Greek prophet

20 **praedīco, -ere, -dīxī, -dictum** - *to foretell, prophesy, predict*

21 **timidus, -a, -um** - *fearful*

Scȳrius, -a, -um - *of Scyros*, a Greek island off Euboea in the middle of the Aegean sea ruled by King Lycomedes

commendō (1) - *to entrust* (someone, something + acc.) *to* (+ dat.)

22 **habitus, -ūs, m.** - *style of dress, apparel*

cēlō (1) - *to hide, conceal*

23 **Pyrrha, -ae, f.** - *Pyrrha*; in Greek pyrrha means "red" or "golden-haired"

capillus, -ī, m. - *hair of the head*

rūfus, -a, -um - *red*

24 **fallax, -ācis** - *deceitful, misleading, deceptive*

25 **mercātor, -ōris, m.** - *merchant, trader*

merx, mercis, f. - *merchandise;* (pl.) *goods*

26 **muliebris, -e** - *womanly, feminine*
27 **incitō** (1) - *to rouse, incite*

clipeus, -ī, m. - *round shield*

hasta, -ae, f. - *spear*

tetigisset - pluperfect subjunctive of **tangō** - *to touch*

28 **nātus, -ī, m.** - *child*

deā: ablative of source

quid (interrogative adv.) - *why?*

dubitō (1) - *to doubt, hesitate*

ēvertō, -ere, -vertī, -versum - *to overturn, sack*

30 **libenter** (adv.) - *gladly, willingly*
33 **gravidus, -a, -um** - *pregnant*

prōdūcō, -ere, -dūxī, -ductum - *to produce, bring forth*

34 **praecox, -ocis** - *precocious, mature at an early age*

GRAMMAR AND COMPREHENSION QUESTIONS

1) What tense is *praedīxerat*?
2) What is the antecedent of *quī*?
3) Why did the maidens call Achilles Pyrrha?
4) What tense and mood is *vēnissent*?
5) What is *omnēs* understood to modify?
6) What case is *Graecīs* and what is its grammatical function?

7) What type of clause is *ut . . . fieret*?
8) What case is *nōmine* and what is its grammatical function?

---

15   Antequam Graecī Trōiam māgnā classe petīvērunt, Ulixēs māgnam calliditātem dēmōnstrāvit cum hērōem Achillem ad bellum allexerit. Nam Thetis, dīvīna māter Achillis, sciēbat fīlium suum, sī umquam Trōiam oppugnāvisset, ibi peritūrum esse. Etiam tum Achillēs erat iuvenis novem annōrum, nōndum barbātus. Vātēs Calchās autem

20   **praedīxerat** Graecōs sine Achille Trōiam nōn victūrōs esse.

        Timida Thetis igitur fīlium suum rēgī Scȳriō commendāvit **quī** Achillem inter virginēs habitū fēmineō cēlāvit. Hae eum nōn Achillem sed Pyrrham iam vocābant, quoniam capillus eī erat rūfus. Cum Graecī Achillem petentēs Scȳrum **vēnissent,** fallax vestis **omnēs** praeter Ulixem

25   dēcēpit. Ulixēs, sē mercātorem esse simulāns, in mercibus muliebribus quaedam arma posuit. Nam intellegēbat haec iuvenem incitātūra esse. Statim cum Achillēs clipeum hastamque tetigisset, huic Ulixēs dīxit: "Nāte deā, quid dubitās īngentem Trōiam ēvertere? Tibi māgna erit glōria." Achillēs tum auxilium suum **Graecīs** prōmīsit et libenter Trōiam

30   nāvigāvit. Itaque Ulixēs effēcit **ut** Achillēs, bellum contrā Trōiānōs gerēns, praeclārissimus hērōs **fieret.**

        (Dum Achillēs in Scȳrō habitat, Dēidamīae, rēgis fīliae, amōre captus est. Deinde Dēidamīa gravida fīlium, **nōmine** Pyrrhum, prōdūxit. Rē vērā Achillēs erat praecox! Posteā Pyrrhus etiam contrā Trōiānōs pugnāvit, sed

35   ibi vocātus est Neoptolemus, nōvus mīles.)

Discussion Questions

    1) Thetis tried to thwart fate when she disguised Achilles. Do you know of other mythological characters who similarly tried to change fate? Is changing fate possible?
    2) What was Ulysses's second disguise?
    3) How did Ulysses craftily reveal Achilles's identity?

36   **Aulide**: locative case, *at Aulis*

      convocō (1) - *to call together, convene*

37   **vīsus est**: a true passive - *was seen*

      serpēns, -entis, m. - *snake, serpent*

      āra, -ae, f. - *altar*

38   **ascendō, -ere, -dī, -sum** - *to go up, climb, ascend*

      nīdus, -ī, m. - *nest*

      octō (indecl. adj.) - *eight*

      pullus, -ī, m. - *chick*

39   **ululō** (1) - *to shriek, wail*

40   **dēvorō** (1) - *to devour, consume*

      mīrābilis, -e - *amazing, wondrous, remarkable*

dictū: supine with *mīrābile*: *amazing to tell*. This use of the supine is quite common. Other examples are: *mīrābile audītū, amazing to hear* and *horribile vīsū, horrible to see*

41   **interpretor** (1) - *to interpret, explain*

      avis, -is, f. - *bird*

42   **vexō** (1) - *to afflict, harass, vex*

      Trōiae: locative case: *at Troy*

      decimus, -a, -um - *tenth*

43   **superō** (1) - *to surpass, overcome, conquer*

      auferō, -ferre, abstulī, ablātum - *to bear away, gain*

Grammar and Comprehension Questions

   1) To whom does *hic* refer?

   2) What form is *ululantem*?

   3) What happened to the serpent after it devoured the chicks?

   4) What case is *novem annōs* and what is its construction?

   5) What tense is *auferēmus*?

Omnibus mīlitibus tandem Aulide convocātīs, deī ōmen mīsērunt: vīsus est māgnus serpēns prope āram in quā Graecī sacrificia faciēbant. **Hic** tum arborem ascendit in quā nīdus erat plēnus octō pullōrum. Serpēns ille eō temporis mōmentō, postquam et pullōs et **ululantem** 40 mātrem dēvorāverat, mīrābile dictū in saxum mūtātus est. Vātēs Calchās statim hoc ōmen interpretātus est: "Sīcut hic serpēns mātrem avem ipsam cum pullīs suīs vexāvit, ita **novem annōs** Trōiae pugnābimus, sed decimō annō et urbem et Trōiānōs superābimus et aeternam glōriam **auferēmus.**" Itaque mox ad lītora Trōiāna nāvigāvērunt.

DISCUSSION QUESTION

1) How do you think the leaders and the troops might have reacted to Calchas's prophecy?

Achilles on Scyros reveals his identity to Ulysses (mosaic,
2nd–3rd century CE; from Zeugma: modern
Gazientep, Turkey) (Public Domain)

Cultural Influences

The entire Trojan War cycle has produced innumerable artistic reflections. The following list is extremely brief but perhaps representative of the breadth of influence. Students and teachers are encouraged to explore the wealth of influence on their own.

Art: many paintings of the discovery of Achilles on Scyros including Anton van Dyck with Peter Paul Rubens, "Achilles Discovered by Ulysses and Diomedes" c. 1617 (Prado, Madrid); Nicolas Poussin, "Achilles and the Daughters of Lycomedes," 1656 (Virginia Museum of Fine Arts); "Discovery of Achilles on Scyros," painting, c. 1650, Museum of Fine Arts, Boston; Erastus Salisbury Field, "The Embarkation of Ulysses,"1900 (Springfield, MA Museum of Fine Arts)

Literature: Robert Herrick, 1627 poem "The Parting Verse, or, Charge to His Supposed Wife" from Ulysses to Penelope.

Music: many operas such as by Alessandro Scarlatti, *Achille e Deidamia*, 1698 and Georg Frederic Handel, *Deidamia*, 1741.

Chapter Two

THE VOYAGE AND THE LANDING:
THE INITIAL COSTS OF WAR

This chapter could be entitled "The Three *P*'s" for Philoctetes, Protesilaus, and Palamedes. All these heroes suffered greatly because of their involvement in the Trojan War. Once the fleet left Aulis, the Greeks sailed to Troy with only one noteworthy incident. Philoctetes, king of a small region near Aulis, possessed the great bow and arrows of Hercules. In the incident described below, the Greeks seemingly lose Philoctetes from the expedition. (He will appear again later!) When the Greeks reached the shores of Troy, the Trojans were armed on the beach ready to resist them. The second episode describes the landing and heroism of Protesilaus which, through extraordinary circumstances, led to his wife Laodamia's tragic act.

Ulysses (the Greek Odysseus) is the hero of Homer's *Odyssey* where he is famous for his cunning; he even introduces himself as "renowned among men for all wiles" (9.20). In the *Iliad* he plays a primarily positive role. In the rest of Greek and Latin literature, however, he is very disreputable. This side of his character is clearly evident in the Palamedes episode. In the first chapter Palamedes saw through Ulysses's feigned madness and thus compelled him to go to Troy. In this episode Ulysses takes vengeance against Palamedes. It is not clear when the episode recounted here occurred, but it is well before the action of the *Iliad*.

The passages below are modeled primarily on the language of Ovid in the Philoctetes episode, Catullus and Ovid in the section on Protesilaus, and Ovid and Hyginus in the Palamedes section.

SOURCES

On Philoctetes: • Homer, *Iliad* 2.716–28 • Sophocles, *Philoctetes* • Apollodorus, *Epitome* 3.27 • Ovid, *Metamorphoses* 13.45–55, 313–335 • Hyginus, *Fabulae* 102

On Protesilaus: • Homer, *Iliad* 2.695–702 • Stasinus, *Cypria* 17 • Apollodorus, *Epitome* 3.29–30 • Catullus 68.74–130 • Ovid, *Heroides* 13, *Ars Amatoria* 3.17–18 • Propertius, *Elegies* 1.19.7–10 • Hyginus, *Fabulae* 103

On Palamedes: • Apollodorus, *Epitome* 3.7–8 • Ovid, *Metamorphoses* 13.34–62, 308–12 • Hyginus, *Fabulae* 105

1 **Aulis, -idis, f.** - *Aulis*; port in eastern Greece

ēgredior, -ī, -gressus sum - *to go out, depart, disembark*

2 **salvus, -a, -um** - *sound, healthy, safe*

3 **vīsus est**: a true passive - *was seen*

dictū: supine with *horribilis* - *dreadful to tell*

pes, pedis, m. - *foot*

Philoctētēs, -ae, m. - *Philoctetes*; warrior king from near Phthia, the kingdom of Achilles

4 **putēscō, -ere** - *to rot, decay, putrify*

taeter, -tra, -trum - *foul, hideous*

5 **Ulixēs, -is, m.** - *Ulysses*; the Greek Odysseus, king of Ithaca

auctor, -ōris, m. - *originator, instigator*

iussū (defective noun; abl. s. m. only) - *at the order of*

arcus, -ūs, m. - *bow*

sagitta, -ae, f. - *arrow*

6 **Lemnos, -ī, f.** - *Lemnos,* an island in the Aegean on the way to Troy from Aulis

expōnō, -ere, -posuī, -positum - *to leave behind*

famēs, -is, f. - *hunger*

frangō, -ere, frēgī, frāctum - *to break, crush*

7 **pannus, -ī, m.** - *rag*

vestiō, -īre, -īvī, -ītum - *to clothe*

avis, -is, f. - *bird*

adsiduus, -a, -um - *continuous, constant*

gemitus, -ūs, m. - *groaning, lamentation*

8 **exsecror, -ārī, -ātus sum** - *to curse*

Grammar and Comprehension Questions

1) What form is *nāvigāntēs* and what does it modify?
2) What tense and voice is *vīsus est*?
3) The form *eī* comes from what demonstrative pronoun? What case and number is it?
4) What case and construction is *Ulixe auctōre*?
5) Who is the subject of *expositus est*?
6) Why did the Greeks abandon Philoctetes on Lemnos?
7) How did Philoctetes survive on Lemnos?
8) What part of speech is *adsiduē*?

Aulide **nāvigāntēs** Graecī in quamdam īnsulam ēgressī sunt. Ibi, dum prō salvā nāvigātiōne deīs sacrificant, prope āram māgnus serpēns **vīsus est**. Serpēns, horribile dictū, pedem Philoctētae percussit. **Eī** grave vulnus mox pūtēscēbat ut Graecī taetrum odōrem ferre nōn possent.

5 **Ulixe auctōre** et iussū Agamemnonis Philoctētēs cum arcū sagittīsque Herculis in īnsulā Lemnō **expositus est**. Ibi morbō fameque frāctus et pannīs vestītus avibus sē alēbat. **Adsiduē** saxa et silvās gemitū movēbat; adsiduē Ulixem exsecrābātur.

DISCUSSION QUESTION

1) In Chapter One there was also a serpent. Is there any similarity to this episode?

10 **prohibeō, -ēre, -uī, -itum** - *to prevent, hinder*

prohibēbant + nē + subj. = *that, from, lest*

praetereā (adv.) - *in addition to, besides, moreover*

sors, sortis, f. - *an oracular response, oracle*

11 **humus, -ī, f.** - *ground, earth, soil*

tangeret: imperfect subj. in relative clause of characteristic; see *Latin for the New Millennium*, Level 2, p. 508.

12 **Prōtesilāus, -ī, m.** - *Protesilaus*; his name in Greek means "first of the people." Hyginus reports his original name may have been Iolaus.

13 **dēsaliō, -īre, -saluī** - *to leap, spring, bound down from*

turba, -ae, f. - *crowd, throng*

necō (1) - *to murder, kill*

14 **hērōs, -ōis, m.** - *hero*

Hector, -oris, m. - *Hector*; chief Trojan warrior, son of King Priam and Hecuba

15 **ēgregius, -a, -um** - *outstanding, exceptional, excellent*

16 **māgnopere** (adv.) - *greatly, exceedingly*

17 **cāsus, -ūs, m.** - *downfall, misfortune*

Lāodamīa, -ae, f. - *Laodamia*; wife of Protesilaus; her name, like her husband's, includes the Greek root for people *lao*; in other versions she is called Polydora (many-gifted).

18 **coniugium, -iī, n.** - *marriage*

anima, -ae, f. - *soul, spirit*

modo (adv.) - *recently, just now*

nūpta, -ae, f. - *married woman, wife*

19 **nōndum** (adv.) - *not yet*

saturō (1) - *to fill, satiate, satisfy*

20 **abrumpō, -ere, -rūpī, -ruptum** - *to break off, cut short*

moneō, -ēre, -uī, -itum - *to warn, advise, remind*

GRAMMAR AND COMPREHENSION QUESTIONS

1) What tense and mood is *ēgrederentur*?
2) What case and number is *mortī*?
3) What did the prophecy say about the first man to land on Troy?
4) The form *hunc* comes from what demonstrative pronoun? What case and number is it?
5) What type of adjective is *pulcherrima*?
6) What type of adjective is *dulcius*? What gender, case, and number is it?
7) What case is *animā*? In what construction is it found?
8) What type of construction is *ut . . . posset*?

Tandem Graecī lītus Trōiae conspexērunt, sed multī armātī Trōiānī

10   prohibēbant nē in lītus **ēgrederentur**. Praetereā sors **mortī** dēsignāverat

Graecum mīlitem quī prīmus humum Trōiae tangeret. Omnēs Graecī

igitur haesitābant, praeter Prōtesilāum quī dē nāve fortiter dēsaluit in

mediam turbam Trōiānōrum. Prōtesilāus necāvit ūnum hostem, tum

secundum tertiumque, at subitō hērōs Hector contrā eum stetit. Hector

15   fortem Prōtesilāum statim necāvit. Posteā prō ēgregiā virtūte omnēs

Graecī **hunc** māgnopere honōrābant.

Sed eō cāsū **pulcherrima** Lāodamīa, uxor Prōtesilāī, āmīsit

coniugium **dulcius** vītā atque **animā**. Modo enim nova nūpta facta erat;

nōndum longō tempōre māgnum amōrem saturāverat **ut** vīvere coniugiō

20   abruptō **posset**. Saepe etiam virum suum monuerat:

DISCUSSION QUESTION

1) Who might you expect to be first off the ship to attack the Trojans?

21 **novissimus** - *last*
    exeō, -īre, -iī, -itum - *to go out, exit*
    īnfēlix, -icis - *unhappy, miserable*

22 **adimō, -ere, -ēmī, -emptum** - *to take away;* as adj. - *dead*
    lūgeō, -ēre, lūxī - *to mourn, lament*
    cēreus, -a, -um - *waxen, made of wax*
    adsiduus, -a, -um - *continuous*

23 **lacrimō (1)** - *to weep, shed tears*
    umbra, -ae, f. - *ghost, shade*
    caecus, -a, -um - *hidden, unseen*

24 **dēnique** (adv.) - *at last, finally*
    misereō, -ēre, -uī (+ dat.) - *to pity, have compassion for*

25 **permittō, -ere, -mīsī, -missum** (+ dat. + inf.) - *to permit, allow*
    intueor, -ērī, -tutus sum - *to gaze at with wonder*

26 **salvus, -a, -um** - *safe, alive*
    gaudeō, -ēre, gāvīsus sum - *to be glad, rejoice*

27 **trānseō, -īre, -iī, -itum** - *to pass by, pass, elapse*
    īnferī, -ōrum, m. pl. - *those below, the dead*
    diffugiō, -ere, -fūgī - *to fly apart, disperse, vanish*

28 **diūtius** (comp. adv.) - *longer*
    percutiō, -ere, -cussī, -cussum - *to strike through*
    comes, -itis, m./f. - *companion*

29 **exstinctus, -a, -um** - *slain, dead*

30 **Palamēdēs, -is, m.** - *Palamedes*
    īrātus, -a, -um (+ dat. of person) - *angry at*
    māchinor, -ārī, -ātus sum - *to devise, contrive, plot*

31 **excōgitō (1)** - *to think out, contrive, devise*

32 **somnium, -iī, n.** - *dream*

33 **clam** (adv.) - *in secret, secretly*
    tabernāculum, -ī, n. - *tent*
    cēlō (1) - *to conceal, hide*

GRAMMAR AND COMPREHENSION QUESTIONS

1) The verb form *exī* is the imperative of what verb?
2) In what sense is Laodamia *prīma*?
3) How did the gods take pity on Protesilaus?
4) What tense of infinitive is *revēnisse*? With *eum* what construction does this form?
5) What construction requires the subjunctive in the clause *quōmodo eum interficeret*?
6) What construction is *sē in somniō monitum esse*? How do you translate *monitum esse* in the context of the perfect verb *dīxit*?
7) What case is *ūnum diem*? What does this case indicate?

"Novissimus dē nāve **exī**." Nunc īnfēlix Lāodamīa **prīma** virum
ademptum lūgēbat. Tenēns cēream imāginem Prōtesilāī adsiduē
lacrimābat. Eōdem tempōre umbra Prōtesilāī in caecīs locīs nōn poterat
esse immemor iūcundae uxoris. Dēnique deī Prōtesilāō miserentēs, eī
25   permīsērunt trēs hōrās domum redīre. Lāodamīa virum suum intuēns
putābat **eum** salvum Trōiā **revēnisse** et māgnopere gaudēbat. At, tribus
hīs hōrīs trānsitīs, umbra in īnferōs retrō diffūgit. Nunc Lāodamīa dolōre
vincta diūtius vīvere nōn poterat; gladiō sē percussit atque ita comes
exstinctī virī ante annōs suōs secūta est.
30   Ulixēs Palamēdī īrātus adsiduē māchinābatur **quōmodo eum
interficeret**. Tandem cōnsilium excōgitāvit: Agamemnonī **dīxit sē in
somniō monitum esse** per **ūnum diem** āmovēre Graeca castra. Castrīs
mōtīs, Ulixēs multum aurum clam in tabernāculō Palamēdis cēlāvit.

Discussion Questions

1) In other versions Laodamia jumps into a fire to kill herself. Why do
   you think she chooses a sword here, which to the ancients seemed
   a more masculine way of death?
2) Can you find similarities between the story of Protesilaus and
   Laodamia and Shakespeare's Romeo and Juliet?

34   **velut** (adv.) - *as if, just as if*

35   **Priamus, -ī, m.** - *Priam;* king of Troy

     prōdō, -ere, -didī, -ditum - *to betray*

37   **postrīdiē** (adv.) - *on the next day*

     prōdūcō, -ere, -dūxī, -ductum - *to bring before, in front of*

     māiestās, -tātis, f. - *treason*

38   **accūsō** (1) (+ acc. of person + gen. of the charge) - *to accuse*

39   **absconditus, -a, -um** - *hidden, concealed*

40   **effodiō, -ere, -fōdī, -fossum** - *to dig up, dig out*

     dēmōnstrō (1) - *to point out, show, demonstrate*

41   **prōditor, -ōris, m.** - *traitor, betrayer*

Grammar and Comprehension Questions

1) What does *missam* modify?

2) *Tantum* correlates with which following word?

3) What gender, number, and case is *eī*?

4) On what condition did the false letter promise gold?

5) What trick did Ulysses use to convince the Greeks that the gold had come from the Trojans?

6) What case is *dolō*? What is its function?

Etiam Trōiānum captīvum coēgit epistulam scrībere velut Palamēdī

35 ā Priamō **missam**. Palamēdeī, sī modo Graeca castra Trōiānīs prōdat, falsa epistula **tantum** aurum **eī** prōmīsit quantum Ulixēs iam cēlāverat. Postrīdiē ad rēgem Ulixēs Palamēdem prōdūxit et eumque māiestātis accūsāvit, cūius crīminis quamquam suspiciōnem Palamēdēs fortiter negābat; Ulixēs tamen rege ad illud tabernaculum ductō absconditum

40 aurum effōdit. Etiam falsam epistulam dēmōnstrāvit. Agamemnōn igitur crēdēns Palamēdem esse prōditōrem innocentem Palamēdem **dolō** Ulixis dēceptum interficī iūssit.

DISCUSSION QUESTION

1) Does the Palamedes story indicate a language barrier between the Greeks and Trojans?

Philoctetes marooned by the Greeks on Lemnos (c. 420 BCE; Metropolitan Museum of Art, New York City) (© Creative Commons 2.5/Marie-Lan Nguyen)

Cultural Influences

Art: Numerous painters have depicted the sufferings of Philoctetes on Lemnos, such as Guillaume-Guillon Lethiere in "Philoctetes on the Desert Island of Lemnos, Scaling the Rocks in Order to Reach a Bird He Has Killed" (1797). Strangely, artistic representations of the Protesilaus and Laodamia theme as well as of Palamedes are rare.

Literature: William Wordsworth, "When Philoctetes in the Lemnian Isle," sonnet in *Poetical Works* (1827). Wordsworth also penned "Laodamia," an 1814 poem in *Poems, Including Lyrical Ballards.*

Music: Many composers have written music to accompany Sophocles's *Philoctetes*, ranging from Etienne Mehul (1788) to Elliott Carter (1936). There have also been operas on the Protesilaus and Laodamia theme by Verazi, Naumann, and others.

Chapter Three

THE QUARREL

The first nine years of the Trojan War were conducted primarily as siege warfare and were essentially a stalemate. There were skirmishes outside the walls, but it seems that the Trojans mainly stayed within their steep walls. The Greek fleet of 1,186 ships was pulled up on the shoreline and formed their encampment. The Greeks, far from their homeland, supplied themselves primarily by attacking nearby cities allied to the Trojans. It was the sacking of one such city, Thebe, that ultimately resulted in the action of Homer's *Iliad*.

The *Iliad*, which describes the action of only about 50 days at the beginning of the tenth year of the war, is part of a much larger epic cycle. Unfortunately, the rest of the cycle—*Cypria, Aithiopis, Ilias Parva, Iliou Persis (The Sack of Ilium)*—has survived only in fragments. Therefore this chapter will begin with the action of the *Iliad*, for it is the tenth year of the war that is by far the most dramatic and most familiar.

HOMER'S *ILIAD*

The rich complexity of Homer's *Iliad* is hard to compress into a few chapters, but the broad outlines of the plot are not that complicated. The theme of the epic is the wrath of Achilles—its cause and its unforeseen and tragic consequences. Homer's story of the war, however, is only the beginning of the mythological narrative. Other writers and artists have added considerably to the details of Homer's story; for instance, the theft of the Palladium, a sacred statue of Athena, is not mentioned in Homer, but is included here because of its importance in Vergil's version of the fall of Troy. The primary source for this chapter is Homer's *Iliad*. When later material is included the notes indicate the source.

The action of the epic takes place on two planes simultaneously: the human and the divine. These two planes often intersect, since many of the heroes are descendants of the gods, who definitely play favorites. Thus the battlefield is crowded with both humans and immortals. Also, there is the matter of fate, which has determined that Troy will fall. Nevertheless, the divine supporters of Troy try their best to thwart the dictates of fate. It is up to Zeus to see that fate is fulfilled.

The *Iliad* begins with an invocation to the Muse to tell the story of the wrath of Achilles. Then Homer immediately turns to the situation that arose after Thebe had been sacked and the booty distributed to the various Greek soldiers according to their worth. As was typical in warfare at this time, women were considered part of the booty. Thus Chryseis, daughter of Chryses, the priest of Apollo, had been captured and given to Agamemnon as his prize. The action of the epic begins as Chryses, carrying the emblems of his high office, comes to the Greek camp to attempt to ransom his daughter.

Sources

Homer, *Iliad* 1 • Hyginus, *Fabulae* 106, 121

A battle from the Trojan War depicted in medieval French style (First Master
of the Bible Historiale of Jean de Berry, France, c. 1390–1400;
Getty Museum, California) (Public Domain)

1 **fīlii Pēleī** - a patronymic, literally "named from the father." In Greek literature children are identified by the father's name, and this device is found very frequently in Homer and other Greek literature.

canō, canere, cecinī, cantum - *to sing*

vastitās, -tātis, f. - *devastation*

īnfandus, -a, -um - *unspeakable, dreadful*

2 **Danaī, -um, m. pl.** - *the Greeks.* The Greeks did not call themselves Greeks (the Roman name for them), but Danaans, Achaians, Argives, etc. In passages from Homer the Greeks will be called Danaans.

3 **deum** - here, gen. pl. contracted

iurgō (1) - *to quarrel*

Apollō, -inis, m. - *Apollo; god of prophecy, music and poetry, archery, medicine and disease (in Homer not the sun god)*

īrātus, -a, -um - *angered, angry*

4 **īnsolenter** (adv.) - *insolently, arrogantly*

ūsus esset: subjunctive to indicate the reason of the subject; here, *treated*

5 **Chrȳsēs, -ae, m.** - *Chryses,* priest of Apollo

6 **Chrȳsēis, -idos, f.** (Greek acc. *Chryseida*) - *Chryseis;* daughter of Chryses

pretium, -iī, n. - *ransom*

redimō, -ere, -ēmī, -emptum - *to buy back, ransom*

7 **laetus, -a, -um** - *happy, glad, joyful*

approbō (1) - *to approve*

praeter (prep. + acc.) - *except*

8 **asper, -era, -erum** - *rough, harsh*

expellō, -ere, -pulī, -pulsum - *to drive out, expel*

revēneris: pluperfect subjunctive with *nē* in a negative command (see *Latin for the New Millennium,* Level 2, p. 151)

9 **insigne, -is, n.** - *distinguishing mark, token, emblem*

prōtegō, -ere, -tēxī, -tēctum - *to protect*

potius (adv.) - *rather*

Mycēnae, -ārum, f. pl. - *Mycenae;* the Greek capital of Agamemnon's kingdom

---

GRAMMAR AND COMPREHENSION QUESTIONS

1) What verbal form is *cane*?
2) Which goddess is referred to as *dea*?
3) What case is *sacerdōte* and why?
4) What construction is *ut . . . redimeret*?
5) What tense is *prōtegent*?
6) What case is *Mycēnīs*?
7) How is *ut* translated with the indicative mood?

Īram Achillis, fīliī Pēleī, **cane, dea**, et vastitātem quae īnfandum dolōrem Danaīs fēcit. Incipe ex quō tempore Agamemnōn et Achillēs inter sē iurgābant. Quis deum effēcit ut inter eōs iurgārent? Apollō, īrātus quod Agamemnōn **sacerdōte** īnsolenter ūsus esset.

5   Nam Chrȳsēs sacerdōs Apollinis ad Graeca castra vēnerat **ut** fīliam suam, Chrȳsēida, plūrimō pretiō **redimeret**. Omnēs Danaī precēs sacerdōtis laetē approbāvērunt—praeter Agamemnonem quī senem sacerdōtem asperē expulit. "Nē umquam," inquit, "ad nāvēs iterum revēneris nam īnsignia deī tē nōn **prōtegent**. Fīliam tuam nōn reddam;
10   potius **Mycēnīs ut** serva labōrābit et moriētur."

Discussion Questions

1) How were priests supposed to be treated? What do you think about Agamemnon's treatment of the priest?
2) What is immediately established about the relationship between Agamemnon and his troops? What sort of a leader is Agamemnon?

The priest Chryses pleads with Agamemnon to release his daughter Chryseis for ransom (mosaic from the House of the Nymphs, 4th century CE; Nabeul [ancient Neapolis], Tunisia) (Public Domain/Habib M'henni)

12 **supplicō** (+ dat.) - *to supplicate, beg*

13 **sagitta, -ae, f.** - *arrow*

14 **īrāscor, -ī, īrātus sum** - *to be angry*

nox, noctis, f. - *night*

ruō, -ere, ruī, rutum - *to rush, hasten*

arcus, -ūs, m. - *bow*

tendō, -ere, tetendī, tentum - *to stretch, extend;* here, *to draw*

15 **bōs, bovis, m./f.** - *ox*

canis, -is, m./f. - *dog*

16 **pestis, -is, f.** - *plague, pestilence*

furō, -ere, furuī - *to rage*

pyra, -ae, f. - *funeral pyre*

flagrō (1) - *to blaze, burn*

17 **novem** (indecl. adj.) - *nine*

vastō (1) - *to lay waste, ravage, devastate*

decimus, -a, -um - *tenth*

pes, pedis, m. - *foot*

18 **concilium, -iī, n.** - *council*

19 **vātēs, -is, m.** - *prophet*

-ve (conj.) - *or*

patefaciō, -ere, -fēcī, -factum - *to make open, disclose, reveal*

20 **praeteritus, -a, -um** - *past*

21 **quoniam** (conj.) - *since*

nē: in clause of fearing: *that, lest* (See *Latin for the New Millennium,* Level 2, p. 506)

22 **irrītō** (1) - *to exasperate, irritate, vex*

prōmittō, -ere, -mīsī, -missum - *to promise*

25 **iactō** (1) - *to brag, boast*

causā (+ preceding genitive) - *for the sake of, because of, on account of*

26 **tractō** (1) - *to treat*

27 **pestifer, -era, -erum** - *pestilential, destructive*

GRAMMAR AND COMPREHENSION QUESTIONS

1) What case is *sacrificiō* and why?
2) What form is *supplicantem*?
3) What case and construction is *novem diēs*?
4) An epithet is the technical term for a phrase such as *pedibus celer,* which is frequently used to describe Achilles. Can you think of other descriptive epithets for Achilles or other characters?
5) What mood is *petamus* and what is the type of construction?
6) The relative pronoun *quī* introduces what type of clause with *patefaciat*?
7) What type of clause is *cūr . . . īrascātur*?
8) What tense is the infinitive *dēfēnsūrum esse*?
9) To whom does *sē* refer?
10) What case is *sacerdōtis suī* and on what does it depend?
11) What case is *pestiferās*?
12) What mood does *dum* take here? How then should you translate it?

Senex māgnopere timēns discessit. Iterum atque iterum Apollinī supplicābat: "Sī umquam tibi **sacrificiō** placuī, effice ut prō lacrimīs meīs sagittae tuae Danaōs pūniant." Deus **supplicantem** sacerdōtem audiēns īrātus est. Ut nox sīc deus dē caelō ruit et arcum tendēns contrā Danaōs

15 plūrimās sagittās mīsit. Prīmum bovēs canēsque Apollō percussit, sed mox et mīlitēs. Pestis ubique furēbat et ubique pyrae flagrābant.

Novem diēs pestis castra vastābat; decimō diē Achillēs **pedibus celer** Danaōs ad concilium convocāvit. "**Petamus**," inquit, "aliquem sacerdōtem vātemve **quī patefaciat cūr** Apollō nōbīs **īrascātur**." Tum

20 Calchās surrexit, quī omnia praeterita, praesentia, futūraque sciēbat. "Quoniam rogās, dīcam cūr Apollō īrascātur, sed vereor nē ego ipse māgnum rēgem irrītem. Ergō tū prōmitte tē mē **dēfēnsūrum esse**; tum vēritātem dīcam." Achillēs respondit: "Tē dēfēndam etiam sī Agamemnonem in animō habēs quī nunc **sē** multō maximum omnium

25 Danaum esse iactat." Tum Calchās: "Apollō **sacerdōtis suī** causā īrāscitur cum eum Agamemnōn īnsolenter tractāverit; nam nec fīliam eius reddidit nec pretium accēpit. Ergō sagittās **pestiferās** deus mittet **dum** rēx fīliam sacerdōtī sine pretiō reddat et māgnum sacrificium deō faciat."

DISCUSSION QUESTIONS

1) What does the fact that Apollo hit the animals first indicate about the understanding of the transmission of plague?
2) Who takes responsibility for solving problems among the Greeks?

29   **ardēns, -entis** - *flaming, blazing*
30   **praedīcō, -ere, -dīxī, -dictum** - *to foretell, prophesy*
30–31 **uxōrī meae**: this is Clytemnestra, the sister of Helen. She will appear in a significant episode later.
31   **antepōnō, -ere, -posuī, -positum** (+ dat.) - *to put before, prefer*
     cōnservō (1) - *to preserve, maintain, conserve*
32   **careō, -ēre, -uī, -itūrus** (+ abl.) - *to lack, be without*
33   **avārus, -a, -um** - *greedy*
35   **triplex, -icis** - *triple, three times*
     quadriplex, -icis - *quadruple, four times*
37   **num** (interrog. adv.) - anticipates the answer "no"
39   **vel . . . vel** - *either . . . or*
     Aiax, -ācis, m. - *Ajax;* the Greek Aias, one of the major Greek warriors, cousin of Achilles
     decet (impersonal verb + acc. + inf.) - *it is becoming, fitting*
40   **num** (interrog. adv. introducing questions expecting the answer "no") - *surely not?*

quis - after *num* = *aliquis*
41   **pāreō, -ēre, -uī** (+ dat.) - *to obey*
42   **iuvō, -āre, iūvī, iūtum** - *to help, aid, assist*
     ēvertō, -ere, -vertī, -versum - *to overturn, sack*
43   **interficiō, -ere, -fēcī, -fectum** - *to kill, murder*
     contumēlia, -ae, f. - *insult, outrage*
     impōnō, -ere, -posuī, -positum - *to place on, impose*
44   **auferō, -ferre, abstulī, ablatum** - *to take away, carry off*
     minor, -ārī, -ātus sum - *to threaten*
     Phthia, -ae, f. - *Phthia;* the kingdom of Achilles in Thessaly, Greece
45   **accumulō** (1) - *to pile up, heap up, accumulate*
47   **exclāmō** (1) - *to shout, scream*
48   **Brīsēis, -idos, f.** (Greek acc. *Brīsēida*) - *Briseis*
49   **tabernāculum, -ī, n.** - *tent, encampment*
50   **vāgīna, -ae, f.** - *sheath*
     percussūrus erat: periphrastic, *was about to . . .*

GRAMMAR AND COMPREHENSION QUESTIONS

1) What construction is *nē . . . caream?*
2) What case and form is *nōbilissime?*
3) What tense and mood is *cēperimus?*
4) What form of what verb is *nōlī?*
5) What case is *ūllō* and why?
6) What tense and mood is *iuvem?*
7) What tense, person, and number is *redībō?* From what verb?
8) What tense, person, and number is *vīs?* From what verb?

Tum Agamemnōn īrā ardēns surrēxit et Calchantī: "Semper mala,"
30 inquit, "mihi praedīcis. Puellam reddere nōlō, quoniam eam uxōrī
meae antepōnō. Tamen hanc reddam ut hunc populum cōnservem.
Ergō mihi dā aliud, aequum praemium, **nē** ego sōlus praemiō **caream**."
Statim Achillēs respondit: "Fīlī Atreī, **nōbilissime** sed etiam avārissime,
quōmodo tibi aliud praemium dabimus? Omnia praemia iam distribūta
35 sunt. Sed, cum Trōiam **cēperimus**, triplicem quadriplicemve praedam
tibi reddēmus." Agamemnōn īrātē respondit: "**Nōlī** temptāre mē
dēcipere. Num crēdis tē praemium tuum cōnservātūrum esse sed mē **ūllō**
caritūrum? Nōn. Aut aliud praemium mihi Danaī dent aut ego praemium
tuum vel Ulixis vel Aiācis capiam. Nam nōn decet mē sōlum carēre."
40 Achillēs īrātus respondit: "Ō impudentissime, **num quis tibi
pārēbit**? Nihil praeter lūcrum cōgitās. Ego nōn Trōiam vēnī quod Trōiānī
mē laesērunt sed ut tē **iuvem**. Prō tē multās urbēs ēvertī et plūrimōs
hostēs interfēcī. At nunc mihi contumēliam impōnis quoniam ā mē
praemium meum auferre mināris. Nunc igitur Phthīam cum mīlitibus
45 meīs **redībō**. Nōn hīc manēbō ut dīvitiās tuās accumulem et mē
īnsolenter tractēs."
"Curre quō **vīs**," Agamemnōn exclāmāvit. "Nōn ego tē diūtius
retinēbō. Multī aliī enim rēgēs mē honōrābunt. Brīsēida, autem,
praemium tuum, ē tabernāculō capiam." Tum Achillēs valdē īrātus
50 gladium ē vāgīnā ēdūcēns Agamemnonem percussūrus erat.

Discussion Questions

1) What other evil had Calchas prophesied to Agamemnon?
2) Whose prize does Agamemnon threaten to take?
3) When Achilles asks *num quis tibi pārēbit* what is he essentially
   doing?
4) What has Achilles done for Agamemnon?

51 **Minerva, -ae, f.** - *Minerva;* the Greek Athena

   adsistō, -ere, -stitī - *to stand by, near*

   Iūnō, -ōnis, f. - *Juno;* wife of Jupiter, the Greek Hera

52 **ambō, -ae, -ō** (adj. + pronoun) (acc. *ambōs*) - *both*

53 **in vicem** (idiom + gen.) - *in return for, in recompense of*

54 **rursum** (adv.) - *back*

   īnserō, -ere, -uī, -tum - *to put back*

56 **celer, -eris, -ere** - *swift*

   tingō, -ere, tinxī, tinctum - *to wet, stain, dye*

   iūrō (1) - *to swear*

57 **aliquandō** (adv.) - *at some time*

   homicīda, -ae, m. - *killer of men, man-slaughtering,* the Homeric epithet for Hector

58 **permultus, -a, -um** - *very many*

   paeniteō, -ēre, -uī (with *ut* clause as the subject) - *to cause regret; it will cause you regret that*

59 **Danaum:** a shortened form of *Danaōrum* that will be used consistently throughout this book

60 **Nestor, -oris, m.** - *Nestor;* aged king of Pylos renowned for his wisdom and speech

   sapiēns, -ntis - *wise*

61 **sūrgō, -ere, -rēxī, -rēctum** - *to rise, stand up*

   sēdō (1) - *to calm*

63 **dīmittō, -ere, -mīsī, -missum** - *to send away, let go, dismiss*

   opus, -eris, n. - *work, task; deed*

   opus est (+ abl.) - *there is need for*

64 **prōvocō** (1) - *to provoke, challenge*

65 **regō, -ere, rēxī, rēctum** - *to rule, guide, direct*

66 **āvertō, -ere, -vertī, -versum** - *to turn aside*

67 **Patroclus, -ī, m.** - *Patroclus,* son of Menoetius, best friend of Achilles

   discēdō, -ere, -cessī, -cessum - *to go away, depart*

68 **dirimō, -ere, -ēmī, -emptum** - *to separate, break off, dissolve*

69 **quī:** relative pronoun in relative clause of purpose: *to*

70 **culpō** (1) - *to blame, censure*

72 **stultus, -a, -um** - *foolish*

   pereō, -īre, -iī, -itum - *to be destroyed, perish*

73 **invītus, -a, -um** - *unwilling, against one's will*

Grammar and Comprehension Questions

1) What verb is *vīsa est*? How is it translated?

2) Who is the subject of *distribuistī*?

3) What construction is *Danaōs . . . cupītūrōs esse*?

4) What is the effect of the imperfect tense *sēdābat*?

5) To whom does *tū* refer?

6) What case are *terrae mīlitumque* and in what construction?

7) What is the function of *quam*? With what word does it connect?

8) What construction is *conciliō diremptō*?

9) What form is *ī*?

10) To whom does *iste* refer? What sort of connotation does it convey?

At statim dea Minerva adsistēns eī sōlī **vīsa est** et dīxit: "Dea Iūnō
mē mīsit; nam vōs ambōs aequāliter amat. Nōlī rēgem interficere. Posteā
rēx in vicem huius īnsolentiae tibi plūrima dōna dabit." Atque Achillēs
gladium in vāgīnam rursum īnseruit et dīxit: "Brīsēida reddam, quoniam
55   eam mihi **distribuistī**. Sed cavē nē aliud quidquam ā mē capere temptēs.
Nam tum sanguis tuus celeriter hoc gladium meum tinget. Nunc iūrō
aliquandō **Danaōs** Achillem māgnopere **cupītūrōs esse** cum homicīda
Hector permultōs mīlitēs interficiat; tum tē paenitēbit ut nūllum
honōrem **optimō Danaum** habērēs."

60   Tum senex rēx Nestor, quī erat multō sapientissimus
ēloquentissimusque Danaum, surrēxit et ambōs rēgēs verbīs **sēdābat**:
"Ego multō senior melius cōnsilium dō. **Tū** nōlī puellam capere quam
Danaī dedērunt. Īram dīmitte, nam Achille opus est. Et tū, Achillēs, nōlī
Agamemnonem potestāte prōvocāre; plus enim **terrae mīlitumque**
65   **quam** tū regit." Sed sapientia verba Nestoris nōn valuērunt, cum īra
animōs vīcisset. Achillēs, cum sē ab aliīs rapidē āvertisset, ē conciliō cum
amīcō Patroclō discessit.

Conciliō diremptō, anxiī Danaī discessērunt. At Agamemnōn
nuntiōs ad tabernāculum Achillis mīsit quī Brīsēida auferrent. Nuntiī
70   īram Achillis timuērunt, sed hērōs eōs amīcē salūtāvit. "Vōs nōn culpō
sed Agamemnonem. **Ī**, Patrocle, Brīsēida addūc et eīs dā. Sed **iste** sciat mē
eum nōn iuvātūrum esse cum stultē agat et Danaī prope nāvēs pereant."
Itaque Patroclus Achillī pārēns Brīsēida ēdūxit quae invīta ībat.

DISCUSSION QUESTIONS

1) Who does Achilles refer to as *optimō Danaum*?
2) How does Achilles treat Agamemnon's messengers? What does this
   treatment indicate about his mental state and his anger?
3) How did Achilles get Briseis? What do we find out about her feelings?

CULTURAL INFLUENCES

The characters of Achilles and Agamemnon have been represented in nearly count-less ways from Homer's day onward. The French Prix de Rome annual competition has often featured scenes from this chapter; e.g., in 1801 the competition subject was "Achilles Receiving the Ambassadors of Agamemnon" (won by Jean-Auguste-Dominique Ingres), in 1810 the subject was "The Wrath of Achilles." Recently Wolf-gang Petersen explored the relationship between Achilles and Agamemnon in the film *Troy* (2004).

Art: In this section the focus is on representations of the Chryseis and Briseis episodes. A recently discovered painting by Luca Ferrari (1605–54) "Agamem-non refusing to allow Chryses to ransom his daughter"; Luca Cambiaso "Apollo, at the Urging of Chryses, attacks the Camp of the Greeks before Troy," fresco (1544); paintings by Claude Lorrain "Seaport with Ulysses restoring Chryseis to Her Father Chryses," (c. 1644) and Joseph-Marie Vien "L'embarquement de Chrys-eis,"(1780–85); Benjamin West paintings "Chryseis Returned to Her Father" (1771?) and "Chryses Invoking the Vengeance of Apollo against the Greeks" (1773). On Briseis: Andrea Schiavone "The Departure of Briseis," painting (1563); Johann Tischbein the Elder, "The Abduction of Briseis from the tent of Achilles," painting (1773); Giovanni Battista Tiepolo frescoes "Minerva Prevents Achilles from Kill-ing Agamemnon" and "Briseis Led to Agamemnon (by Eurybates and Talthybius)" (1757); Antonio Canova plaster relief "Achilles Returning Briseis (to Agamemnon's Messengers)" (1787–90). Other bas-reliefs on the same theme by Thorwaldsen and Rude. George Frederick Watts, "Achilles and Briseis" fresco (1858). Paul Manship, "Briseis" bronze statue (1916–18).

Music: The complicated feelings of Briseis have been the subject for operas and ballets with music by composers such as Lotti, Bianchi, Basili, Taglioni and Goldmark. Curiously an opera "L'Ira di Achille" by Gaetano Donizetti from 1817 was never performed.

Chapter Four

ACHILLES'S REQUEST

After Achilles and his Myrmidons withdrew from the battle, the Greeks led by Ulysses returned Chryseis to Chryses, and Apollo lifted his curse. Nonetheless all was far from well in the Greek camp. Achilles, upset at the loss of Briseis, then asked his mother, the sea goddess Thetis, to make an extraordinary request of Zeus that will have enormous consequences for the rest of the epic and for Achilles himself. This chapter describes the request and its immediate aftermath. Some of the episodes that follow Achilles's request in Homer's narrative would be more fitting earlier in the war, such as single combat between Menelaus and Paris, yet they contribute to the energy of the narrative.

SOURCE

Homer, *Iliad* 1–3

1 **lacrimō** (1) - *to weep*

2 **quoniam** (conj.) - *since*

3 **pariō, -ere, peperī, partum** - *to beget, produce, give birth to*

saltem (adv.) - *at least*

decet (impersonal verb + acc. + inf.) - *it is becoming, fitting*

Iuppiter, Iovis, m. - *Jupiter, Jove; king of the gods, the Greek Zeus*

tonō (1) - *to thunder*

paulum (adv.) - *to a small extent, a little*

5 **contumēlia, -ae, f.** - *insult, indignity, affront*

impōnō, -ere, -posuī, -positum - *to place on, burden with, apply*

ēmergō, -ere, -mersī, -mersum - *to come up out of, emerge*

Thetis, -idis, f. - *Thetis*, mother of Achilles, a Nereid (sea goddess)

iuxtā (prep. + acc) - *very near, close to*

6 **adsideō, -ēre, -sēdī, -sessum** - *to sit by, near*

cōnsōlor, -ārī, -ātus sum - *to console, comfort, solace*

7 **reficiō, -ere, -fēcī, -fectum** - *to restore, make good, repair*

8 **dēsidērium, -iī, n.** - *desire, petition, request*

dummodo (conj. + subj.) - *provided that, so long as*

9 **invīsus, -a, -um** - *hated, hateful*

10 **rursum** (adv.) - *back*

pellō, -ere, pepulī, pulsum - to push, drive

11 **agnōscō, -ere, -nōvī, -nitum** - *to recognize, acknowledge*

13 **ēducō** (1) - *to bring up, rear, nourish*

vērō (adv.) - *truly, in fact*

14 **maestus, -a, -um** - *unhappy, sad, mournful*

16 **pugna, -ae, f.** - *fight, battle*

17 **proficīscor, -īscī, -fectus sum** - *to set out, depart*

supplicō (1) - *to supplicate, beg* (The supplicant knelt and embraced the knees of the person begged with one hand and his chin with the other hand.)

19 **sollicitus, -a, -um** - *troubled, anxious, disturbed*

haesitō (1) - *to hesitate, be in doubt*

nē - after verb of fearing *timēbat* translate - *that* (see *Latin for the New Millennium*, Level 2, p. 506)

20 **irrītō** (1) - *to provoke, vex, enrage*

faveō, -ēre, fāvī, fautum (+ dat.) - *to favor, support*

dēnique (adv.) - *at last, finally*

21 **adnuō, -ere, -nuī, -nūtum** - *to nod*

tremō, -ere, tremuī - *to tremble*

Grammar and Comprehension Questions

1) To what does *praemiō meō captō* refer?

2) What tense and mood is *det*? What verb is it from?

3) What mood is *adiuvet*? What does that mood convey here?

4) What case is *Danaōs* and what word agrees with it?

5) To whom does *suam* refer?

6) What tense is *erit*?

7) What is Thetis's request? Why is Zeus reluctant?

8) What gender is *potēns* and what does it modify?

Postquam nuntiī Brīsēida cēpērunt, Achillēs lacrimāns prope lītus
sedēns mātrem saepe invocābat. "Quoniam mē mortālem brevī vītā
peperistī, saltem decet Iovem tonantem mē honōrāre. At nunc nē paulum
quidem mē honōrat; nam Agamemnōn, **praemiō meō captō**,
5   contumēliam mihi impōnit." Ē marī ēmersit Thetis et iuxtā fīlium suum
adsēdit. Achillem omnia narrantem Thetis cōnsōlābātur. Sed Achillēs, "Sī
mē amās," inquit, "in honōre meō reficiendō adiuvābis. Ad Olympum ī et
Iovem ōrā ut mihi dēsīderium meum **det**. Dummodo Danaī, praesertim
invīsus Agamemnōn, nūllum honōrem mihi habeant, Iuppiter Trōiānōs
10   **adiuvet**. Morientēs **Danaōs** rursum ad nāvēs pellat ut Agamemnōn
dēmentiam **suam** agnōscat quod nūllum honōrem optimō Danaum
habuit."

Trīstis Thetis respondit: "Cūr tē ēducāvī? Vērō tē malō fātō peperī,
nam nunc vīta tua **erit** brevis maestaque. Ad Olympum tamen ībō;
15   fortasse Iuppiter vōtum tuum dabit. Tū prope celerēs nāvēs manēns, ab
omnibus pugnīs dēsiste sed īram contrā Danaōs tenē." Dea ad Olympum
profecta est ubi Iovem sōlum invēnit; supplicāns deum rogāvit ut fīlium
honōrāret. "Trōiānōs firmēs dum Danaī dignum honōrem fīliō meō dent."
Iuppiter sollicitus haesitābat; nam timēbat nē Iūnōnem irrītaret quae
20   Danaōs maximē favēret. Dēnique autem Iuppiter caput **potēns** adnuit et
omnis Olympus tremuit.

Discussion Questions

1) What do you think about Achilles weeping? Is this unheroic or
unmanly?
2) Why does Achilles particularly resent his short life and his
mortality?
3) Achilles asks Zeus to give help to his the enemy. In military terms
what does Achilles's request constitute? What might one label
Achilles?
4) Why does Thetis seem to mourn her son while he is alive?

22 **perficiō, -ere, -fēcī, -fectum** - *to carry out, accomplish, complete*

23 **somnium, -iī, n.** - *dream*

Nestor, -oris, m. - *Nestor;* aged Greek king of Pylos; excellent speaker and advisor. In *Iliad* 11.631–36 Homer describes a weighty, magnificent golden cup with a double base and two golden doves on top. Such an object has been found at Mycenae.

25 **oppugnō (1)** - *to fight against, attack, assail*

26 **gaudeō, -ēre, gāvīsus sum** - *to be glad, rejoice*

27 **mīrābilis, -e** - *amazing, wondrous, remarkable*

28 **experior, -īrī, -pertus sum** - *to test, try, experience*

statuō, -ere, -uī, -ūtum - *to decide*

queror, -ī, questus sum - *to complain*

29 **patior, -ī, passus sum** - *to suffer, endure*

31 **laetus, -a, -um** - *happy, glad, joyful*

ruō, -ere, ruī, rutum - *to rush*

fīniō, -īre, -īvī, -ītum - *to end, terminate*

32 **infectus, -a, -um** - *not achieved, not fulfilled*

33 **conventus, -ūs, m.** - *assembly, meeting*

repellō, -ere, reppulī, -pulsum - *to drive back, push back*

GRAMMAR AND COMPREHENSION QUESTIONS

1) What construction is *ut . . . perficeret*?
2) What case is *ipsō diē* and what does it indicate?
3) What is the first principal part of *gāvīsus est*? What type of verb is it?
4) What is the first principal part of *questus est*?
5) What gender, number, and case is *multa et horrenda*? What English word must you understand with the two adjectives?
6) What tense is *permittet*?
7) What mood is *nāvigēmus*? What is its construction?
8) What mood and tense is *fīnītum esset*? Note that *nisi* follows. What type of conditional construction is this?

Mox Iuppiter cōnsilium finxit **ut** vōtum Achillis **perficeret**. Ad
Agamemnonem falsum somnium, figūram simillimam Nestorī, mīsit.
Haec imāgō perfectam victōriam contrā Trōiam prōmīsit sī **ipsō diē**
25   rēx urbem oppugnāvisset. Agamemnōn ē somnō excitātus māgnopere
gāvīsus est et omnēs ducēs convocāvit. Somniō narrātō, eōs hortātus est
ut hostēs statim oppugnārent. At prīmō, mīrābiliter, Agamemnōn Danaōs
mīlitēs experīrī statuit. Omnibus mīlitibus convocātīs **questus est**:
"Novem annōs Trōiae manentēs **multa et horrenda** passī sumus. Iuppiter
30   nōbīs Trōiam capere nōn **permittet**. Nunc igitur domum **nāvigēmus**."
Statim omnēs mīlitēs laetī ad nāvēs ruērunt. Tum bellum vērō **fīnītum
esset** et fātum fuisset infectum, **nisi** Minerva Ulixem excitāvisset. Nam
mīlitēs fortiter reprehendit et ad conventum rursum reppulit.

DISCUSSION QUESTIONS

    1) What did the dream promise Agamemnon?
    2) How did the ancients interpret dreams? How does this reaction
       compare to modern interpretation?
    3) What extraordinary action did Agamemnon take at the assembly?

34 **nōnne** (interrogative adv. introducing questions expecting the answer "yes") - *don't?*

35 **ignāvus, -a, -um** - *cowardly*

36 **incitō** (1) - *to rouse, stir*
pudor, -ōris, m. - *shame*

37 **oppōnō, -ere, -posuī, -positum** - *to station opposite*
Paris, -idis, m. - *Paris*; prince of Troy
aciēs, -ēī, f. - *line of battle*
prōsiliō, -īre, -uī - *to leap forward, rush forward*

38 **prōvocō** (1) - *to call forth, challenge*

39 **rapiō, -ere, rapuī, raptum** - *to seize, carry away, steal*
ulcīscor, -ī, ultus sum - *to take revenge*

40 **prōdeō, -īre, -iī, -itum** - *to come forward, advance*

simulac (adv.) - *as soon as*
vicissim (adv.) - *in turn*

41 **cēlō** - *to hide, conceal*

42 **utinam** (adv. + subj. to express impossible wish) - *would that, I wish that*
certus, -a, -um - *certain, sure, definite*

43 **dērīdeō, -ēre, -rīsī, -rīsum** - *to deride, laugh at, make fun of*
num (interrog. adv. introducing questions expecting the answer "no") - *surely not?*

44 **audeō, -ēre, ausus sum** - *to dare*

45 **rectus, -a, -um** - *straight, right*

46 **utercumque, utracumque, utrumque** - *whichever (of two)*

GRAMMAR AND COMPREHENSION QUESTIONS

1) What construction follows *intellegitis?*
2) What case is *vōs?*
3) What case is *pudōre?* What word governs it?
4) To whom does *quem* refer?
5) What case is *male?*
6) What type of clause is *cuius uxor cēpistī?*

Ulixēs: "Nōnne **intellegitis**," inquit, "māgnum rēgem vōs experīrī?
35   Iam quidem īrāscētur quod vōs tam ignāvōs dēmōnstrātis. Nunc igitur ad
pugnam **vōs** incitāte." Tum mīlitēs **pudōre** mōtī sē armāvērunt.

Iam tandem, Danaīs Trōiānīsque oppositīs, Paris ex aciē prōsiluit ad
pugnam optimōs Danaōs prōvocāns, **quem** Menelāus vidēns māgnopere
gaudēbat. Nunc enim ā Paride prō Helenā raptā sē ultūrum esse putābat.
40   Itaque prōdiit. Sed simulac Paris Menelāum vicissim vīdit, tremēns
refūgit et inter Trōiānōs sē cēlāvit. At frāter Hector Paridem fortiter
reprehendit: "**Male** Paris, utinam nē tū umquam nātus essēs. Certē Danaī
nōs dērīdent putantēs tē esse optimum mīlitem nostrum. Num contrā
Menelāum **cuius uxor cēpistī** pugnāre ausus es?" Paris tum respondit:
45   "Rectē mē reprehendistī. Nunc igitur ego sōlus contrā Menelāum
pugnābō. Utercumque alterum vincit et Helenam et omnia **bona** ē
Mycēnīs auferet."

DISCUSSION QUESTIONS

1) What do you think about Paris's challenge to single combat? Is it
consistent with his character? What kind of warrior is Paris?
2) How did Hector feel about his brother?
3) What did the *bona* consist of?

48   **Priamus, -ī, m.** - *Priam;* king of Troy

48–49   **iūs iūrandum, -ī, n.** - *oath*

50   **iūrō** (1) - *to swear*

51   **adversus, -a, -um** - *facing, opposite*

        pugnātor, -ōris, m. - *fighter, combatant*

52   **hasta, -ae, f.** - *spear*

        scūtum, -ī, n. - *shield*

53   **prōtegō, -ere, -texī, -tectum** - *to cover, protect*

54   **poena, -ae, f.** - *penalty, punishment*

        poenās dare (idiom) - *to pay the penalty*

        perfodiō, -ere, -ōdī, -ossum - *to pierce, perforate*

55   **celer, -eris, -ere** - *swift*

        dēclīnō (1) - *to turn away, aside, to swerve*

        vītō (1) - *to avoid*

56   **galea, -ae, f.** - *helmet*

        horribile dictū: another use of an adjective plus the supine - *dreadful to say*

        frangō, -ere, frēgī, fractum - *to break, shatter*

58   **lōrum, -ī, n.** - *strap;* translate here as *chinstrap*

59   **frustror, -ārī, -ātus sum** - *to cheat of his hopes, frustrate, disappoint*

60   **āēr, āeris, m.** - *air, thin air*

        ēvānēscō, -ere, ēvānuī - *to vanish, fade away, disappear*

61   **cubiculum, -ī, n.** - *bedroom*

        attonitus, -a, -um - *astonished, stunned*

62   **poscō, -ere, popōscī** - *to demand, call for*

        intercēdō, -ere, -cessī, -cessum - *to intervene, interfere*

64   **pareō, -ēre, -uī** (+ dat.) - *to obey*

65   **Pandarus, -ī, m.** - *Pandarus,* Trojan archer

        praecordia, -ōrum, n. pl. - *midriff, abdomen*

66   **vexō** (1) - *to attack constantly, harry, trouble*

Grammar and Comprehension Questions

1) What case is *cēterīs Trōiānīs?* Why?
2) What case, number, and gender is *hunc?* To whom does it refer?
3) To whom does *eius* refer?
4) What tense is *trahēbat?* What sense does the tense convey here?
5) What construction is *ut . . . tenēret?*
6) What case is *deae?* Why?

Gaudēns Menelāus hanc pugnam accēpit, sed Priamum petīvit ut iūs

iūrandum faceret; nam **cēterīs Trōiānīs** nōn crēdēbat. Mox, sacrificiīs

50 factīs, Priamus Menelāusque iūs iūrandum iūrāvērunt. Omnēs mīlitēs

adversī sedentēs duōs pugnātōrēs ācriter spectābant.

Prīmum Paris hastam iēcit quae medium scūtum Menelāī percussit,

sed scūtum **hunc** prōtexit. Deinde, cum Menelāus Iovem ōrāvisset ut

Paris morte poenās daret, hastam iēcit. Hasta scūtum Paridis perfōdit sed

55 Paris celeriter sē dēclīnāns mortem vītāvit. Menelāus gladium ēdūcēns

incurrit et galeam **eius** percussit. Horribile dictū, gladius fractus est.

Tum īrātus galeam ipsam rapiēns Paridem ad castra Danaum **trahēbat**,

quem lōrum galeae strangulābat. Observāns Venus lōrum subitō frēgit **ut**

rēx vacuam galeam **tenēret**. Frustrātus Menelāus galeā ad Danaōs

60 iactā iterum impetum fēcit. Mīrābile dictū, Paris in āerem ēvānuit; nam

Venus hunc tollēns ad cubiculum tulerat. Attonitus Menelāus Helenam

omniaque bona poposcit. Deī autem intercessērunt nē bellum dēsineret.

Ē caelō volāns Minerva similis hominī vīsa est et Trōiānum Pandarum

hortāta est ut ad Menelāum sagittam mitteret. **Deae** parēns, Pandarus

65 Menelāum in praecordiīs vulnerāvit (sed eum nōn interfēcit). Omnēs

Danaī, praesertim Agamemnōn, graviter vexātī Trōiānōs ferōciter

oppugnāvērunt. Itaque bellum iterum coepit.

DISCUSSION QUESTIONS

1) Why does Venus help Paris?
2) Can the actions of Venus be explained without divine intervention?
   Are they believable to a modern audience? Similarly, are the
   actions of Minerva believable?

Cultural Influences

Art: on Thetis: paintings by Giovanni Battista Tiepolo, "Thetis Consoling Achilles" (1757), and Jean Auguste Dominique Ingres, "Jupiter et Thétis" (1811). On the single combat: paintings by Francois Boucher "Venus Saves Paris from the Fury of Menelaus" (c. 1765), Henry Fuseli, "Aphrodite Carries Paris Off after His Battle with Menelaus" (1766–80), Angelica Kauffman "Hector Reproaching Paris" (1775), Louis-Jean-Francois Lagrené, "Preparations for the Combat of Paris and Menelaus" (1780–81).

Chapter Five

BATTLE: THE *ARISTEIA* OF DIOMEDES; THE TROJAN HEROES: AENEAS, HECTOR

After the truce was broken, the battle raged fiercely. In Achilles's absence, on the Greek side the Argive King Diomedes, inspired by Minerva, fought most valiantly and even wounded two gods who supported the Trojans, Venus and Mars. The fifth book of the *Iliad* focuses on Diomedes's deeds of valor, termed *aristeia* in Greek. The Trojan Aeneas urged Pandarus, the truce-breaker, to fight with Diomedes, but Diomedes then killed Pandarus. This chapter begins as Aeneas, standing astride the body of Pandarus, tries to protect the body and weapons of his ally. This scene will be echoed several more times in the epic. Later in this chapter we will enter the walls of Troy with Hector where in a series of meetings he converses with his mother, Queen Hecuba, Paris and Helen, and finally his wife Andromache with their child Astyanax.

SOURCE

Homer, *Iliad* 5–6

1   **Aenēās, -ae, m.** (acc. *Aenēan*)
- *Aeneas*; son of Venus and
Anchises, Trojan warrior, future
founder of the Roman people

    Diomēdēs, -is, m. - *Diomedes*;
Argive king

2   **spoliō** (1) - *to strip, remove*

    leō, -ōnis, m. - *lion*

    super (prep. + acc) - *above, over*

3   **feriō, -īre** - *to strike*

    coxa, -ae, f. - *hip*

    os, ossis, n. - *bone*

    genu, -ūs, n. - *knee*

4   **cālīgō, -inis, f.** - *mist, fog*

5   **amplector, -plectī, -plexus sum** - *to
take, clasp, embrace*

6   **palla, -ae, f.** - *mantle, cloak*
in rectangular shape worn
particularly by women

7   **portō** (1) - *to carry*

    trānsfīgō, -ere, -fīxī, -fīxum - *to
pierce through, drive or thrust
through*

8   **sanguis**: The gods do not have blood
like humans but *ichor* which
makes them immortal.

    ululō (1) - *to howl, yell*

    āter, ātra, ātrum - *black, dark*

9   **cēlō** (1) - *to hide, conceal*

    adfor, -fārī, -fātus sum - *to speak to,
address*

10   **Diōnē, -ēs, f.** - *Dione*; mother of
Venus. (In other early myths
Venus has no mother.)

11   **intereā** (adv.) - *meanwhile*

    ter (adv.) - *three times*

12   **prōtegō, -ere, -texī, -tēctum** - *to
cover, protect*

15   **sānus, -a, -um** - *sound, healthy*

    aciēs, -ēī, f. - *line of battle*

    Mars, Martis, m. - *Mars*; god of war

19   **concurrō, -ere, -currī, -cursum** (+
dat.) - *to engage in battle with, fight*

    prehendō, -ere, -hendī, -hensum -
to grasp, take hold of

    impellō, -ere, -pulī, -pulsum - *to
drive in*

20   **saucius, -a, -um** - *wounded*

    decem (indecl. adj.) - *ten*

    mille (indecl. adj. in s.) - *thousand*

     mīlia, -ium, n. pl. - *thousands*

Grammar and Comprehension Questions

1) What type of clause does *timēns nē* introduce?

2) What literary device is *ut leō*?

3) What is the antecedent of *quod*?

4) What tense and mood are the verbs in *mortuus esset, nisi . . .
amplexa esset . . . tēxisset*? What type of condition is this?

5) What type of construction is *ut . . . possent*?

6) How does *quae* help you determine whom Diomedes is
commanding?

7) What case is *terrā*? What is its function?

8) What tense is *oppugnātūrus*?

9) What tense and mood is *concurrerit*?

Aenēās, **timēns nē** Diomēdēs corpus Pandarī caperet et arma
spoliāret, **ut leō** super corpus stābat. Sed Diomēdēs māgnō saxō sublātō
in Aenēan iēcit, **quod** feriēns coxam Aenēae os frēgit. Aenēās genibus
terram petīvit atque cālīgō oculōs obscūrāvit. Tum hērōs **mortuus esset,**
5 **nisi** māter Venus grave perīculum vidēns fīlium manibus **amplexa esset**
et pallā **tēxisset ut** Danaī eum vidēre nōn **possent.** Sed cum Venus fīlium
ē pugnā portāret, Diomēdēs secūtus manum deae hastā trānsfīxit ut
sanguis flueret. Illa ululāns Aenēan dēmīsit, sed Apollō eum ātrā cālīgine
cēlāvit. Tum Diomēdēs adfātus est: "Cēde tū **quae** es expers bellī."
10 Lacrimāns dolōre Venus ad Olympum celeriter fūgit ubi māter Diōnē eam
cūrāvit. Intereā **terrā** Diomēdēs in Apollinem ter incurrit; sed Apollō
Aenēan prōtegēns monuit: "Cēde. Nōlī deōs pugnāre." Iste pedem statim
rettulit. Deus Aenēan ad templum suum portāvit cūrāvitque. Tum Apollō
imāginem Aenēae finxit quam ad pugnam mīsit ut Danaōs dēciperet.
15 (Posteā sānum Aenēan ad aciem remīsit.) Apollō etiam Martem hortātus
est ut prō Trōiānīs pugnāret. Sed Diomēdēs Hectorem **oppugnātūrus**
aliquem deum esse cum eō intellēxit et pedem igitur retulit. Tamen
Minerva Diomēdem hortāta est ut deum oppugnāret. Cum ille Martī
concurrerit, dea ipsa hastam prehendēns in abdōmen deī impellere
20 adiūvit. Iste saucius tantā vōce clāmāvit quantā novem aut decem mīlia
virōrum.

DISCUSSION QUESTIONS

1) Does Aeneas, the founder of the Roman race, look heroic here?
2) Can Diomedes see Venus?
3) The usual epithet of Venus is "smiling." What contrasting actions
   describe her here?
4) What might you call the *imāgō* of Aeneas? What is its purpose?
5) What does it indicate about Diomedes that he is able to wound even
   Mars?

22 **permultus, -a, -um** - *very many*

23 **Hector, -oris, m.** - *Hector*; eldest son of King Priam and Queen Hecuba, chief Trojan warrior

25 **praecipuus, -a, -um** - *exceptional, special*

    iuvō, -āre, iūvī, iūtum - *to help, aid, assist*

26 **aciēs, -ēī, f.** - *line of battle, battle line*

    obvius, -a, -um - *opposite*

        obviam īre (+ dat.): *to meet*

27 **libāmen, -inis, n.** - *libation, drink offering*

28 **sordēs, -is, f.** - *dirt, filth*

    foedō (1) - *to soil, make filthy, pollute*

    rogātiō, -ōnis, f. - *request*

29 **māgnificus, -a, -um** - *magnificent, splendid, sumptuous*

    dōnō (1) (+ acc. of person, + abl. of gift) - *to give, present to*

    acerbus, -a, -um - *harsh, bitter*

30 **āvertō, -ere, -vertī, -versum** - *to turn away*

31 **persuadeō, -ere, -suāsī, -suāsum** (+ dat.) - *to persuade*

33 **ignāvia, -ae, f.** - *cowardice*

34 **apud** (prep. + acc) - *at, by*

    occurrō, -ere, -currī, -cursum (+ dat.) - *to run to meet*

GRAMMAR AND COMPREHENSION QUESTIONS

1) What form is *faciendum*? In what construction with *est*?
2) What gender, number, and case is *ea*?
3) Why did Hector refuse to drink or make a libation?
4) What noun does *intrāns* modify?
5) What does Helen feel about her husband Paris?
6) What construction is *sē . . . parāre*?

Cum Danaī fortissimē pugnārent et permultōs Trōiānōs vulnerārent
interficerentque, Helenus, vātēs Trōiānōrum, frātrem Hectōrem vocāvit:
"Ad urbem redī et mātrem rogā ut fēminās convocet. Nam Minervae
25   praecipuum dōnum **faciendum est** ut fortasse nōbīs iuvet." Hector igitur
aciē relictā mox Trōiam intrāvit ubi Hecuba obviam eī iit. **Ea** vīnum
praebēns rogāvit ut biberet et libāmen Iovī faceret, sed ille nōlēbat, quod
sordēs bellī sē adhūc foedābat. Tum, cum rogātiōnem frātris nuntiāverat,
Hecuba fēminaeque māgnificā pallā deam dōnāvērunt; acerba dea autem
30   caput ab eīs āvertit.

Deinde Hector domum Paridis **intrāns** huic persuadēbat ut ad
proelium redīret. Ibi Helenam etiam invēnit, quae coniugem suum
propter ignāviam reprehendit. Sed Paris respondit **sē** redīre nunc **parāre**
et prōmīsit sē apud portās Hectorī mox occursūrum esse.

Discussion Questions

1) What sense does it make for the Trojans to send their best warrior
on an errand into Troy?
2) What do we discover about Hector's character when he refuses to
make a libation without first purifying himself?
3) What is offered to Minerva? When Minerva turns her head aside,
what does this action reveal about her?
4) Do you think Paris would have returned to the battle without the
urging of Helen and Hector?

35 **Andromacha, -ae, f.** - *Andromache*; wife of Hector

36 **trepidus, -a, -um** - *filled with alarm, fearful*

moenia, -ium, n. pl. - *walls of a city*

37 **Astyanax, -actis, m.** - *Astyanax*; means Lord of the City, which was a nickname. His given name was Skamandrios, after the local river.

39 **īnfēlix, -icis** - *ill-fated, unfortunate, unhappy*

40 **miseror, -ārī, -ātus sum** - *to pity*

viduus, -a, -um - *widowed*

patior, -ī, passus sum - *to suffer, endure*

41 **septem** (indecl. adj.) - *seven*

42 **servitūs, -tūtis, f.** - *servitude, slavery*

redigō, -ere, -ēgī, -actum - *to drive, compel, reduce*

remaneō, -ēre, -mānsī, -mānsum - *to remain, stay*

44 **pudeō, -ēre, -uī, -itum est** (most frequently 3rd person impersonal + acc.) - *it fills with shame, makes ashamed*

ignāvus, -a, -um - *cowardly*; here substantive, *a coward*

45 **frōns, frontis, f.** - *front*

in fronte prīmā: *at the front of the battle, in the forefront*

46 **adipiscor, -piscī, adeptus sum** - *to obtain, acquire, win*

aliquandō (adv.) - *at some time, one day*

49 **antequam** (conj.) - *before*

50 **cristātus, -a, -um** - *crested with horse hair*

51 **abhorreō, -ēre, -uī** - *to recoil from*

brācchium, -iī, n. - *arm*

complector, -ctī, -plexus sum - *to hold in the arms, embrace, enfold*

52 **precor, -arī, -ātus sum** (+ acc. of person) - *to pray to, entreat*

praestāns, -antis - *surpassing others, outstanding, excellent, exceptional*

validus, -a, -um - *strong, powerful*

53 **regō, -ere, rēxī, rēctum** - *to rule*

dicant: impersonal third person pl. - *let them say*

56 **cōniciō, -ere, -iēcī, -iectum** - *to hurl*

57 **effugiō, -ere, -fūgī, -fugitūrus** - *to flee from, escape*

GRAMMAR AND COMPREHENSION QUESTIONS

1) What is the nominative singular of *vīrēs*?
2) Why is Hector *omnia* to Andromache? What is her history? (As a side-note, her mother was ransomed out of servitude but then died.)
3) What construction is *Trōiam cāsūram esse*?
4) What word correlates with *tanta*?
5) What is Hector's greatest concern?
6) The form *moriar* is ambiguous: either future or subjunctive. Assuming it is subjunctive, what is its type and force?
7) What frightens Astyanax?
8) What is the effect of the imperfect tense in *cōnsōlābātur*?
9) What construction is *hīs dictīs*?

35   Dēnique Hector domum rediit ut uxōrem Andromacham invenīret,
sed illa trepida proelium dē moeniīs spectāns aberat. Itaque Hector
ad portās rediit ubi uxōrem īnfantemque fīlium Astyanactem invēnit.
Lacrimāns Andromacha ad eum cucurrit et ōrābat eum ad pugnam nōn
redīre. "**Vīrēs** tuae tē interficient, quī nec parvum fīlium nec īnfēlicem
40   mē miserāris. Mox Danaī tē interficient et ego vidua patiar. Nam tū es
omnia mihi, quoniam Achillēs patrem septemque frātrēs interfēcit atque
mātrem in servitūtem redēgit. Itaque hīc in moeniīs remanē." Hector
respondit: "Mihi tuī et fīliī nostrī maxima cūra est. Sed mē māgnopere
pudēret sī similis ignāvō pugnam vītārem.

45   "Nam fortis esse et in fronte prīmā pugnāre didicī; sīc māgnam
glōriam mihi patrīque adipiscor. Certē crēdō aliquandō **Trōiam cāsūram
esse**, sed nōn **tanta** mihi est cūra patris vel mātris vel etiam frātrum
quī multī morientur quanta tuī, quam lacrimantem in servitūtem aliquī
Danaus auferret. **Moriar** antequam hoc videam." Tum Hector
50   fīlium tollere temptāvit, sed Astyanax timēns cristātam galeam ab eō
abhorruit. Rīdēns pater galeam remōvit et fīlium brācchiīs complectēns
Iovem precātus est: "Effice ut hic puer, fīlius meus, sit praestāns, validus,
Trōiamque regat et dicant hunc esse māiōrem quam patrem." Ita precāns
fīlium ad brācchia uxōris cārae reddidit et lacrimās eius vidēns
55   **cōnsōlābātur**: "Misera Andromacha, cūr tantum prō mē dolēs? Nēmō mē
in mortem cōniciet nisi fātum est, quod nec fortis nec ignāvus effugere
potest." **Hīs dictīs**, Hector ad pugnam sed Andromacha domum rediit.

DISCUSSION QUESTIONS

1) Can Hector realistically keep out of the battle? Can he protect his
   family by staying within the walls?
2) How does Hector compare to Paris as a warrior and a person?
3) What effect does Hector's smile create in the episode?
4) What poignancy is there in the prayer for Astyanax? Do you know
   what happens to him?

Cultural Influences

Diomedes's wounding of Venus and her complaints to Jupiter were a popular theme for painters; see works by Garofalo, Johann Loth, Gabriel-Francois Doyen, Jacques-Louis David, Antoine Callet, Jean-Auguste-Dominique Ingres, and Nicolas Gosse.

Numerous operas, tragedies, and ballets (ranging from Euripides to Martha Graham) have explored the theme of the suffering of Andromache, although most of these focus on later episodes in her story. As *The Oxford Guide to Mythology in the Arts* notes "One of the most popular episodes from the *Iliad* in postclassical painting, literature, and music is Hector's final farewell to Andromache and their young son, Astyanax" (493). Representative writers and artists on this theme range from Dante and Chaucer in literature to the multiple sculptures of Giorgio de Chirico. Similarly the relationship between Helen and Paris has inspired artistic creativity throughout the centuries, but most of these efforts focus on the abduction or escape from Sparta, not on their relationship later in Troy.

Hector's farewell to Andromache (Hektor-Denkmal Moers, 2012; chateau park of Moers, Germany) (© Creative Commons 3.0/Panoraminchen)

Chapter Six

THE EMBASSY TO ACHILLES

After Hector returned to the battle, he immediately challenged any Greek to single combat. The Greek warriors were reluctant but, shamed by Nestor, finally some volunteered and Ajax was chosen. The two fought valiantly all day, but at nightfall neither was the victor. The two then exchanged gifts indicating their respect for one another. That night the Trojans held a council at which one of the leaders suggested that they return Helen and the treasure that Paris had stolen. Paris refused to return Helen but agreed to return the treasure. The Greeks later refused this offer. Meanwhile, the Greeks also held a council and decided to build a protective ditch and rampart (long overdue, it would seem). The two sides agreed to a truce to bury the dead.

At the dawn of the next day Jupiter weighed the scales of fate, which indicated favor for the Trojans (as promised to Achilles). With Hector pursuing, the Greeks were driven back to the ditch. For the first time the Trojans decided to camp for the night on the plain rather than to retreat to the safety of their walls. At another Greek assembly Agamemnon wept before his troops and said that they should return home. Diomedes, however, refused to leave until their mission was accomplished. Nestor suggested that the leaders hold a private meeting; there he advised Agamemnon to send an embassy to Achilles and offer him great gifts if he would return to the battle. Surprisingly, Agamemnon agreed, even admitting that he had been mad to quarrel with Achilles for the sake of a woman. He offered more than a king's ransom in gifts if Achilles returned to battle; but he also wanted Achilles to acknowledge that he himself was kinglier. Nestor answered that no one could reject such gifts and, to ensure that Achilles would accept them, he recommended that three warriors go to Achilles: Ulysses, renowned for his clever speaking; Ajax, a great warrior and Achilles's cousin; and Phoenix, Achilles's tutor and, in essence, foster-father. This chapter begins as these three arrive at the camp of Achilles.

SOURCE

Homer, *Iliad* 9

2 **lyra, -ae, f.** - *lyre* (musical stringed instrument)

increpō, -āre, -uī, -itum - *to sound, pluck*

praeda, -ae, f. - *booty, plunder, spoil*

3 **laus, laudis, f.** - *praise*

4 **dēmiror, -ārī, -ātus sum** - *to be utterly astonished at, be amazed*

exsiliō, -īre, -uī - *to leap up, jump up*

studiōsus, -a, -um - *eager*

5 **hospitium, -iī, n.** - *hospitality*

praebeō, -ēre, -uī, -itum - *to offer, give, provide*

cēna, -ae, f. - *dinner, meal*

perficiō, -ere, -fēcī, -fectum - *to accomplish, complete*

6 **incipiō, -ere, -cēpī, -ceptum** - *to begin*

nuntiō (1) - *to announce, report*

7 **incendō, -ere, -cendī, -cēnsum** - *to set fire to, kindle, burn*

minor, -ārī, -ātus sum - *to threaten*

obsecrō (1) - *to beg, implore*

8 **exitium, -iī, n.** - *destruction, ruin*

sērō (adv.) - *late, too late*

acerbus, -a, -um - *bitter, grievous*

paenitēbit: impersonal verb + acc.: *it will affect with regret, you will regret*

9 **meminī, meminisse** (defective verb occurs only in perfect but with present sense) - *to remember*
Mementō: singular imperative

caveō, -ēre, cāvī, cautum - *to beware, avoid*

10 **temperantia, -ae, f.** - *moderation, self-control, temperance*

11 **dīmittō, -ere, -mīsī, -missum** - *to send away, dismiss, let go*

dōnō (1) - *to give x* (abl.) *to y* (acc.)

12 **texō, -ere, -uī, -itum** - *to weave*
texendī: genitive gerund - *weaving*

perītus, -a, -um (+ gen.) - *practised, skilled in, expert at*

praetereā (adv.) - *in addition to that, besides, moreover*

vīgintī (indecl. adj.) - *twenty*

13 **spolium, -iī, n.** (usually pl.) - *spoil, booty*

regnum, -ī, n. - *kingdom*

14 **nūpta, -ae, f.** - *bride*

postrēmō (adv.) - *finally*

intactus, -a, -um - *untouched, undamaged*

15 **fīniō, -īre, -īvī, -ītum** - *to finish, conclude*

callidus, -a, -um - *clever*

postulō (1) (+ acc. + inf.) - *to demand*

rēgālis, -e - *kingly*

GRAMMAR AND COMPREHENSION QUESTIONS

1) Precisely identify the form *āctūrōs esse*. What is its first principal part?
2) What was Hector threatening to do?
3) What tense and mood is *dīxerit*? In what construction?
4) What form is *ūtere*? Remember that this is a deponent verb.
5) What tense and mood is *capta erit*?
6) What part of Agamemnon's speech did Ulysses omit?

Cum trēs lēgātī accēderent, Achillem cum Patroclō sedentem invēnērunt. Achillēs lyram increpābat, quam praedam ex urbe captā cēperat, et laudēs clārōrum virōrum canēbat. Cum lēgātōs vīdisset, dēmirātus ille exsiluit atque eōs studiōsē salūtāvit. Statim māgnum
5   hospitium, vīnum cibumque, eīs praebuit. Cēnā perfectā, Ulixēs dīcere incēpit. Nuntiāvit hostēs miserōs Danaōs in mare mox **āctūrōs esse**, Hectorem autem nāvēs incendere minārī. Tum Ulixēs illum obsecrāvit: "Danaōs adiuvā, nōs ex exitiō servā. Sī sērō adiuvēs, acerbē tē paenitēbit. Mementō quae verba pater tibi nāvigātūrō Trōiam **dīxerit**: 'Cavē īram et
10   temperantiā **ūtere**.' Sed tū haec oblītus es. Dēnique Agamemnōn īram nunc dīmīsit et etiam tē maximīs dōnīs dōnāre vult: aurō, argentō, equīs, septem fēminīs texendī perītīs. Praetereā vīgintī captīvās fēminās atque plūrima spolia praebet cum Trōia **capta erit**. Etiam partem rēgnī suī et fīliam nūptam tibi praebet. Postrēmō Brīsēida intactam reddet." Ulixēs
15   fīnīvit; callidē nōn nuntiāvit Agamemnonem postulāre sē rēgāliōrem vocārī.

Discussion Questions

1) Is Achilles's choice of booty what you would have expected?
2) What is the theme of Achilles's song? Can he gain this if he refuses to fight?
3) Are you surprised that Agamemnon relents from his anger?
4) What do you think of the generosity or extravagance of his promised gifts?
5) Do you think Achilles is interested in marrying into Agamemnon's family?

17 **iste, ista, istud** - *that one* (often in a derogatory or sarcastic sense)

ōdī, odisse (defective verb in perfect with present sense) - *to hate*

sentiat ... dīcat: subjunctives in relative clause of characteristic (See *Latin for the New Millennium*, Level 2, p. 508)

19 **grātiās agere** (+ dat. of person) (idiom) - *to thank*

īnsolenter (adv.) - *arrogantly, haughtily, insolently*

20 **occurrō, -ere, -currī, -cursum** (+ dat.) - *to hurry to meet, meet*

adsiduus, -a, -um - *continuous, constant*

perīclitor, -ārī, -ātus sum - *to be in danger, run a risk*

reportō (1) - *to take back, carry back*

21 **trādō, -ere, -didī, -itum** - *to hand over, deliver*

23 **rapiō, -ere, rapuī, raptum** - *to seize*

24 **quidem** (postpositive adv.) - *indeed*

bellum gerere (idiom) - *to wage war*

nōnne (interrogative adverb introducing questions expecting the answer "yes") - *is it not?*

25 **num** (interrogative adverb introducing questions expecting the answer "no") - *do?*

Atrīdēs, -ae, m. - *son of Atreus* (patronymic for Agamemnon and Menelaus)

26 **dehonestō** (1) - *to dishonor*

implōrō (1) - *to ask for help, implore*

prorsum (intensive adv.) - *altogether, completely*

29 **praesidium, -iī, n.** - *protection*

30 **crās** (adv.) - *tomorrow*

30–31 **lūx, lūcis, f.** - *light*

prīmā lūce: *at dawn*

31 **Phthīa, -ae, f.** - *Phthia*, home of Achilles in Thessaly, Greece

32 **impudēns, -ntis** - *shameless*

dēficiō, -ere, -fēcī, -fectum - *to withhold service from, desert*

33 **fraudō** (1) - *to cheat, defraud*

deciēns (indecl. noun + gen.) - here understood to be abl. - *ten times*

vīciēns (indecl. noun + gen.) - here understood to be abl. - *twenty times*

34 **luō, -ere, -uī** - *to pay, atone for*

GRAMMAR AND COMPREHENSION QUESTIONS

1) Why does Achilles use *istum* instead of *illum*? To whom does *istum* refer?
2) What case is *mē* with *ūsus est*?
3) What has happened to the spoils from the cities Achilles sacked?
4) What is the force of the different tenses in *rapuit et tenet*?
5) What mood is *implōret*? In what construction?
6) What mood are *servet* and *repellat*? What word introduces their construction?
7) How does Achilles claim Hector behaved when he himself was not fighting?
8) What case is *prīmā lūce*? In what construction?

Achillēs Ulixī respondit: "**Istum** ōdī quī aliud sentiat sed aliud dīcat. Mē Agamemnōn nōn persuādēbit quoniam mihi pugnantī hostēs suōs prō sē nūllās grātiās ēgit. Nunc **mē** etiam īnsolenter **ūsus est**. Mors ignāvō
20   et fortī mīlitī pariter occurrit. In pugnā adsiduē perīclitāns nihil reportō. Vīgintī et trēs urbēs prō istō cēpī, ē quibus plūrima spolia istī trādidī. Sī aliquid parvum tenēbam, hoc mihi satis faciēbat. At nunc ā mē sōlō praemium meum, fēminam cordī meō cāram, iste **rapuit et tenet**. Cūr quidem Danaī cum Trōiānīs bellum gerunt? Nōnne prō pulchrā Helenā?
25   Num Atrīdae sōlī uxōrēs suās amant? Nunc quoniam mē iste dēcēpit et dehonestat, mē numquam posteā **implōret**. Istum prorsus cōgnōvī; mē nōn persuādēbit."

"Cōnsilium ā tē, Ulixēs, et aliīs petat, quōmodo nāvēs ā igne **servet** et Hectorem **repellat**. Cum ego pugnārem, Hector ā praesidiō murōrum
30   longē exīre nōlēbat. Nunc cum Hectore pugnāre nōlō. Crās etiam, **prīmā lūce**, Phthīam nāvigābō. Ergō haec verba Agamemnonī omnibusque Danaīs nuntiā, ut aliī Danaī īrātī ā istō impudentī dēficiant, quī amicōs fraudat. Dōna eius contemnō. Sī deciēns aut vīciēns donōrum mē dōnet, Agamemnōn animum meum nōn plācēbit dum hanc contumēliam luat."

DISCUSSION QUESTIONS

1) Did Ulysses's speech have any positive effect?
2) How do you view Achilles's opinions of the equality of death in the context of the heroic ethic?
3) What sort of behavior is Achilles advocating among the Greek soldiers? What might you call this?

35	rēs - here, *possessions*		sileō, -ēre, -uī - *to be silent*
	anima, -ae, f. - *breath*		**dūrus, -a, -um** - *harsh, strong*
36	**ēmittō, -ere, -mīsī, -missum** - *to send out, let go, release*	45	**Pēleus, -ī, m.** - *Peleus;* king of Phthia and father of Achilles
37	**remaneam pugnemque:** subjunctives in subordinate clause in indirect statement	46	**indoctus, -a, -um** (+ gen.) - *untrained, unskilled in*
		47	**orbus, -a, -um** - *childless*
38	**sīn** (conj.) - *but if, if however*	49	**reprimō, -ere, -pressī, -pressum** - *to hold in check, repress, check*
39	**adsequor, -sequī, secūtus sum** - *to gain, win*		
		50	**velut** (adv.) - *just as*
	moneō, -ēre, -uī, -itum - *to advise, warn*	51	**tantum** (used as adverb) - *so much*
			etsī (conj.) - *even if*
40	**accendō, -ere, -cendī, -cēnsum** - *to stir up, arouse, inspire*	52	**haudquāquam** (adv.) - *not at all*
43	**stupefactus, -a, -um** - *stunned, amazed*		

Grammar and Comprehension Questions

1) In what construction are the infinitives *peritūrum esse, cōnsecūtūrum,* and *adsecūtūrum esse*? What introduces the construction?
2) What type of form is *dūrissimē*?
3) What type of construction is *ut . . . docērem*?
4) Why did Phoenix consider Achilles to be like a son?
5) What case is *dōnīs*? What is its function?
6) What tense and mood is *reppuleris*?
7) How has Jupiter honored Achilles?
8) What type of construction does *utrum* introduce?

35   "Multās rēs habeō et plūrēs cōnsequī possum; sed anima vītae

semel ēmissa recipī nōn potest. Māter mea dīxit duās sortēs mihi esse: sī

hīc remaneam pugnemque, mē **peritūrum esse**, sed aeternam glōriam

cōnsecūtūrum; sīn ad patriam redeam, nōn māgnam glōriam sed longam

vītam mē **adsecūtūrum esse.** Itaque aliōs moneō: domum rursum

40   nāvigāte, quoniam Iuppiter Trōiam dēfendit et Trōiānōs mīlitēs accendit.

Ergō īte et hoc respōnsum Danaīs nuntiāte; sed Phoenix, sī vult, mēcum

remaneat et Phthīam crās redeat."

    Hīs dictīs, trēs lēgātī stupefactī silēbant; nam Achillēs **dūrissimē**

dīxerat. Tandem Phoenix dīcere incēpit. "Sī īrātus domum redīre

45   dēcrēvistī, quōmodo ego, fīlī, hīc rēmanēbō? Nam Pēleus mē tēcum

ēmisit **ut** tē, indoctum pugnandī, fortissimē pugnāre et ēloquentissimē

dīcere **docērem.** Tum ut pater tē tōtō corde amābam, quoniam mē orbum

futūrum esse cōgnōveram. Itaque tē fīlium meum habēbam. Achillēs,

māgnam īram reprimē, nam etiam deī **dōnīs** movērī possunt.

50   Sī cum dōnīs ad pugnam nunc redīs, Danaī tē velut deum honōrābunt;

sīn sine dōnīs sērō redīs, nōn tantum tē honōrābunt etsī ignem ā nāvibus

reppuleris."

    Achillēs respondit: "Phoenix, pater, tālī honōre haudquāquam

indigeō; Iuppiter enim mē iam honōrat. Nōlī prō Agamemnone ōrāre

55   nē mē offendās. Sed hīc remanē et prīmā lūce cōnstituēmus **utrum** crās

domum redeāmus."

DISCUSSION QUESTIONS

1) Do you find Achilles's refusal to help selfish?
2) What unusual information does Achilles have about his own life?
3) What are Achilles's choices?
4) Is it true that Jupiter is defending Troy?
5) Do you find a change of tone between the speeches of Ulysses and
     Phoenix?

58 **praestat** (impersonal + inf.) - *it is better*

59 **obdūrescō, -ēscere, -uī** - *to harden*
pretium, -iī, n. - *blood price*
caedō, -ere, cecīdī, caesum - *to kill, murder*

60 **implācābilis, -e** - *that cannot be placated, relentless, implacable*
atquī (conj.) - *and yet, but yet*

61 **propitius, -a, -um** - *well-disposed, favorable, gracious*
es: singular imperative, *be*

63 **prūdēns, -ntis** - *sensible, prudent*
apud - *in the presence of, among*
reminiscor, -ī - *to recall to mind, recollect, remember*

66 **incendō, -ere, -cendī, -cēnsum** - *to set fire to, ignite*

68 **concilium, -iī, n.** - *council*
importūnus, -a, -um - *unfavorable, troublesome, grim*

69 **recūsō** (1) - *to reject*
in grātiam redīre: *to become reconciled*

Grammar and Comprehension Questions

1) What gender, number, and case are *haec mala*? What is their grammatical function?
2) What gender is *permulta alia*? Of what might the *permulta alia* consist?
3) What tense and mood follows *dum*? How then do you translate it?
4) What signal has Achilles established for his return to fighting?

Embassy to Achilles (Phoenix and Ulysses on the left of Achilles; Kleophrades painter, c. 480 BCE; Staatliche Antikensammlungen, Munich, Germany) (Public Domain)

Dēnique Aiāx locūtus est. "Ulixēs, eāmus. Nam nihil effēcimus.
Haec mala Danaīs celeriter nuntiāre praestat. Achillēs contrā nōs sē
obdūruit. Eum nōn intellegō; nam homō pretium caesī fīliī accipit,

60   sed is prō ūnā fēminā nōs in implācābilī odiō habet. Atquī **tibi** septem
fēminās praebēmus, et **permulta alia**. Propitius es; nōs, sociōs tuōs quī tē
honōrant, nunc aestimā et iuvā."

Achillēs respondit: "Omnia haec verba prūdentia videntur, at tamen
animus meus adhūc furit cum contumēliam apud Danaōs reminīscar. Ī

65   et hoc istī nuntiā: ad pugnam nōn redībō **dum** Hector oppugnāns nāvēs
meās incendat. Tum pugnābō; ibi Hector repellētur."

Itaque duo lēgātī ad Agamemnonem redīvērunt, sed Phoenix
remānsit. Ulixēs et Aiāx conciliō haec importūna nuntiāvit. "Achillēs
dōna recūsat et in grātiam nōn redībit." Tum ducēs Danaī trīstēs

70   dēspērābant.

Discussion Questions

1) Whom does Ajax first address? Why?
2) What is Ajax's style of speaking?
3) In Ajax's speech to whom does *tibi* change the address?
4) What conflict of behavior do you see in Achilles's response to Ajax?
5) Does Ajax's speech accomplish anything?
6) How successful was the embassy?

Chapter Seven

Spy Missions

After the failure of the embassy to Achilles, a sleepless Agamemnon wanted to call another council. Menelaus, also sleepless, met his brother and suggested that they send scouts into the Trojan camp to discover their plans. At the council Nestor repeats this suggestion. Diomedes volunteers and chooses Ulysses to accompany him, because he is crafty and the goddess Minerva protects him. Meanwhile, in the Trojan camp Hector also calls a council and suggests a spy mission into the Greek camp. He wants to know whether the Greeks are guarding their ships as before, or if they intend to flee. Dolon, eager to win the offered reward of a chariot and fine horses, volunteers. He asks for the horses of Achilles himself! This spy episode is a precursor of Vergil's story of Nisus and Euryalus in *Aeneid* 9. Also, the scene prepares for the negative treatment of Ulysses in many Greek authors, such as Sophocles, and in Vergil. The narration here begins as each warrior dresses for his mission.

SOURCE

Homer, *Iliad* 10

1 **Diomēdēs, -is, m.** - *Diomedes;* Greek hero, king of Argos

galērus, -ī, m. - *a cap or hat made of animal skin*

dē: abl. of source: *from, of*

taurus, -ī, m. - *bull*

induō, -ere, -duī, -dūtum - *to put on*

scorteus, -a, -um - *leather, made of leather*

2 **dēns, dentis, m.** - *tooth*

aper, aprī, m. - *wild boar*

> **galērum dentibus aprī aptum:** such artifacts have been found at Mycenae and in Crete dating from the 14th century BCE.

Dolon, -ōnis, m. - *Dolon;* Trojan spy (his Greek name means *trick, deceit*)

sagum, -ī, n. - *cloak,* especially a *military cloak*

lupus, -ī, m. - *wolf*

3 **mustēla, -ae, f.** - *weasel*

4 **leō, -ōnis, m.** - *lion*

vagor, -ārī, -ātus sum - *to wander, prowl*

ardea, -ae, f. - *heron*

5 **precor, -ārī, -ātus sum** (+ acc. + inf.) - *to pray to*

6 **approbō** (1) - *to approve*

campus, -ī, m. - *plain, open space*

cadāver, -eris, n. - *dead body, corpse, cadaver*

sternō, -ere, strāvī, strātum - *to strew, spread*

furtim (adv.) - *secretly, stealthily*

8 **cēlō** (1) - *to hide, conceal*

praetereō, -īre, -iī, -ītum - *to pass by, go past*

incurrō, -ere, -currī, -cursum - *to rush at, charge at, attack*

9 **tergum, -ī, n.** - *back*

> **ā tergō**: *from behind*

10 **pulsō** (1) - *to beat, pound*

11 **iactō** (1) - *to throw, hurl*

cōnsultō (adverbial) - *on purpose, intentionally*

feriō, -īre - *to strike, hit*

sistō, -ere, stetī, statum - *to stop*

12 **fuga, -ae, f.** - *flight, escape*

revertor, -ī, -versus sum - *to turn round, back*

13 **crepitō** (1) - *to chatter, rattle*

balbūtiō, -īre - *to stammer*

vīvus, -a, -um - *alive, living*

pretium, -iī, n. - *price*

14 **redimō, -ere, -ēmī, -emptum** - *to buy back, ransom*

Grammar and Comprehension Questions

1) How do the nouns *sagum* and *pellem* relate to one another?
2) What word does *missae* modify?
3) What is the effect of changing to the present tense with *intrant*?
4) What mood does *dum* take? How then is *dum* translated?
5) What exact form is *celerius*?
6) What case is *māgnō pretiō*? What is its grammatical function?

Hērōs Diomēdēs galērum dē pelle taurī induit; Ulixēs scorteum galērum dentibus aprī aptum. Trōiānus Dolōn **sagum pellem** lupī et galērum dē pelle mustēlae induit. Diomēdēs Ulixēsque Graeca castra discessērunt ut duo leōnēs vagantēs. Vōce ardeae ā Minervā **missae**
5   ductī sunt. Ulixēs igitur Minervam precātus est eōs adiuvāre; Diomēdēs precem etiam approbāvit. Campum cadāveribus strātum **intrant**. Furtim prōgredientēs aliquem accēdentem vident. Statim Ulixēs Diomēdēsque dēcernunt sē in tenebrīs cēlāre **dum** ille praetereat. Nam volunt incurrere illum ā tergō et capere inter Graeca castra et sē. Cum Dolōn pedēs
10   pulsantēs ā tergō audiat, **celerius** currit, sed Danaī etiam celerius currunt. Tum Diomēdēs hastam iactāns eum cōnsultō nōn ferit et clāmat: "Siste fugam vel haec secunda hasta tē feriet." Dolōn stāns revertēnsque Danaōs videt et, dentibus timōre crepitantibus, balbūtit: "Vīvum mē capite. Pater mē **māgnō pretiō** redimet."

DISCUSSION QUESTIONS

1) Why did Odysseus and Diomedes not wear their normal helmets?
2) Do you think the difference in material of the three warriors' equipment is significant? How might his material characterize each?
3) Why didn't Diomedes kill Dolon with his first throw?

17   **genū, -ūs, n.** - *knee*
     tremō, -ere, -uī - *to tremble, quake*
19   **age**: (idiom) - *come, come on*
20   **dispōnō, -ere, -posuī, -positum**
     - *to distribute, arrange, set out,*
     organize
21   **statiō, -ōnis, f.** - *post, military*
     position
     explicō (1) - *to make clear, known*
22   **Thrax, Thrācis, m.** (also adj.) -
     Thracian, from Thrace, area at the
     north of the Aegean sea west of
     the Hellespont
     Rhēsus, -ī, m. - *Rhesus*, king of
     Thrace. (There had been an
     oracle that if Rhesus and his
     horses drank from the Trojan
     river Scamander they would
     be invincible. Thus Minerva,
     the Greek supporter, wanted to
     eliminate them from the war.)

     nūper (adv.) - *recently*
23   **candidus, -a, -um** - *bright, white*
     nix, nivis, f. - *snow*
     currus, -ūs, m. - *chariot*
     aureus, -a, -um - *of gold, golden*
25   **ater, atra, atrum** - *black, dark, grim,*
     dreadful
     dīmittō, -ere, -mīsī, -missum - *to let*
     go, dismiss
26   **praestāns, -ntis** - *exceptional,*
     excellent
27   **speculor, -ārī, -ātus sum** - *to spy,*
     reconnoiter
     sīn (conj.) - *but if, if however*
     noceō, -ēre, -uī, -itum (+ dat.) - *to*
     harm, hurt, damage

GRAMMAR AND COMPREHENSION QUESTIONS

    1) What construction is *genibus trementibus*?
    2) What other word correlates with *utrum* in this construction?
    3) What case and function is *eīs*?
    4) What is the antecedent of *cuī*?
    5) What verb must you understand in the phrase *cuī . . . arma* to
        complete the meaning?
    6) To whom does *sē* refer?
    7) What gender, number, and case is *praestantia*?

15   Nunc Ulixēs respondit: "Nōlī timēre nec mortem cōgitāre. Sed
        nōbīs dīc cūr hīc vēnerīs." Dolōn **genibus trementibus:** "Hector mē in
        errōrem indūxit; nam equōs Achillis mihi prōmīsit, sī inveniam **utrum**
        Danaī nāvēs adhūc dēfendant an fugere in animō habeant." Ulixēs rīsit.
        "Māgnifica dōna sunt equī Achillis. At nunc age, haec mihi exactē dīc: ubi
20   Hector est? Ubi Trōiānī mīlitēs et sociī dispositī sunt? Quae cōnsilia **eīs**
        sunt?" Tum Dolōn omnēs statiōnēs Trōiānōrum et sociōrum explicāvit.
        Addidit autem Thrācēs mīlitēs cum rēge Rhēsō nūper vēnisse, **cui**
        pulcherrimī equī candidiōrēs nive atque māgnificus currus et aurea **arma.**
        Dēnique ōrāvit ut sē līberārent cum **sē** omnia vērē dīxisse invēnissent.
25   Sed Diomēdēs ātrī vultū locūtus est: "Dīmitte spem fugae, quamquam
        praestantia nōbīs nuntiāvistī. Nam sī tē līberāverimus, iterum
        speculāberis. Sīn nunc moriēris, numquam iterum nōbīs nocēbis."

Discussion Questions

1) How do you interpret Ulysses's smile?
2) What do you think of Dolon placing the blame on Hector? How does
   this affect your impression of him?
3) Why does Dolon give the information about Rhesus, for which he
   was not asked?

28   **mentum, -ī, n.** - *chin*

     tangere mentum: to touch or grasp the chin, especially by the beard, was part of the formal gesture of supplication, which also involved encircling the knees with the other hand.

     supplicō (1) - *to supplicate, beg, ask for mercy*

29   **collum, -ī, n.** - *neck*

     pulvis, -eris, m. - *dust*

30   **spoliō** (1) - *to strip, strip off*

     arcus, -ūs, m. - *bow*

31   **tropaeum, -ī, n.** - *trophy,* made by hanging the enemy's armor from a tree or on a cross-like post

32   **quō** (adv.) - *to where*

33   **fessus, -a, -um** - *exhausted, wearied*

     duodecim (indecl. adj.) - *twelve*

34   **ovis, -is, f.** - *sheep*

     caper, -prī, m. - *goat*

     -ve (conj.) - *or*

     intereā (adv.) - *meanwhile*

36   **purgō** (1) - *to clear*

     negōtium, -iī, n. - *trouble*

37   **somniō** (1) - *to dream*

38   **spolium, -iī, n.** - *spoil, booty*

39   **onustus, -a, -um** - *laden, weighed down*

40   **levō** (1) - *to lighten, relieve*

GRAMMAR AND COMPREHENSION QUESTIONS

1) What happens to the head of Dolon?
2) What did the Greeks do with Dolon's equipment?
3) With what word does *fessōs* agree?
4) Why were the Thracians so weary?
5) What poetic device is *ut leō . . . incurrēns*?
6) How do you translate *medius*? Where was Rhesus?
7) What case is *videntēs* and with which word does it agree?

Dolōn tum tangere mentum eius temptābat ut supplicāret, sed
Diomēdēs collum illius gladiō percussit, et caput in pulverem cecidit. Duo
30   mīlitēs sagum galērumque spoliāvērunt atque arcum hastamque cēperunt
ut tropaeum Minervae facerent. Ulixēs deam ita precātus est: "Dūc
nōs quō Thrācēs equīque iacent." Ductī ā deā mox ad Thrācēs, itinere
proeliōque **fessōs**, accessērunt. Diomēdēs ā Minervā firmātus duodecim
Thrācēs interfēcit **ut leō** in ovēs caprōsve **incurrēns**. Intereā **medius**
35   Rhēsus dormiēbat; equī hunc circumībant. Ulixēs per cadāverēs viam
purgābat ut equōs nūllō negōtiō dūceret. Deinde Rhēsum, quī dē aliquō
malō somniābat, decimum et tertium Diomēdēs interfēcit. Dum cōgitant
utrum plūria spolia capiant, Minerva Diomēdī Ulixīque locūta est: "Ad
nāvēs redīte." Deae pārentēs spoliīs onustī rediērunt. Danaī eōs **videntēs**
40   gaudēbant. Itaque animī Danaum māgnopere levābantur.

DISCUSSION QUESTIONS

1) How trustworthy were Ulysses's words?
2) What was the ancient view about killing a suppliant? Was Dolon
technically a suppliant?
3) Do you think there is any significance that Rhesus is Diomedes's
thirteenth victim?

Cultural Influences

Art: Painting by Anthony van Dyck, (Patroclus with) "The Horses of Achilles" (1650/1700 or later). The Museum of Fine Arts, Boston houses an enormous painting (124" x 129.5") by Henri Regnault (1868), "Automedon with the horses of Achilles." Automedon was Achilles's charioteer. The museum also has a number of preliminary sketches. Gustave Mercier produced a print with the same title. There is a Graeco-Roman era intaglio ring of Odysseus, Dolon, and Diomedes in which Dolon supplicates Odysseus while Diomedes stands ready with his sword. J.H.W. Tischbein engraved "Diomedes and Odysseus Capturing Dolon."

Literature: Dante in *Inferno, Canto* 26.55–63 depicts Ulysses and Diomedes wrapped in a single flame. There are drawings of this scene by Sandro Botticelli (1490s), and John Flaxman (c. 1792), and a watercolor by William Blake (1824–27).

Dolon as a spy attempts to conceal himself by wearing a wolf pelt (c. 460 BCE; Louvre Museum, Paris, France) (© Creative Common 3.0/Saiko)

Chapter Eight

A Deadly Suggestion

After the spy missions, day dawns and the battle recommences. With Agamemnon leading the way, the Greeks charge. Hector receives a divine message not to fight until Agamemnon is wounded, which soon occurs. Thus Hector re-enters the battle and is opposed by Diomedes and Ulysses. Diomedes is wounded by Paris (a surprising development) and retreats. Ulysses is surrounded by Trojans and wounded; Menelaus and Ajax rescue him. Now three of the greatest Greek warriors are unable to fight, and the situation looks increasingly desperate. Then Machaon, the Greek physician, is wounded and taken back to the ships by Nestor. Achilles, himself also an expert healer taught by the centaur Chiron, was watching from his camp. Here he asks Patroclus to go to Nestor's tent to see if the wounded warrior is really Machaon.

Source

Homer, *Iliad* 11

1 **Menoetius, -iī, m.** - *Menoetius;* father of Patroclus

2 **genū, -ūs, n.** - *knee*

supplicō (1) - *to supplicate, beg, ask for mercy*

3 **tergum, -ī, n.** - *back*

4 **Machāon, -onos, m.** (Greek acc. **Machāona**) - *Machaon;* the main Greek physician

5 **saliō, -īre, -uī, saltum** - *to jump, leap*

6 **prehendō, -ere, -dī, -sum** - *to take hold of, grasp*

8 **īrācundus, -a, -um** - *prone to anger, hot-tempered, irascible*

11 **alicuī innocentī**: dative with *īrāscitur*

12 **cūrae Achillī**: datives in the double dative construction (see *Latin for the New Millennium*, Level 2, p. 494) - a dative of purpose plus a dative of the person involved

nihil (adv.) - *not at all, in no way*

misereor, -ērī, -itus sum - *to pity, feel sorry for*

15 **dēnuō** (adv.) - *for a second time, again, anew*

GRAMMAR AND COMPREHENSION QUESTIONS

1) What word needs to be understood with *locūtus* to complete the meaning?
2) *Fīlī Menoetiī* is a patronymic. Who else is referred to by his patronymic?
3) What form is *ventūrōs esse*? In what construction?
4) Do you find it unusual that the physician was actively fighting on the battlefield?
5) What type of pronoun is *quem*?
6) What tense and mood are *redūxistī*? In what construction?
7) What gender is *hoc* and to what does it refer?
8) What mood follows *dum* and how therefore is it translated?
9) What signal hinted at here in *dum nāvēs ignī cōnsumantur* might inspire Achilles to fight again?
10) What tense and mood are *essem*? In what construction?

Patroclō Achillēs **locūtus**: "**Fīlī Menoetiī**, mihi cāre, nunc cōgitō
Danaōs ad genua mea **ventūrōs esse** ut supplicent. At ad Nestorem
curre et rogā quem vulnerātum ē proeliō redūcerit. Ā tergō crēdō hunc
esse Machāona, sed faciem nōn vīdī." Amīcō pārēns Patroclus
5   ad tabernāculum Nestoris cucurrit. Nestor eum vidēns dē sēde saluit
et manum prehendēns indūxit et eum sedēre ōrāvit. Patroclus autem
negāvit. "Nōn sedēbō, optime. Mihi nōn persuadēbis. Praeclārus
īrācundusque est Achillēs quī mē mīsit. Nam cōgnōscere voluit **quem**
vulnerātum ē proeliō **redūxistī**. Nunc quoniam intellegō Machāona
10   vulnerātum esse, **hoc** Achillī nuntiābō. Ipse enim cōgnōvistī quam ille sē
gerat: interdum alicuī innocentī īrāscitur." Tum Nestor respondit: "Cūr
nunc Danaī cūrae Achillī sunt? Nihil intellegit quanta mala patiāmur.
Achillēs, etsī fortis, dē Danaīs nihil cūrat neque miserētur. Exspectatne
dum nāvēs ignī cōnsumantur aut omnēs Danaī occidāmur? Utinam
15   dēnuō adulēscēns **essem** qualis eram cum ferōcēs hostēs vincēns māgnam
glōriam cōnsequerer."

DISCUSSION QUESTIONS

1) How does Achilles want the Greeks to treat him? Does this make
sense in the context of the embassy?
2) Why would the wounding of the physician Machaon be particularly
significant?
3) What does it indicate when Nestor quickly rises from his chair at
Patroclus's appearance?
4) How do Patroclus's comments characterize Achilles? Is this
characterization consistent with his behavior so far?

18 **impatiēns, -ntis** (+ gen.) - *impatient (of)*
   mora, -ae, f. - *delay*
   reverenter (adv.) - *with respect, respectfully*
   conclūdō, -ere, -clūsī, -clūsum - *to conclude, finish*
19 **sōlitārius, -a, -um** - *alone, lonely*
20 **sērō** (adv.) - *late, too late*
   comes, -itis, m. - *companion, associate, friend*
   Mementō: singular imperative of *meminī*
22 **genus, -eris, n.** - *birth, parentage*
   nātū (abl. s. m.) - *by/in birth, age*
23 **oportet** (impersonal + acc. + inf.) - *it is right, proper that*
   prūdēns, -ntis - *prudent, sensible*

25 **quodsī** (conj.) - *but if*
   praedictum, -ī, n. - *prediction, prophecy*
26 **saltem** (adv.) - *at least*
   Myrmidonēs, -um, m. pl. - *Myrmidons;* the warriors of Achilles, named for their descent from ants! See Ovid, *Metamorphoses* 7.517–657 for the story.
27 **recēdō, -ere, -cessī, -cessum** - *to withdraw, draw back*
28 **integer, -gra, -grum** - *unimpaired, fresh*
   colligō, -ere, -lēgī, -lectum - *to gather together, assemble*
   sē colligere: *to pull oneself together, refresh, recover*

GRAMMAR AND COMPREHENSION QUESTIONS

1) What construction is *Nestore longam historiam dīcente*?
2) Why does Patroclus continue to listen to Nestor's long-winded story?
3) What person and number is *audīvimus*? Who is the subject?
4) What case is *genere*? What is the function of the case here?
5) What gender, number, and case is *haec*? To what does it refer?
6) What word does *gerentem* modify?
7) What is the ruse that Nestor is trying to engineer against the Trojans?
8) Why is it essential that Patroclus wear the arms of Achilles?

Nestore longam historiam dīcente, Patroclus, quamquam impatiēns morae, reverenter audiēbat. Nestor tum conclūsit: "Tum omnēs virī Nestorem honōrābant. At sōlitārius Achillēs virtūte suā fruētur et
20 multum et sērō flēbit cum omnēs comitēs mortuī sint. Mementō quae verba tibi pater dīxerit cum tē Achillemque Trōiam mīserit. Nam Ulixēs et ego haec **audīvimus.** 'Achillēs **genere** nōbilior est; tū autem nātū senior es. Vīrēs illius etiam multō māiōrēs, sed oportet tē illī prūdenter dīcere et bene monēre.' Sed **haec** oblītus es. Iam nunc tē audiēns Achillēs
25 persuādērī potest. Quodsī propter aliquod praedictum in proelium nōn reveniet, rogā ut tē saltem arma Achillis **gerentem** cum Myrmidonibus ēmittat. Fortasse Trōiānī tē esse Achillem putābunt et recēdent. Nam tū integer plūrimōs mīlitēs in Trōiam repellere poteris ut Danaī sē colligere possint." Tum Patroclus excitātus ad Achillem recurrit.

DISCUSSION QUESTIONS

1) Why does Nestor decide to tell a long-winded story of his own valor to Patroclus? What else might be going on in his mind?
2) What moral do you draw from Nestor's story?
3) Who else reminded someone of his father's words on the departure from Phthia?
4) Has there been some other *praedictum* that is keeping Achilles from battle?
5) How does Nestor appeal to Patroclus himself?

Achilles tends to the wounded Patroclus (Sosias painter, c. 500 BCE; Staatliche Antikensammlungen, Berlin, Germany) (Public Domain)

Chapter Nine

THE HEROIC CODE AND JUPITER'S EDICT

Homer does not immediately allow the audience to see the results of Nestor's suggestion. As Patroclus hastens from Nestor's tent, he meets a wounded friend who asks him for first aid. Patroclus cannot refuse and thus is delayed. During this delay Homer, in Books 12–15, shows Jupiter fulfilling his promise to Achilles. The situation becomes significantly worse for the Greeks. The Trojans are massed outside the new Greek fortifications. Jupiter decides to give glory to his mortal son Sarpedon, lord of the Lycians, since he is soon doomed to die. In the first part of this chapter, Sarpedon speaks to his battle-companion Glaucus about their duty as warriors and leaders.

After this speech Sarpedon grabbed hold of the battlement and wrenched away a great portion. This was the first breach in the Greek defenses. The battle raged about the walls with significant casualties on both sides. At the end of Book 12 (half-way through the epic) Hector hurled a monstrous stone against the Greek gate. The gate splintered, and, as Hector burst into the Greek camp, he called to the other Trojans to follow and burn the Greek ships. Of course, the Greeks are fated to defeat Troy, and in Books 13–14 the pro-Greek gods, in defiance of Jupiter, wreak havoc upon the Trojan troops. (Juno has seduced Jupiter and caused him to be put to sleep to keep him out of the action!) During the melee Hector is wounded by Ajax. As Book 15 opens, Jupiter wakens and is enraged to find what the gods have engineered while he slept. He then delivers an edict that summarizes much of the rest of the epic. His speech is the second part of this chapter.

SOURCE

Homer, *Iliad* 12, 15

2 **pōculum, -ī, n.** - *cup, drinking vessel*
suāvis, -e - *sweet, pleasant, tasty*
pinguis, -e - *rich, fertile*
Lyciī, -ōrum, m. pl. - *the Lycians, allies of the Trojans from what is now southern Turkey*

3 **nostrum est** (idiom + inf.) - *it is our duty*
frōns, frontis, f. - *brow, forehead*
in fronte prīmā (idiom) - *in the first rank*

4 **dūrus, -a, -um** - *harsh, hard*

5 **ignāvus, -a, -um** - *cowardly*
ovis, -is, f. - *sheep*
vescor, -ī (+ abl.) - *to feed on, enjoy*

7 **fingō, -ere, finxī, fictum** - *to imagine, suppose*

fugientēs: *avoiding, escaping, surviving*
iuvenis, -is, m. - *youth*

9 **niger, -gra, -grum** - *black, dark*
mānēs, -ium, m. pl. - *spirits of the dead, shades*

10 **circumstō, -stāre, -stetī** - *to stand round, surround*
āvertō, -ere, -vertī, -versum - *to turn away, aside; keep off, avert*
pergō, -ere, -rexī, -rectum - *to continue, proceed*

11 **tradō, -ere, -didī, -ditum** - *to give over, surrender*

Grammar and Comprehension Questions

1) What case is *nōs*? What is its function?
2) What are the benefits of being a hero?
3) What tense is *loquētur*?
4) On what word does *posse* depend?
5) What mood and tense are *pugnārem* and *hortārer*? Why? What does the mood indicate? Consider this question in the context of the previous sentence.
6) What inspires Sarpedon to fight?

"Glauce, cūr tē mēque omnēs aliī honōrant? Nam nōbīs optimam carnem, pōcula suāvis vīnī, et pinguēs agrōs Lyciī dant. **Nōs ut** immortālēs habent. Ergō nostrum est in fronte prīmā Lyciōrum locum stāre et dūrī proeliī partem capere. Itaque aliquis Lyciōrum **loquētur**:

5 'Vērē hī dominī nostrī nōn sunt ignāvī quī pinguibus ovibus vescuntur et suāve vīnum bibunt, quoniam fortēs in fronte prīmā Lyciōrum pugnant.' Finge, amīce, nōs hoc bellum fugientēs semper vīvere immortālēs iuvenēs **posse**. Tum nec ego in prīmā fronte **pugnārem** nec tē **hortārer** ut pugnēs et glōriam cōnsequāris. At nunc, cum innumerābilēs nigrī mānēs nōs

10 circumstent, quōs nēmō āvertere vel fugere potest, pergēmus. Aut glōriam prō nōbīs quaerēmus aut eam aliīs tradāmus."

DISCUSSION QUESTIONS

1) What does Sarpedon fantasize for himself and Glaucus? Can you think of similar fantasies?
2) What does Sarpedon sense surrounds them? What might this indicate about his sense of his future?

12 **Phoebus, -ī, m.** -*Phoebus,* an epithet of Apollo that means "shining" in Greek

sagittārius, -ī, m. - *archer, bowman*

sānus, -a, -um - *sound, healthy*

13 **īnspīrō** (1) - *to breathe into*

14 **dēbilis, -e** - *enfeebling, strengthless*

pavor, -ōris, m. - *sudden fear, terror, fright*

sternō, -ere, strāvī, strātum - *to scatter, strew*

15 **revertor, -ī, -versus sum** - *to turn round and go back, retreat*

17 **Sarpēdōn, -onis, m.** - *Sarpedon;* king of the Lycians, son of Zeus

18 **inde** (adv.) - *then, next*

20 **adsistō, -ere, -stitī** - *to stand by, near*

21 **perficiō, -ere, -fēcī, -fectum** - *to complete, accomplish*

adnuō, -ere, -uī, -ūtum (+ dat.) - *to nod assent to, agree to, grant*

22 **praedātor, -ōris, m.** - *plunderer, pillager*

GRAMMAR AND COMPREHENSION QUESTIONS

1) What mood is *īnspīrēs*?
2) What is the antecedent of *quī?*
3) What tense is *occīdet?*
4) What tense is *occīdit?*
5) What do the *cōnsiliīs Minervae* refer to?
6) What tense is *perfecta erit?*
7) To what does *eī* refer?

Hera and Zeus on his throne on Mt. Ida (Temple E at Selinus, Sicily, mid-6th century BCE; Brooklyn Museum, New York) (© Creative Commons 2.5/Giovanni Dall'Orto)

Iuppiter prōnuntiat: "Phoebe Apollō, illūstris **sagittārī, sānō** Hectorī
vīrēs **inspīrēs** ut dolōris oblīvīscatur, **quī** eum nunc fatīgat. Hector,
proelium iterum intrāns, dēbilem pavōrem in Danaīs sternat
15 ut revertantur et in fugam ad nāvēs Achillis agantur. Deinde Achillēs
comitem Patroclum ēmittet. Sed eum hastā illūstris Hector **occīdet,**
postquam ille plūrimōs et splendidum Sarpēdonem, fīlium meum
occīdit. Prō Patroclō īrātus Achillēs tum Hectorem occīdet. Inde pugnam
ā nāvibus repellam dum Danaī Trōiam **cōnsiliīs Minervae** capiant. Ante
20 īram nōn dēsinam nec sīnam ūllum deum Danaōs adsistere dum prex
Achillis **perfecta erit.** Nam **eī** adnuī illō diē cum Thetis genua amplectāns
honōrem Achillī, praedātōrī urbium, orāret."

DISCUSSION QUESTIONS

1) In what other context do you find the word *sagittārius*?
2) What does the word *sānō* indicate will happen to Hector?
3) Where will the Greek rout end?
4) Why did Thetis embrace Jupiter's knees?
5) What epithets do you find in this selection?
6) How active a role does Jupiter play in the action?
7) Does Homer leave any room for suspense in the remainder of the
   epic?

Chapter Ten

PATROCLUS DONS THE ARMOR OF ACHILLES

After Jupiter's edict, much of the action of the previous two books is undone. Apollo heals Hector and leads him back into the battle. The Trojans re-enter the Greek camp and are on the point of setting fire to the ships. Here finally Homer returns to Patroclus and the suggestion of Nestor. The request that Patroclus makes and that Achilles grants seems simple enough, but it leads to tremendous consequences that play out in the remainder of the epic. The action sets in motion a domino effect as one death on the battlefield triggers another and another. This reading begins as Achilles meets Patroclus returning to his tent.

SOURCE

Homer, *Iliad* 16

1 **parvulus, -a, -um** (diminutive) - *tiny, very little*

2 **miseror, -ārī, -ātus sum** (+ gen.) - *to pity, feel sorry for*

   ob (prep. + acc.) - *on account of, because of*

3 **gemō, -ere, -uī, -itum** - *to groan*

5 **saucius, -a, -um** - *wounded*

   cuī tēcum aliquid est: idiom, *Who can do anything with you?*

6 **tantopere** (adv.) - *so greatly*

   immītis, -e - *harsh, merciless, unfeeling*

   quodsī (conj.) - *but if*

   praedictum, -ī, n. - *prophecy, prediction*

7 **Myrmidonēs, -um, m. pl.** - *the Myrmidons*; the people of Achilles, named for their descent from ants!

8 **colligō, -ere, -ēgī, -ectum** - reflexive use: *to pull oneself together, recover*

9 **integer, -gra, -grum** - *untouched, unhurt, whole*

10 **simplex, -icis** - *innocent, naive*

    perniciēs, -ēī, f. - *destruction, ruin*

11 **sollicitus, -a, -um** - *troubled, anxious*

12 **vexō** (1) - *to trouble, upset*

aequālis, -is, m./f. - *an equal*

13 **auctōritās, -tātis, f.** - *position of authority, influence*

    praeteritus, -a, -um - *past, bygone, over*

14 **habēbō** (idiom with *praeteritum*) - *I will consider*

    atquī (conj.) - *but, and yet, nevertheless*

    profiteor, -ērī, -fessus sum - *to state openly, declare, avow*

16 **induō, -ere, -duī, -dūtum** - *to put on, don, wear*

    cupidus, -a, -um (+ gen.) - *desirous of, eager for*

17 **incendō, -ere, -cendī, -censum** - *to set fire to, inflame*

    reditus, -ūs, m. - *homecoming, return*

18 **dētrimentum, -ī, n.** - *damage, detriment, loss*

19 **satisfaciō, -ere, -fēcī, -fectum** - *to give satisfaction, make amends for*

21 **minuō, -ere, -uī, -ūtum** - *to lessen, diminish*

    oportet, -ere, oportuit (impersonal; + acc. + inf.) - *it is fitting, right*

22 **obruō, -ere, -ruī, -rutum** - *to overwhelm, crush*

GRAMMAR AND COMPREHENSION QUESTIONS

1) What mood is *īrāscar*? In what construction?

2) What mood is *possint*? What use of the mood is this?

3) What gender, number, and case is *hoc*? To what does it refer?

4) What gender, number, and case is *istī*? To whom does Achilles refer?

5) What gender and case is *istī* here? What is its grammatical function?

6) What tense and mood is *reppuleris*?

7) What case is *tibi*? Why?

8) What is Achilles's wish for himself and Patroclus?

"Patrocle, cūr flēs ut parvula puella? Aliquod malum in Phthīā audīvistī? Aut Danaum miserāris quī ob dēmentiam suam moriuntur?" Gemēns Patroclus respondit: "Fīlī Peleī, multō praeclārissime Danaum, Achillēs, nōlī īrāscī. Tantus dolor Danaīs accidit. Omnēs fortissimī

5 ducēs sauciī pugnāre nōn possunt. At tū, Achillēs, cuī tēcum aliquid est? Nē tantopere **īrāscar**! Immītis es. Quodsī propter aliquod praedictum pugnāre nōn vīs, mē saltem cum Myrmidonibus ēmitte. Et arma tua mihi dā ut Trōiānī mē esse tē fortasse putent et recēdent. Ita Danaī sē colligere **possint**. Nam nōs integrī plūrimōs mīlitēs Trōiam repellere possint." Ita

10 simplex Patroclus supplicābat, sed mortem perniciemque suam ōrābat.

Graviter sollicitus Achillēs respondit: "Quid dīcis? Nam **hoc** animum acriter vexat, cum aliquis aliquō aequālī īnsolenter ūtātur et praemium recipit quia **istī** māior auctōritās est. Tamen hoc praeteritum nunc habēbō. Semper īrāscī in animō nōn habēbam. Atquī professus sum mē

15 īram nōn dēsitūrum esse dum pugna ad nāvem meam perveniat. Itaque māgnifica arma mea indue et Myrmidonēs proeliī cupidōs ēdūc. Nē **istī** nāvem nostram incendentēs reditum nostrum auferant. Sed mihi parē ut māgnam glōriam mihi cōnsequāris et Danaī mihi prō dētrimentō satisfaciant. Cum ignem ā nāvibus **reppuleris**, revenī. Quamquam

20 Iuppiter glōriam tibi det, sine mē **tibi** nōn pugnandum est. Ita enim honōrem meum minuēs. Nōn oportet tē mīlitēs contrā Trōiam dūcere nē aliquī deus tē obruat. Utinam tū egoque sōlī Trōiam capiāmus."

DISCUSSION QUESTIONS

1) Is Achilles's criticism of Patroclus for weeping justified?
2) What bad news might Patroclus have heard from Phthia?
3) Does Achilles know that Nestor made the suggestion?
4) Did it seem to you that Achilles intended his anger to be temporary?
5) How does the suggestion allow Achilles to save face? Why does he agree?
6) Does Achilles seem selfish in his commands to Patroclus? Or does he simply want to share glory with his friend? Or is he worried about him fighting alone?

23 **sudō** (1) - *to sweat, perspire*
    spīritus, -ūs, m. - *breath, breathing*
    aegrē (adv.) - *with difficulty, hardly,
    scarcely*
24 **adstō, -stāre, -stitī** - *to stand near*
25 **cuspis, -idis, f.** - *sharp point, tip*
    dirimō, -ere, -ēmī, -emptum - *to
    separate, cut off*
    inermis, -e - *unarmed, defenseless*
26 **edax, -ācis** - *voracious, devouring,
    destructive*
    femor, -oris, n. - *thigh*
27 **proficīscor, -ī, -fectus sum** - *to set
    out, start*
28 **sūmō, -ere, sūmpsī, sumptum** - *to
    take, take up*
29 **ocrea, -ae, f.** - *greave* (protection for
    lower leg)
    lōrīca, -ae, f. - *corselet* (chest
    protector)
    aēneus, -a, -um - *made of bronze,
    bronze*
30 **scūtum, -ī, n.** - *shield*
31 **adloquor, -quī, -cūtus sum** - *to
    speak to, address*

32 **meminī, meminisse** (defective verb)
    - *to remember*
33 **invītus, -a, -um** - *unwilling*
    ad: *by, near*
    retineō, -ēre, -tinuī, -tentum - *to
    keep, retain*
35 **commoveō, -ēre, -mōvī, -mōtum** -
    to stir up, rouse
    instruō, -ere, -struxī, -structum - *to
    equip, draw up*
37 **praecipuus, -a, -um** - *special,
    exceptional*
    pōculum, -ī, n. - *cup*
    arca, -ae, f. - *chest, box*
    impleō, -ēre, -plēvī, -plētum - *to fill
    up*
40 **īnspīrō** (1) (+ dat.) - *to breathe in,
    infuse*
41 **inviolātus, -a, -um** - *unharmed,
    uninjured*
43 **concēdō, -ere, -cessī, -cessum** - *to
    allow, grant*

Grammar and Comprehension Questions

1) To what prior actions does *haec* refer?
2) What form is *proficīscere*? (See *Latin for the New Millennium*, Level 2, p. 508.)
3) What construction is *nāvēs . . . nōn dēlendae sunt*?
4) Why didn't Patroclus take Achilles's spear?
5) What type of subjunctive are both *pugnēmus* and *redeāmus*?
6) What attitude does Achilles reveal that his own Myrmidons had towards him?
7) How did Jupiter honor Achilles in the past?
8) Who is meant by *comitem*?

Intereā Aiax sudāns et spīritum aegrē dūcēns contrā Hectorem et
Trōiānōs vix nāvēs dēfendēbat. Tum Hector adstāns hastam eius gladiō
25 percussit ut cuspis dirimerētur. Nunc inermis hērōs recessit. Trōiānī
edācem ignem in nāvēs iēcērunt. **Haec** vidēns Achillēs femora manibus
percussit et clāmāvit: "**Proficīscere**, Patrocle. **Nāvēs** nostrae igne **nōn
dēlendae sunt**. Arma sūme. Ego Myrmidonēs convocābō."

Patroclus arma Achillis induit: ocreās, lōrīcam, galeam, et aēneum
30 gladium scūtumque sūmpsit; sed hastam eius nōn sūmpsit—nam sōlus
Achillēs hāc ūtī poterat. Tum Achillēs Myrmidonēs adlocūtus est:
"Meminī vōs contrā mē diū murmurāre: 'Īrātus nostrī nōn miserāris
quoniam nōs invītōs ad nāvēs retinēs. Aut **pugnēmus** aut domum
redeāmus.' At nunc tempus est cum Trōiānīs pugnāre." Ita animōs
35 mīlitum commōvit, quī ad pugnam sē instruxērunt.

Sed Achillēs in tabernāculum recessit ut Iovem precārētur.
Praecipuum pōculum ex arcā sustulit, vīnō implēvit et vocāvit: "Iuppiter
omnipotēns, cum ante precātus sim, audiēns mē honorāvistī. Nunc etiam
precem meam tribue. Ego ipse ad nāvēs remaneō, sed **comitem** meum
40 cum omnibus Myrmidonibus ēmittō. Eī vīrēs īnspīrēs ut māgna glōria
eum sequātur. Sed, cum ille ignem ā nāvibus reppulerit, inviolātus cum
armīs et omnibus comitibus ad mē reveniat." Sīc precātus est, et Iuppiter
eum audīvit. Prīmam precem concessit, sed secundam negāvit. Achillēs
tum pōculum reposuit et exīvit ut proelium spectāret.

Discussion Questions

1) What acts as a signal to Achilles so that he immediately sends
Patroclus into battle?
2) What was Patroclus supposed to do when he had quenched the fire?
3) Was Achilles aware that Jupiter refused the second part of his
prayer?

45   **vorax, -ācis** - *ravenous, insatiable*

     lupus, -ī, m. - *wolf*

     pugnātum - acc. or first supine (See *Latin for the New Millennium*, Level 2, p. 323.)

     exitūrī erant: periphrastic construction: *were about to . . .*

46   **mementōte** (pl. imperative + gen.)

48   **quod**: *that*

49   **habēret**: in subjunctive to express the view of the subject of the sentence

51   **tremefaciō, -ere, -fēcī, -factum** - *to cause to tremble; to tremble, quiver*

52   **dīmittō, -ere, -mīsī, -missum** - *to let go, give up*

53   **revertor, -ī, -versus sum** - *to return*

55   **vītō** (1) - *to avoid*

     dēpellō, -ere, -pulī, -pulsum - *to drive off, away; to get rid of*

     sōlum (adv.) - *only*

56   **partim** (adv.) - *partly*

     ūrō, -ere, ussī, ustum - *to burn, destroy by fire*

     īnsequor, -sequī, -secūtus sum - *to pursue (with hostile intent)*

57   **ōrdō, -inis, m.** - *order*

     ruō, -ere, ruī, rutum - *to rush*

     fossa, -ae, f. - *ditch, trench*

     retrōrsum (adv.) - *backwards*

     trānsgredior, -ī, -gressus sum - *to cross, go over*

59   **moenia, -ium, n. pl.** - *walls of a city*

Grammar and Comprehension Questions

1) What case and in what construction is *nōbīs*?
2) Who does Patroclus mean by *optimō Danaum*?
3) What tense is *dīmīsisse*?
4) What prevented all the Trojans from fleeing?
5) What is the antecedent of *quī*?

45   Myrmidonēs ut vorācēs lupī pugnātum exitūrī erant. Eōs Patroclus
        adlocūtus est: "Comitēs Achillis, fortēs este; virtūtis mementōte. **Nōbīs**
        honor Achillī, praeclārissimō Danaum, dandus est. Nam ita Agamemnōn
        dēmentiam suam cognōscet, quod nūllum honōrem **optimō Danaum**
        habēret."

50   Tum Patroclus Myrmidonēsque Trōiānōs fortiter oppugnāvērunt, quī
        videntēs arma Achillis et Myrmidonēs tremefaciēbantur. Nam putāvērunt
        Achillem ipsum īram **dīmīsisse** et in amīcitiam cum Agamemnone
        reversum esse. Prīmus Patroclus hastam iēcit quae Trōiānum ducem
        percutiēns occīdit. Deinde ā nāvibus Trōiānī fugiēbant ut mortem

55   vītārent. Statim Patroclus ardentem ignem dēpulit. Sōlum ūna nāvis
        partim usta erat. Tum ferōx fiēbat pugna. Danaī Trōiānōs īnsequēbantur
        quī nūllō ōrdine ruēbant. Hector aliīque fossam retrōrsum trānsgressī
        sunt; aliī fossā retinēbantur. Praesertim Patroclus impetum dūxit ut
        Danaī permultōs hōstēs occīderint et reliquī ad moenia repulsī sint.

DISCUSSION QUESTIONS

  1) Does Patroclus resent Achilles's instructions at all?
  2) What does Patroclus choose as the focus or purpose of their mission?
  3) How much emphasis does Homer place in the narrative on the
     quenching of the fire?

Achilles sacrificing to Zeus (Jupiter) for Patroclus's safe return (picture
47 of the Ambrosian *Iliad*, 5th–6th c. CE; Biblioteca
Ambrosiana, Milan, Italy) (Public Domain)

Chapter Eleven

A Chain of Death Begins

The Greeks and Patroclus, wearing Achilles's armor, have pushed the Trojans back toward their walls in front of which the battle now rages. Patroclus has not allowed the Trojans to flee into their city and escape death. In the midst of the carnage the Lycian King Sarpedon, the foremost Trojan ally, rallies his men. Sarpedon, however, is soon fated to die. In this Book 16 Homer brings us to the divine plane where, in an extraordinary scene, Jupiter laments his son's death. The death of Sarpedon is pivotal because it is the first of a number of parallel death scenes. One death triggers another as the epic continues.

Source

Homer, *Iliad* 16

1 **Sarpēdōn, -onis, m.** - *Sarpedon;* son of Zeus, Lycian king allied with the Trojans

Lyciī, -ōrum, m. pl. - *the Lycians;* allies of the Trojans from what is now southern Turkey

pudor, -ōris, m. - *feeling of shame, shame, sense of honor*

2 **concurrō, -ere, -currī, -cursum** - *to run together, charge, contend, fight*

4 **vultur, -uris, m.** - *vulture*

7 **heu** (interj.) - *alas*

8 **dubium, -iī, n.** - *doubt*

in dubiō esse (idiom): *to be in doubt*

maestus, -a, -um - *sad, mournful, stern*

11 **damnō** (1) - *to condemn, doom*

12 **praetereā** (adv.) - *moreover, further, in addition*

13 **immō** (adv.) - *on the contrary, rather*

14 **spīritus, -ūs, m.** - *breath; spirit, soul*

15 **portō** (1) - *to transport, carry*

16 **sepeliō, -īre, -īvī, sepultum** - *to dispose of a corpse in the proper fashion, bury, burn*

sepulcrum, -ī, n. - *tomb, grave*

lapis, -idis, m. - *stone, tomb-stone*

17 **sanguineus, -a, -um** - *bloody* (The gods did not actually have blood in their veins, but a substance called *ichor* which made them immortal. Nonetheless, Homer uses the word for blood in describing these tears.)

18 **effundō, -ere, -fūdī, -fūsum** - *to pour forth, shed*

19 **occurrō, -ere, -currī, -cursum** - *to meet or confront in a hostile manner, go to oppose (one another)*

20 **Thrasymēlēs, -is, m.** - *Thrasymeles;* a Lycian soldier

22 **ultrā** (prep. + acc.) - *beyond, past*

volō (1) - *to fly*

armus, -ī, m. - *the forequarter or shoulder* (of an animal)

trānsfīgō, -ere, -fīxī, -fīxum - *to pierce through*

23 **ululō** (1) - *to scream, howl*

pulvis, -eris, m. - *dust*

currus, -ūs, m. - *chariot*

24 **Automedōn, -onis, m.** - *Automedon;* the charioteer of Achilles

habēna, -ae, f. - *rein*

abscindō, -ere, -scidī, -scissum - *to cut off, away, shear*

GRAMMAR AND COMPREHENSION QUESTIONS

1) What case is *vōbīs*? What is its grammatical function?
2) What verbal form is *este*?
3) What construction is *quis sit*?
4) What tense is *moritūrus est*?
5) What what prior word does *an* correlate?
6) What tense is *redūxeris*?
7) What use of the subjunctive is *moriātur*?
8) What is the antecedent of *quae*?
9) What is the antecedent of *quī*?

Sarpēdōn Lyciīs clāmāvit: "Nūllus **vōbīs** est pudor? Quō curritis? Nunc ferōcēs **este**. Ego ipse contrā hunc mīlitem concurram ut inveniam **quis sit**. Nam is multōs Trōiānōs māgnīs vīribus occīdit." Hīs dictīs, Sarpēdōn dē currū dēsiluit. Tum Patroclus etiam dēsiluit. Ut duo vulturēs

5   clāmantēs concurrērunt.

Intereā Iuppiter ab Olympō spectāns fīliī suī miserābātur. Iūnōnem adlocūtus est: "Heu, Sarpēdōn, mihi cārissimus, fātō manū Patroclī **moritūrus est**. Cor meum in dubiō est utrum eum ē maestō proeliō ēripiam et vīvum in Lyciā dēpōnam, **an** permittam ut manū Patroclī

10   vincatur." Iūnō statim respondit: "Quāle verbum dīxistī? Cupis aliquem mortālem ā morte redūcere? Diū enim fātō is damnātus est. Hoc faciās, at aliī deī tē nōn approbābunt. Praetereā sī hunc vīvum **redūxeris**, alius deus fīlium suum ē proeliō ēripere etiam cupiet. Immō. Sī eum amās, nunc **moriātur** ut fātum est. Sed, cum vīta spīritusque eum reliquerint,

15   Mortem tranquillumque Somnum mitte ut eum ad Lyciam portent. Ibi frātrēs Lyciīque eum sepelient sepulcrō et lapide honorantēs. Tālis mortuīs est honor." Tum Iuppiter uxōrī pāruit, sed sanguineās lacrimās prō cārō fīliō effūdit.

Nunc Patroclus Sarpēdonī occurrit. Prīmum Patroclus hastam in

20   Thrasymēlem, comitem Sarpēdonis, iēcit, **quae** abdōmen percussit ut Thrasymēlēs vīribus āmissīs mortuus sit. Tum Sarpēdōn hastam iēcit, sed hasta ultrā Patroclum volāns armum Pēdasī, equī Achillis, trānsfīxit, **quī** ululāns in pulverem cecidit. Aliī equī igitur movēre currum nōn poterant. Sed Automedōn periculum vidēns habēnās Pēdasī abscīdit ut aliī equī

25   līberātī sint. Sarpēdōn alterā hastā iactā frūstrā sōlam terram percussit.

DISCUSSION QUESTIONS

1) What does the Olympian scene tell us about the relationship between Jupiter and fate?
2) From Juno's comments, what can you infer about the relationship between Jupiter and the other gods?

27 **quercus, -ūs, f.** - *oak-tree*
    lacerō (1) - *to tear, scratch*
28 **Glaucus, -ī, m.** - *Lycian commander*
    bellātor, -ōris, m. - *warrior, fighter*
28–29 **tibi . . . pugnandum est**: passive periphrastic with dative of agent - *you must fight*
29 **incitō** (1) - *to rouse up, incite*
30 **pudeō, -ēre, -uī** - *to fill with shame, make ashamed*
32 **afficiō, -ere, -fēcī, -fectum** - *to affect, stir, move*
    bracchium, -iī, n. - *arm* (here in Greek accusative of respect, a more poetic usage; see *Latin for the New Millennium*, Level 2, p. 495) - *as to his arm, wounded in his arm*
33 **precor, -ārī, -ātus sum** (+ dat.) - *to pray to*

34 **ubicumque** (conj.) - *wherever*
35 **effluō, -ere, -fluxī** - *to run out, flow out*
    dēsinō, -ere, -sivī, -situm - *to cease, leave off*
36 **firmus, -a, -um** - *firm, steady*
41 **stetit**: from **sistō, -ere, stetī, statum** - *to cause to stop, check, stop*
    īnspīrō (1) - *to infuse with, to inspire*
43 **adstō, -stāre, -stitī** - *to stand by, near*
44 **omnīnō** (adv.) - *wholly, altogether, entirely*
45 **conficiō, -ere, -fēcī, -fectum** - *to destroy, consume, waste*
46 **dominus, -ī, m.** - *lord, master*
47 **subveniō, -īre, -vēnī, -ventum** (+ dat.) - *to come to the assistance of, help*
48 **dēdecorō** (1) - *to dishonor, maltreat*

GRAMMAR AND COMPREHENSION QUESTIONS

    1) What form of what verb is *es*? (Hint: it is not the regular second singular indicative.)
    2) What case is *vulnus*? What is its function?
    3) Why does Glaucus rejoice?
    4) What case is *comitum*? Why?
    5) What type of construction does *nē* introduce?

Nunc Patroclus secundā hastā cor Sarpēdonis percussit. Hērōs ut ingēns quercus cecidit sanguineum pulverem digitīs lacerāns, et cārum comitem vocāvit: "Cāre Glauce, quī es in virīs bellātor, nunc tibi hastā gladiōque maximē pugnandum est. Prīmum necesse est Lyciōs incitāre
30   ut prō Sarpēdone pugnent. Nam tē semper pudēbit sī Danaī arma mea spoliāverint. Sed fortis **es** et comitēs nostrōs incitā." Hīs dictīs, Sarpēdōn animam ēmīsit. Glaucus autem dolōre affectus est, quod bracchium vulnerātus Sarpēdonem dēfendere nōn poterat. Apollinī igitur precātus est: "Audī mē, Apollō. Ubicumque es, audīre mē dolentem potes. Nam
35   bracchium mihi vulnerātum est neque sanguis effluere dēsinit. Hastam firmē tenēre nōn possum ut contrā hostēs pugnāre nōn possim. Nunc optimus vir mortuus est cuius corpus dēfendere nōn possum. Hoc **vulnus** igitur sānā et vīrēs mihi dā ut horter Lyciōs prō corpore Sarpēdonis pugnāre."
40   Glaucus ita precātus; Apollō eum audīvit. Statim dolōrem āvertit, sanguinem stetit, Glaucō māgnās vīrēs īnspīrāvit. Iam sānus Glaucus gaudēbat. Statim omnēs Lyciōs incitābat ut prō Sarpēdone pugnārent. Posteā Trōiānōs incitābat, praesertim Aenēan et Hectorem. Adstāns Hectorem adlocūtus est: "Hector, iam **comitum** omnīnō oblītus es, quī
45   prō tē longē ā amīcīs patriāque pugnant. Vīrēs nostrās conficimus, sed tū nōs nōn adiuvās. Nunc Sarpēdōn, dominus Lyciōrum, cecidit ā Patroclō percussus. Itaque mihi subvenī **nē** Danaī māgnifica arma Sarpēdonis spolient et corpus dēdecorent. Nam īrāscuntur nōbīs quī tot Danaōs occīdimus."

Discussion Questions

1) What importance did the ancients attach to the rescue of the body? How does this relate to modern cultural beliefs and practices?
2) Does Glaucus justly accuse Hector? Has Hector forgotten his allies?
3) Is the fight actually on Hector's behalf, as Glaucus claims?

50 **ob** (prep. + acc.) - *on account of, for*

51 **peregrīnus, -a, -um** - *foreign*

52 **utrimque** (adv.) - *on both sides*

54 **niger, -gra, -grum** - *dark, black*

55 **operiō, -īre, -uī, -tum** - *to cover over, conceal*

60 **dēbilis, -e** - *enfeebled, weak, strengthless*

61 **impōnō, -ere, -posuī, -positum** - *to put in*

refugiō, -ere, -fūgī - *to turn back and flee, run away*

62 **imperō** (1) (+ dat.) - *to give orders to, command that*

64 **abluō, -ere, -luī, -lūtum** - *to wash off, wash away*

ambrosia, -ae, f. - *ambrosia,* the food of the gods that also has the power to preserve

unguō, -ere, ūnxī, ūnctum - *to smear, anoint, rub*

65 **decōrus, -a, -um** - *becoming, handsome, fine*

vestiō, -īre, -īvī, -ītum - *to clothe, dress*

geminus, -a, -um - *twin*

68 **īnsequor, -sequī, -secūtus sum** - *to pursue (in a hostile manner)*

modo (adv.) - *only*

mandātum, -ī, n. - *order, command, instruction*

70 **caedo, -ere, cecīdī, caesum** - *to kill*

71 **ter** (adv.) - *three times*

72 **acclīvis, -e** - *upward sloping*

scandō, -ere - *to climb, mount, scale*

73 **quartum** (adv.) - *for the fourth time*

minor, -ārī, -ātus sum - *to threaten, meance*

75 **patruus, -ī, m.** - *uncle*

simulō (1) - *to simulate, imitate*

76 **Age** (idiomatic imperative) - *go on!*

77 **dīrigō, -ere, -rexī, -rectum** - *to guide, steer*

GRAMMAR AND COMPREHENSION QUESTIONS

1) What happens to the corpse of Sarpedon?
2) What type of construction is *quam optimum esset*?
3) What are the two choices Jupiter contemplates? Which choice does he make?
4) What case is *mortālī mente*? Why
5) What tense and mood is *cēpissent*? In what construction?
6) In what guise does Apollo speak to Hector?

50   Dum Glaucus haec dicit, Trōiānī trīstissimī ob Sarpēdonem dolēbant,
qui quamquam peregrīnus prō Trōiānīs tam fortiter pugnāverat. Ferōcēs
Trōiānī, Hectore dūcente, Danaōs oppugnāvērunt. Tum mīlitēs utrimque
prō corpore Sarpēdonis tam ācriter pugnābant ut permultī mortuī sint.
Maestus Iuppiter autem nigram noctem dēmīsit. Ut mox corpus Sarpēdonis

55   nōn etiam vidērī posset cadāveribus armīsque opertum. Nunc Iuppiter
cōgitābat **quam optimum esset** Patroclum occīdere: utrum eō tempore
Hector occīderet eum pugnantem ut corpus raperet et arma Achillis
spoliāret, an deus ipse pugnam augēret et māiōrem glōriam Patroclō daret.
Tandem hoc cōnsilium optimum vidēbatur: ut Patroclus Trōiānōs repelleret

60   et permultōs occīderet. Itaque prīmum Iuppiter dēbilem animum in Hectore
imposuit ut Trōiam refugeret et aliīs Trōiānīs Lyciīsque ut sequerentur
imperāret. Iam Danaī māgnifica arma Sarpēdonis spoliāvērunt. Sed
Iuppiter Apollinem adlocūtus est: "Cāre Phoebe, dēscende et corpus
Sarpēdonis ēripe. Sanguine in flūmine ablūtō, eum ambrosiā ungue et

65   decōrīs vestibus vestī. Tum geminī Somnus et Mors eum ad Lyciam
portent ut fratrēs Lyciīque sepelient sepulcrō et lapide honorantēs."
     Hīs dictīs, Apollō patrī pāruit. Sed Patroclus māgnō clāmōre
Trōiānōs īnsequēbātur. Sī modo mandātīs Achillis pāruisset, fortasse
mortem vītāvisset. Sed mēns Iovis semper fortior est **mortālī mente**. Tum

70   Patroclus permultōs Trōiānōs cecīdit. Trōiam quidem Danaī **cēpissent**
nisi Apollō in ingentī turre stetisset Trōiānōs adiuvāns. Ter Patroclus
acclīvem mūrum scandere temptāvit; ter Apollō eum repulit. Cum
Patroclus quartum temptāvit, Apollō mināns vocāvit: "Cēde, Patrocle.
Tibi nōn fātum est Trōiam capere, nec Achillī ipsō, quī quam tū multō

75   melior est." Patroclus igitur recessit. Nunc Apollō faciem patruī simulāns
Hectorem hortātus est: "Hector, cūr pugnāre dēsīvistī? Nōn oportet. Age!
Equōs contrā Patroclum dīrige. Apollō tē hunc occīdere permittat."

Discussion Question

1) Why do you think Death and Sleep are said to be twins?

78 **aurīga, -ae, m.** - *charioteer*

79 **perturbō** (1) - *to throw into confusion*

80 **praetereō, -īre, -īvī, -itum** - *to go past, pass by*

80–81 **dē currū dēsiluit**: In the normal course of battle warriors rode around in their chariots until they met a worthy opponent. Then they dismounted and fought.

84 **occidō, -ere, -cidī, -cāsum** - *to set*

ante sōlem occāsum: *before sunset, near sunset*

87 **obstō, -stāre, -stitī, -stātum** (+ dat.) - *to stand in the way of, obstruct*

saeptus, -a, -um - *enclosed, wrapped*

nebula, -ae, f. - *mist, fog, cloud*

88 **aggredior, -ī, -gressus sum** - *to approach, assault*

palma, -ae, f. - *palm of the hand*

pellō, pellere, pepulī, pulsum - *to strike*

89 **torqueō, -ēre, torsī, tortum** - *to whirl, twist, spin*

torquērentur: in a middle sense: *spun (themselves)*

90 **umerus, -ī, m.** - *shoulder*

dēcidō, -ere, -dī - *to fall down, fall off*

91 **lōrīca, -ae, f.** - *corselet, breastplate*

attonitus, -a, -um - *stunned, stupefied, paralysed*

imbēcillus, -a, -um - *weak, feeble*

membrum, -ī, n. - *limb*

92 **iaculum, -ī, n.** - *javelin*

93 **cōram** (adv.) - *face to face, openly*

94 **saucius, -a, -um** - *wounded*

inermis, -e - *unarmed, defenseless*

95 **adventō** (1) - *to approach, draw near (in a hostile manner)*

infīgō, -ere, -fīxī, -fīxum - *to drive in, impale*

98 **vescor, -ī** (+ abl.) - *to feed on, eat*

99 **scīlicet** (adv.) - *certainly, surely*

100 **tingō, -ere, tinxī, tinctum** - *to wet, color, stain*

Grammar and Comprehension Questions

1) What weapon does Patroclus use against Hector?
2) What case and construction is *tōtum diem*?
3) Who is *Similis deō bellī*?
4) What did Euphorbus do after he hit Patroclus?
5) What case does *in* take here? What is its meaning?
6) What tense is *dēvastātūrum esse*? How do you translate this in the context of *sperāvistī*?
7) What case is *tibi*? What governs this case?

His audītīs Hector aurīgae imperāvit ut equōs propelleret. Intereā
Apollō Danaōs māgnopere perturbāvit. Hector cēterōs Danaōs
80   praeterīvit, Patroclum sōlum quaerēns. Patroclus Hectore vīsō dē currū
dēsiluit. Tum māgnum saxum sustulit iēcitque, quod nōn Hectorem sed
aurīgam percussit ut dē currū caderet. Statim Hector dē currū dēsiluit et
cum Patroclō prō corpore aurīgae ferōciter pugnābat. **Tōtum dīem** prō
corpore Danaī Trōiānīque contendēbant; sed, ante sōlem occāsum, tum
85   Danaī iam fortiōrēs corpus dētraxit et arma spoliāvit. Deinde Patroclus
in Trōiānōs incurrit. **Similis deō bellī** ter māgnō clāmōre incurrit, sed
cum quartum incurrerit, Apollō ipse eī obstitit. Saeptus nebulā deus
Patroclum ā tergō aggressus prīmum tergum ingentī palmā pepulit ut
oculī torquērentur. Iam galeam dēiēcit, ut sub pedibus equōrum volveret.
90   Hasta in manū Patroclī fracta est; dē umerīs ingēns scūtum dēcidit.
Apollō etiam lōrīcam frēgit. Attonitus Patroclus imbēcillīs membrīs
stabat. Tum ā tergō Trōiānus Euphorbus Patroclum iaculō percussit,
deinde iaculō ēreptō fūgit. Nam nōlēbat Patroclum cōram pugnāre.

Nunc Patroclus saucius inermisque mortem vītāre temptābat, sed
95   Hector adventāns hastam **in** abdōmen īnfīxit. Patroclus cecidit. Omnēs
Danaī terrōre perturbābantur. Hector stāns super Patroclum laetus victor
adlocūtus: "Patrocle, fortasse **sperāvistī** tē Trōiam **dēvastātūrum esse**.
Stulte! Nunc vulturēs tē vescentur. Achillēs, quamquam praeclārissimus,
tē adiuvāre nōn poterat. **Tibi** exeuntī scīlicet imperāvit: 'Nōlī revenīre dum
100   pectus Hectoris sanguine tīnxeris.' Tālibus verbīs tibi stultō persuāsit."

DISCUSSION QUESTIONS

1) If Patroclus had heeded Achilles's warning could he have avoided death?
2) Do the human warriors act of their own free will?
3) How do Apollo and fate interact in this episode?
4) Can the actions in the disarming of Patroclus be explained by other than divine means?
5) Does striking from behind conform to the heroic code?
6) Who owns this helmet? Has it ever been treated this way before?

101 **glōrior, -ārī, -ātus sum** - *to boast*

102 **exuō, -ere, -uī, -ūtum** - *to take off, strip off*

103 **domō, -āre, -uī, -itum** - *to subdue by war, overcome, defeat*

105 **circumstō, -stāre, -stetī** - *to stand around, surround*

107 **volitō (1)** - *to fly about, flit, flutter*

108 **lūgeō, -ēre, lūxī, luctum** - *to mourn, grieve over, lament*

inferī, -ōrum, m. pl. - *the inhabitants of the underworld, the dead*

109 **praedīcō, -ere, -dīxī, -dictum** - *to predict, foretell*

110 **calx, calcis, f.** - *heel*

111 **ēvellō, -ere, -vellī, -vulsum** - *to tear out, pull out*

incēdō, -ere, -cessī - *to proceed on foot, advance*

Grammar and Comprehension Question

1) Who does Patroclus credit with the victory over him?

At nunc moriēns Patroclus respondit: "Iam potes glōriārī. Iuppiter
victōriam tibi dedit—et Apollō quī arma dē umerīs exuit ut mē facile
domuerit. Fātum cum Apolline mē occīdit. Deinde Euphorbus mē
percussit. Tū tertius mē interfēcistī. Nunc haec verba in mente pōne. Tū
105   ipse nōn diū post vīvēs. Iam mors fātumque tē circumstant. Manū māgnī
Achillis moriēris."

His dictīs, Patroclus mortuus est. Volitāns anima iuventūtem
relinquēns et fātum lugēns in īnferōs refūgit. Hector tamen Patroclum,
quamquam mortuum, adlocūtus est: "Cūr mortem meam praedīcis? Quis
110   scit utrum Achillēs hastā meā percussus moriātur?" Tum calce corpus
premēns hastam ēvellit et in pugnam iterum incessit.

DISCUSSION QUESTIONS

1) Does Patroclus's final speech undermine Hector's heroism?
2) Does Hector pay any attention to Patroclus's prophecy in death?
3) Has your attitude towards Hector, established in Chapter 5, changed
   after this episode?

Cultural Influences

Two painters have depicted the body of Sarpedon being carried by Sleep and Death (Henry Fuseli, c. 1803; William Blake Richmond, 1877). More recently, Sarpedon has been featured in a number of interesting roles. There is a brilliantly colored Sarpedon butterfly in Southeast Asia, which is featured on an Australian stamp. There is also an asteroid, 2223 Sarpedon. In 1944 a U.S. battle damage repair ship was christened the U.S.S. Sarpedon (alas, broken up for scrap in 1989). Finally, Lord Sarpedon is a character in the science fantasy game Warhammer set in about 40,000 CE. This varied wealth of reference demonstrates the power of these ancient myths. Sarpedon seems to represent both power and beauty.

Sarpedon's body carried by Hypnos (Sleep) and Thanatos
(Death) (Euphronios Krater, c. 515 BCE; Metropolitan
Museum of Art, NYC) (Public Domain)

Chapter Twelve

THE ARMS OF ACHILLES

After killing Patroclus, Hector immediately sought to kill Automedon, Achilles's charioteer, and gain control of Achilles's immortal horses. Meanwhile Menelaus sheltered Patroclus's body which Euphorbus boldly claimed. After a brief skirmish Menelaus killed this "second" slayer of Patroclus. Then Hector, inspired by Apollo, went to confront Menelaus, who retreated to look for Ajax to aid him. This chapter begins as Menelaus appeals to Ajax for help in rescuing Patroclus's body.

SOURCE

Homer, *Iliad* 17

1   **hūc** (adv.) - *to this place, hither*
    eundem: gerundive of *eō, īre,*
        understand *est.* Uses dative of
        agent (*nōbīs*) - *we must go*
2   **libenter** (adv.) - *willingly*
    cōnsentiō, -īre, -sēnsī, -sēnsum - *to*
        agree
4   **tropaeum, -ī, n.** - *trophy* (made by
        hanging the enemy's armor from a
        tree or cross-like post)
    māgnae glōriae sibi: double dative
        or dative of purpose construction
        (see *Latin for the New Millennium,*
        Level 2, p. 494) - literally: *for great*
        glory for himself
5   **frōns, -ntis, f.** - *forehead, brow*
    contrahō, -ere, -traxī, -tractum - *to*
        draw together, contract
    fronte contractō: *with a frown,*
        scowl
    increpitō (1) - *to rebuke, reproach*
6   **vīsū**: supine from *videō, -ēre*
    dēficiō, -ere, -fēcī, -fectum - *to fail,*
        be ineffective, be lacking

8   **perīclitor, -ārī, -ātus sum** - *to be in*
        danger, run a risk
9   **grātiās agere** (idiom + dat.) - *to*
        thank
13 **bellātor, -ōris, m.** - *warrior, fighter*
    immō (conj.) - *on the contrary, rather*
16 **molestus, -a, -um** - *troublesome,*
        annoying
    anteā (adv.) - *before, formerly*
17 **horreō, -ēre, -uī** - *to shudder at,*
        tremble at
19 **este**: plural imperative of *sum, esse*
20 **redūcō, -ere, -dūxī, -ductum** - *to*
        recall, bring back
21 **quibus . . . spoliāvī**: acc. of person,
        abl. of thing removed
22 **adsequor, -sequī, -secūtus sum** - *to*
        overtake, catch up with
    exuō, -ere, -uī, -ūtum - *to take off,*
        remove
23 **dōnō** (1) - (+ acc. of person, abl. of
        thing) - *to give, gift*

GRAMMAR AND COMPREHENSION QUESTIONS

1) Whose armor is this?
2) What form is *pugnandō*?
3) With what word does *perīclitantibus* agree?
4) Who is the understood subject of *spoliāretur*?
5) What type of subjunctive is *restituant*?
6) To what does *haec* refer?
7) What kind of construction does *utrum* introduce?

"Hūc, Aiax, nōbīs eundum ut nūdum corpus Patroclī ad Achillem reportēmus. Arma enim Hector spoliāvit." Aiax libenter cōnsēnsit.

Iam Hector māgnifica arma servīs trādiderat ut Trōiam ferrent. Nam spērābat haec tropaeum māgnae glōriae sibi futūra esse. At Glaucus,

5   dominus Lyciōrum, fronte contractō Hectorem increpitābat: "Hector, vīsū splendide, in **pugnandō** multō dēficis. Nunc cōgitā quōmodo tū Trōiānīque urbem vestram cōnservāre possītis, quoniam nēmō Lyciōrum contrā Danaōs prō vōbīs pugnāre iam vult. Nam nōbīs **perīclitantibus** nūllās grātiās ēgistis. Dūre, Sarpēdonem, comitem sociumque, relīquistī

10   ut ā Danaīs **spoliārētur**. At nunc domum redībimus et Trōia mox dēlēbitur. Quodsī Trōiānīs ūllae vīrēs remanent, corpus Patroclī in urbem celeriter ferētis. Tum Danaī māgnifica arma Sarpēdonis **restituant**. Nam tālis est bellātor, multō maximus, cuius comes interfectus es. Immō, **haec** nōn faciēs, quoniam tū contrā Aiācem etiam nōn stābis, quī multō melior

15   est quam tū."

Hector respondit: "Glauce, cūr hoc molestum verbum dīxistī? Anteā tē prūdentem esse cōgitābam. Ego impetum nōn horreō. Mē pugnantem spectā. Adstāns disce **utrum** ignāvus sim an aliquem Danaum ferōciter pugnantem occīdam." Deinde Trōiānōs Lyciōsque clāmāvit: "Virī este,

20   comitēs; validam virtūtem redūcite dum pulchra arma praeclārī Achillis induō, quibus victor Patroclum spoliāvī." Tum Hector servōs arma ad urbem ferentēs celeriter adsecūtus est. Paulō dēcēdēns armīs suīs exūtīs dīvīna arma Achillis induit, quibus deī Peleum dōnāverant.

Discussion Questions

1) What motivates Glaucus's reproach?
2) How does the scene between Glaucus and Hector parallel an earlier scene among the Greeks?
3) What kind of transaction is Glaucus suggesting?
4) What was Hector's initial intention regarding the arms of Achilles? What motivated him to change his mind?

24 **aether, -eris, m.** - *heaven, the upper air*

dēspectō (1) - *to look down on, over*

quassō (1) - *to shake*

25 **colloquor, -quī, -cūtus sum** (+ *cum* + abl.) - *to talk to, converse with*

heu (interj.) - *alas*

27 **mītis, -e** - *gentle, mild*

28 **fās** (indecl. neuter noun) - *that which is right, permissible*

in praesēns: (idiom) - *for the present*

30 **adnuō, -ere, -nuī, -nūtum** - *to nod*

33 **praesum, -esse, -fuī, -futurus** (+ dat.) - *to be at the head of, be in charge of*

34 **ignōrō** (1) - *to have no knowledge of, be ignorant of*

36 **mandātum, -ī, n.** - *order, command, instruction*

obsequor, -quī, -cūtus sum (+ dat.) - *to comply with, follow, obey*

37 **arbitrium, -iī, n.** - *decision, choice, will*

omnīnō (adv.) - *at all*

GRAMMAR AND COMPREHENSION QUESTIONS

1) With what word does *induentī* agree?
2) Why didn't Achilles know that Patroclus had died?
3) To whom does *hunc* refer?
4) To what does *tantum malum* refer?

Cum rēx aetheris Iuppiter haec dēspectāret, caput quassāns sēcum
25   collocūtus est: "Heu, miser Hector. Nunc dē morte nōn cōgitās, quae
tamen tibi dīvīna arma praeclārissimī virī **induentī** adstat. Multī aliī hunc
horrent. At nunc huius comitem **fortem mītemque** occīdistī et arma
spoliāvistī, quod **nōn fās** erat. Tamen in praesēns māgnās vīrēs tibi dabō
quod ē proeliō domum nōn redībis nec Andromacha ē manibus tuīs
30   māgnifica arma Achillis accipiet." Iuppiter dīxit et adnuit. Itaque Hector
arma Achillis gerēns proelium iterum intrāvit. Prō corpore Patroclī
terribilis pugna facta est. Aiax Menelāusque Danaīs, Aenēās Hectorque
Trōiānīs praeerant.

Intereā Achillēs ignōrābat Patroclum mortuum esse quoniam
35   proelium prope moenia Trōiae spectāre procul nōn poterat. **Hunc** autem
mandātīs suīs obsecūtūrum esse crēdiderat. Praetereā ante hoc māter sua
arbitrium Iovis saepe patefēcerat; sed iam **tantum malum** omnīnō nōn
dīxerat.

DISCUSSION QUESTIONS

1) What are Jupiter's feelings towards Hector?
2) How is Patroclus characterized? Is *fortem mītemque* an oxymoron?
3) Why shouldn't Hector have taken the arms? Why is it *nōn fās*?

40 **abstō, -stāre, -stetī, -statum** - *to stand at a distance, keep at a distance*

caedō, -ere, cecīdī, caesum - *to kill*

41 **perpetuō** (adv.) - *without interruption, continuously*

42 **quasi** (adv. or conj.) - *as if*

44 **num** (interrogative adv.) - anticipates the answer "no"

omnibus animālibus: ablative of comparison with *miserrimus*

45 **attamen** (conj.) - *but still, nevertheless*

46 **permittō, -ere, -mīsī, -missum** - *to permit, allow*

membrum, -ī, n. - *limb*

47 **Automedōn, -ontis, m.** - *Automedon, the charioteer of Achilles*

salvus, -a, -um - *sound, healthy, safe*

48 **occidō, -ere, -cidī, -cāsum** - *to set (of the sun)*

49 **etiamnum** (particle) - *even now, still*

50 **admoneō, -ēre, -monuī, -monitum** - *to advise, urge*

Antilochus, -ī, m. - *Antilochus*, close friend of Achilles

52 **foedus, -a, -um** - *grievous, atrocious, vile*

54 **lūgeō, -ēre, lūxī, luctum** - *to mourn, grieve over, lament*

GRAMMAR AND COMPREHENSION QUESTIONS

1) What tense and mood is *cecidisset*?
2) What case and number is *eōrum*? Why?
3) How long will Jupiter permit the Trojans to kill the Greeks?
4) Who is the subject of *mitteret*?

40 Equī Achillis autem hoc malum cognōvērunt: quōmodo Patroclus
in pulvere **cecidisset** ab Hectore occīsus. Nunc immōbilēs abstābant
et perpetuō flēbant. Nōlēbant aut ad nāvēs aut in proelium redīre, sed
quasi monumentum stābant et lacrimās dēmittēbant. Spectāns miserōs
equōs Iuppiter **eōrum** miserātus est: "Miserī, cūr vōs immortālēs mortālī
dedimus? Num ut paterēminī? Nam ex omnibus animālibus in terrīs
45 marīque homō est miserrimus. Attamen Hector in currū vōs nōn aget;
hoc nōn permittam. At nunc vīrēs in membrīs vestrīs impōnam ut
Automedontem salvum ē proeliō referātis. Trōiānīs permittam ut Danaōs
occīdant dum ad nāvēs adveniant, dum sōl occidat."

Iove haec dīcente, proelium etiamnum furēbat. Tum Aiax Menelāum
50 admonuit ut nuntium Antilochum, fīlium Nestoris, ad Achillem **mitteret**.
Itaque Menelāus Antilochum adlocūtus est: "Antiloche, audī dē mē
foedum nuntium: **optimum Danaum**, Patroclum, cecidisse. Ergō celeriter
ad nāvēs Achillis curre. Fortasse nūdum corpus ēripere poterit. Hector
arma spoliāvit." Hīs dictīs, Antilochus māgnopere lugēbat et flēbat, sed
55 tamen ad nāvēs cucurrit. Dēnique, Aiāce adiuvante, Menelāus corpus
Patroclī ā Trōiānīs ēripuit. Etiamnum et Trōiānī et Danaī ferōciter
pugnābant.

Discussion Questions

1) What do you think about Jupiter's comments on the nature of mankind?
2) What signal does Jupiter give regarding Trojan success?
3) Who has usually been referred to as *optimus Danaum*?
4) What difficulty might there be for Achilles in returning to battle immediately?

Menelaus holding the body of Patroclus (late 1st century CE Roman copy
of Greek original, c. 240–230 BCE, with subsequent modern restorations
and additions; Loggia dei Lanzi in Piazza della Signora, Florence,
Italy) (© Creative Commons 3.0/Guillaume Piolle)

Chapter Thirteen

ACHILLES'S CHOICE

While the battle continues to rage and the Greeks are pushed back toward their ships, Antilochus as a messenger approaches Achilles's tent. As Achilles sees him approaching, a sense of foreboding overcomes him. This chapter depicts Achilles's reaction to Patroclus's death, the decision he makes, and the new arms he receives. The description of his new shield prefigures Vergil's depiction of Aeneas's new shield in *Aeneid* 8.

SOURCE

Homer, *Iliad* 18, 19

1   **heu** (interj.) - *alas*

3   **quondam** (adv.) - *once, formerly*

    patefaciō, -ere, -fēcī, -factum - *to reveal, make known*

4   **certus, -a, -um** - *certain, sure, definite*

    īnfēlix, -icis - *unhappy, unfortunate, unlucky*

5   **atquī** (conj.) - *but, and yet, nevertheless*

7   **Antilochus, -ī, m.** - *Antilochus*; son of Nestor, friend of Achilles

8   **foedus, -a, -um** - *dreadful, horrible, vile*

10 **āter, -tra, -trum** - *black, dark*

    involvō, -ere, -uī, -ūtum - *to enclose, envelop, overwhelm*

    sordidus, -a, -um - *dirty, filthy*

12 **spargō, -ere, sparsī, sparsum** - *to sprinkle, spatter*

    validus, -a, -um - *strong, mighty, powerful*

13 **laniō** (1) - *to tear*

14 **adversus, -a, -um** - *facing, opposite*

    cohibeō, -ēre, -uī, -itum - *to restrain, check*

    iugulō (1) - *to kill by cutting the throat, kill*

    atrōciter (adv.) - *violently, bitterly, ferociously*

15 **plōrō** (1) - *to utter a cry of grief or pain, wail*

    profundus, -a, -um - *deep*

16 **lāmentor, -ārī, -ātus sum** - *to wail, lament, lament for*

17 **integer, -gra, -grum** - *whole, untouched, unblemished*

18 **peperī**: from *pariō*

19 **excipiō, -ere, -cēpī, -ceptum** - *to take back, receive*

21 **ēmergō, -ere, -mersī, -mersum** - *to come out of the water, emerge*

24 **turpis, -e** - *shameful, base*

GRAMMAR AND COMPREHENSION QUESTIONS

1) What kind of construction does *utinam . . . nē* govern?
2) What construction is *mē vīvō*? What must you understand to complete its meaning?
3) What did Achilles order Patroclus to do?
4) What mood and tense is *accidisset*? In what construction?
5) What type of literary device is *ātra nūbēs dolōris*?
6) What type of construction is *ut . . . spargerētur*?
7) Why did Antilochus restrain Achilles's hands?
8) What is *redeuntem* understood to modify?
9) What type of clause is *ut . . . repellerentur et . . . paterentur*?

Achillēs tum mīrātus est: "Heu, quam Danaī ad nāvēs repelluntur! **Utinam** deī malōs dolōrēs mihi **nē** efficiant quōmodo māter mihi quondam patefēcit. Nam dīxit, **mē vīvō**, fortissimum Danaum manibus Trōiānōrum peritūrum esse. Certē fortis fīlius Menoetiī periit. Īnfēlix!

5   Atquī iussī eum, igne exstīnctō, ad nāvēs redīre, nōn contrā Hectorem pugnāre."

Tum Antilochus advēnit et lacrimāns Achillī nuntiāvit: "Heu, fīlī Peleī, foedum nuntium audiēs. Utinam hoc nē **accidisset**! Patroclus cecidit. Prō nūdō corpore māgna pugna fit. Hector arma spoliāvit."

10   Hīs dictīs, **ātra nūbēs dolōris** Achillem involuit. Cum sordidum pulverem manibus sūmpsisset super caput faciemque fūdit **ut** tunica ātribus cineribus **spargerētur**. Ipse validus in pulvere iacēns capīllōs manibus laniābat. Adversus Antilochus cum eō lūgēbat et manūs Achillis cohibuit; nam timēbat nē Achillēs sē iugulāret. Tum hērōs atrōciter

15   plōrāvit, quem Thetis dīvīna māter in profundō marī audīvit. Tum dea etiam exclāmāvit et sorōribus lāmentāta est: "Audīte mē, sorōrēs, ut dolōrēs meōs cognōscātis. Heu, misera ego. Fīlium integrum validumque, praeclārissimum hērōum peperī. Eum Trōiam celeribus nāvibus ēmīsī; at nunc **redeuntem** ad patriam numquam excipiam. Dum autem vīvit et

20   sōlem videt, eum lūgentem adiuvāre nōn possum. Tamen ībō ut cārum fīlium videam et lāmentantem audiam." Itaque dea ē marī ēmersit et ad Achillem vēnit. Rogāvit: "Cūr, fīlī, dolēs? Dīc, nihil cēlāns. Haec ā Iove facta sunt quōmodo tū ipse precātus es, **ut** omnēs Danaī prō iniūriā tuā ad nāvēs **repellerentur et** turpiter **paterentur**."

DISCUSSION QUESTIONS

1) How did you expect Achilles to react to the news of Patroclus's death?
2) Why doesn't Achilles immediately cry out?
3) What English word is derived from *pulvis, -eris, m.*?
4) Why does Thetis lament?
5) Does Thetis comfort Achilles at all? Or does she rather let him know the consequences of his request?

28–29 **quibus . . . dōnāverant**: ablative of
       gift
30   **utinam**: introduces a mixed tense
       unfulfilled wish (thus contrary to
       fact)
       etiamnum (adv.) - *even now, still, yet*
31   **posthāc** (adv.) - *from this time, from
       now on, hereafter*
33   **poena, -ae, f.** - *punishment, penalty*
       luō, -ere, -ī - *to suffer (a punishment),
       to pay*
37   **occidō, -ere, -cidī, -cāsum** - *to fall,
       fall down*
       subveniō, -īre, -vēnī, -ventum (+ dat.)
       - *to come to the assistance of, help*
38   **haudquāquam** (adv.) - *by no means,
       in no way, not at all*

       inūtilis, -e - *useless*
40   **ēvānēscō, -ere, -uī** - *to vanish, fade
       away*
41   **irrītō** (1) - *to provoke, vex*
       aegrē (adv.) - *painfully, with
       difficulty, reluctantly*
42   **interfector, -ōris, m.** - *slayer, killer*
43   **quandōcumque** (rel. adv.) - *at
       whatever time, whenever*
       dēcernō, -ere, -crēvī, -crētum - *to
       decide, determine*
45   **dētineō, -ēre, -uī, -tentum** - *to
       detain, hold, keep from*

Grammar and Comprehension Questions

1) What use of *quam* is this?
2) What case is *omnia*? In what construction?
3) When Achilles says *hunc perdidī* whom does he ultimately blame for
   Patroclus's death?
4) What form is *vīsū*?
5) What case and number is *mortālis*? To whom does it refer?
6) What mood and tense is *vīveres*? Why?
7) What mood and tense is *dūxisset*? What idiom is understood here
   with the verb *dūcō*?
8) What case is *tibi*? In what construction?
9) What form is *brevius*? What meaning does it convey?
10) How does *inūtile onus* fit in the grammatical structure of the
    sentence?
11) What tense and mood do you think *āmittam* is? What other
    possibility is there?

25   Tum graviter gemēns Achillēs respondit: "Māter mea, omnia haec
        Iuppiter effēcit. Sed **quam** mihi plācet, cum Patroclus, cārus comes
        perierit, quem plus quam **omnia**, etiam vītam meam amābam? **Hunc**
        perdidī, et Hector ingentia arma, **vīsū** mīrābilia, spoliāvit, quibus deī
        Peleum dōnāverant istō diē quō **mortālis** tē deam in mātrimōnium dūxit.
30   Utinam cum aliīs deīs etiamnum **vīveres** et Peleus aliquam mortālem
        dūxisset. At nunc fīlium tuum numquam posthāc domī accipiēs, ut prō
        morte meā plūrimum **tibi** dolendum sit. Nam nōlō vīvere, nisi prīmum
        Hector hastā meā interfectus prō Patroclō occīsō poenās luerit."
        Lacrimāns Thetis respondit: "Tum, fīlī, **brevius** tempus vīvēs,
35   quoniam post mortem Hectoris mox morīrī tibi fātum est." Graviter
        sollicitus Achillēs respondit: "Mihi mox moriendum est, cum comitī
        meō occidentī nōn subvēnerim. Nunc procul ā patriā periit quod eum
        haudquāquam dēfendī. Ut **inūtile onus** hīc sedeō, quamquam in proeliō
        fortissimus Danaum sum. In cōnsiliō aliī meliōrēs sunt.
40   Utinam discordia inter et deōs et mortālēs ēvānēscat! Ita Agamemnōn
        mē irrītāvit. Etsī vexātus tamen hanc īram aegrē **āmittam**. Nunc ībō ut
        istum interfectōrem Patroclī īnsequar. Tum mortem meam accipiam
        quandōcumque Iuppiter dēcernet. Herculēs enim, cārissimus Iovī,
        mortem effūgere nōn poterat. At nunc glōria mihi quaerenda est. Nōlī ā
45   proeliō mē dētinēre, quamquam mē amās. Mihi nōn persuadēbis."

Discussion Questions

1) What does Achilles wish Peleus had done? What inference does this
   lead to about himself?
2) How has Achilles's opinion of himself changed?
3) Considering that it is a life or death decision, does Achilles deliberate
   much while making his choice?
4) Does Achilles truly curb his anger?

47   **glōrior, -ārī, -ātus sum** - *to glory, pride oneself*

50   **Volcānus, -ī, m.** - *Vulcan; god of the forge and handicraft*

for, fārī, fātus sum - *to speak*

52   **Īris, -idis, f.** - *Iris; messenger of the gods, a rainbow*

53   **surgō, -ere, surrēxī, surrēctum** - *to get up, arise*

formīdolōsus, -a, -um - *terrifying, dangerous*

54   **terreō, -ēre, -uī, -itum** - *to terrify, frighten*

55   **ignōrō** (1) - *to have no knowledge, be ignorant of*

56   **vetō, -āre, -uī, -itum** - *to forbid*

59   **fossa, -ae, f.** - *ditch, trench*

60   **ostentō** (1) - *to present to view, exhibit, display publicly*

62   **clangō, -ere** - *to scream, clang*

tuba, -ae, f. - *war trumpet*

63   **aureus, -a, -um** - *made of gold, golden*

cingō, -ere, cinxī, cinctum - *to encircle*

incendō, -ere, -cendī, -cēnsum - *to kindle, light*

65   **fragor, -ōris, m.** - *roar, din*

attonitus, -a, -um - *stunned, stupefied*

67   **comitor, -ārī, -ātus sum** - *to go along with, accompany, attend*

mātūrē (adv.) - *early*

Grammar and Comprehension Questions

1) How do you translate *dum* in the construction with *videās*?
2) What construction is *Iove aliīsque deīs ignōrantibus*?
3) What gender, number, and case is *ipsa*?
4) The phrase *Iovī cārus* is what type of literary device?
5) What sort of literary device is *quasi clangēns tuba*?
6) What gender, number, and case is *eī*? In what construction?
7) What effect does Achilles's appearance have on the Trojans?
8) With what does *ferentibus* agree?
9) Who is the implied subject with which *lacrimāns* agrees?
10) What type of construction is *Achillem redisse*?

Tum Thetis respondit: "Fortiter comitem dēfendere est bonum. At Trōiānī splendida arma Peleī tenent; Hector haec arma gerēns glōriātur, sed nōn diū glōriābitur quoniam mors eum etiamnum circumstat. Sed nōlī in proelium intrāre **dum** mē ad tē revenientem **videās**. Nam prīmā

50 lūce nova praeclārissima arma tibi ā Volcānō facta feram." Sīc fāta ad caelum discessit.

Sed tum Īris ā Iūnōne missa ad Achillem adlocūtus est: "Surge, fīlī Peleī, formīdolōssimus virōrum. In fronte nāvium stā ut terrēns Trōiānōs repellās." Sed Achillēs: "Quis tē mīsit?" Īris respondit: "Iūnō mē mīsit,

55 **Iove aliisque deīs ignōrantibus**." Tum Achillēs: "Quōmodo sine armīs in proelium reveniam? Māter mea autem vetuit mē in proelium redīre dum māgnifica arma ā Volcānō facta ferēns **ipsa** reveniat."

Īris respondit: "Ita. Omnia haec cognōvimus. Sed ad fossam ī et tē Trōiānīs ostentā ut fortasse territī impetūs dēsinant." Hīs dictīs, Īris

60 discessit, sed Achillēs **Iovī cārus** surrēxit. Itaque in mūrō prope fossam stetit et maximā vōce clāmāvit **quasi clangēns tuba**. Eī caput Minerva aureā nūbe cingēns ārdente flammā incendit. Cum Trōiānī flammam vīderint vōcemque audīverint, territī terga vertērunt. Ter Achillēs clāmāvit, ter Trōiānī ignī et fragōre attonitī fūgērunt. Tum Achillēs

65 Danaīs occurrit Patroclum ē proeliō **ferentibus**. **Lacrimāns** corpus ad tabernāculum comitātus est. Dea Iūnō sōlem mātūrē occidere etiam coēgit.

Intereā Trōiānī terrēbantur **Achillem redisse**, quī diū ē pugnā āfuerat.

DISCUSSION QUESTIONS

1) Is it unusual that Achilles has face-to-face communication with the goddess Iris?
2) What happens to Achilles's head? What does this signify? Can you think of other similar images?

71 **Pōlydamās, -antos, m.** - *Polydamas;* Trojan warrior and counselor

intrā (prep. + acc.) - *within, inside*

74 **aufugiō, -ere, -fūgī** - *to flee from, run away from*

75 **uter, -tra, -trum** - *which (of two)*

76 **campus, -ī, m.** - *field, plain*

78 **atrox, -ōcis** - *dreadful, violent*

effrēnātus, -a, -um - *unrestrained, incessant*

79 **ambō, -ae, -ō** (pl. adj. + pronoun) (dat. + abl. m. *ambōbus*) - *both*

solum, -ī, n. - *soil, ground*

tingō, -ere, tinxī, tinctum - *to wet, color, stain*

80 **sepeliō, -īre, -eluī, -ultum** - *to dispose of a corpse in the proper fashion, bury, burn*

81 **rogus, -ī, m.** - *funeral pyre*

duodecim (indecl. adj.) - *twelve*

in praesentī (idiom) - *for the present*

84 **ocrea, -ae, f.** - *greave* (protection for lower leg)

lōrīca, -ae, f. - *corselet, chest protector*

adsentiō, -īre, -sēnsī, -sēnsum - *to agree, approve*

85 **officīna, -ae, f.** - *workshop*

callidē (adv.) - *expertly, skillfully, artfully*

fingō, -ere, finxī, fictum - *to form, fashion, make*

86 **fabricō** (1) - *to fashion, forge*

87 **ōra, -ae, f.** - *rim, border*

Ōceanus, -ī, m. - *Ocean;* the Titan god whose waters were thought to surround the world

lūna, -ae, f. - *the moon*

88 **stella, -ae, f.** - *star*

Grammar and Comprehension Questions

1) What type of construction is *uter vincat*?
2) What case and construction is *tōtam noctem*?
3) What case does *in* take? How is it translated?
4) What does Achilles vow about Patroclus's burial?
5) What case is *omnia haec*? What is its grammatical function?
6) What case are *aurō argentōque*? What use of the case is this?

70   Pōlydamās Trōiānōs monuit ut sē intrā moenia reciperent. Sed
Hector reprehendēns: "Recipere mihi nōn placet, quoniam iam Patroclō
occīsō māgnam victōriam perfēcī et Danaōs ad nāvēs reppulī. Prīmā lūce
bellum iterum gerēmus. Ego Achillem nōn aufugiam sed eī resistam. Tum
vidēbitis **uter vincat**." Hīs audītīs omnēs Hectorem approbābant ut
75   exercitus in campō remanēret.

Tōtam noctem Danaī Patroclum lugēbant, praesertim Achillēs,
quī **in** pectus cārī amīcī atrōcēs manūs imposuit effrēnātē lacrimāns.
"Fātum est nōbīs ambōbus hīc Trōiānum solum tingere, quoniam domum
numquam redībō. Sed tē nōn sepeliam dum ad tē arma et caput Hectoris
80   feram. In rogō tuō duodecim Trōiānōs captīvōs interficiam. In praesentī
hīc iacēbis ā tristibus fēminīs lamentātus."

Intereā Thetis Volcānum rogāvit ut nova arma Achillī faceret:
galeam, ocreās, lōrīcam et scūtum. Volcānus celeriter adsēnsus ad
officīnam redīvit. **Omnia haec** deus callidē finxit, sed praesertim
85   ēlegantissimum, ingēns graveque scūtum **aurō argentōque** fabricāvit.
Ōram flūmine Ōceanī cinxit. Tum terram, caelum, mare, sōlem, lūnam,
stellāsque addidit. In mediō scūtō duās urbēs finxit.

DISCUSSION QUESTIONS

1) What does Achilles intend to do to Hector? What will he do to
   twelve Trojan captives?
2) What women might these be who are lamenting over Patroclus?
3) What would a shield normally depict on its front? For instance, see
   Athena's shield as depicted on many vases and sculptures. Such
   devices are called apotropaic since they are meant to "turn away"
   or frighten the enemy.

89   **festus, -a, -um** - *of festival, festal*
     iūdicium, -ī, n. - *court*
90   **obsideō, -ēre, -sēdī, -sessum** - *to besiege, blockade*
91   **pinguis, -e** - *rich*
92   **aratrum, -ī, n.** - *plow*
     describō, -ere, -scripsī, -scriptum - *to represent, fashion*
     vītis, -is, f. - *grape-vine*
     pastor, -ōris, m. - *shepherd*
     lātrō (1) - *to bark*

     canis, -is, m./f. - *dog*
93   **pavimentum, -ī, n.** - *paved surface, floor*
     saltō (1) - *to dance*
98   **quīn (conj.)** - *but rather, instead*
99   **increpō (1)** - *to rattle, clang, clash*
100 **firmus, -a, -um** - *steady, firm, unwavering*
101 **flagrō (1)** - *to blaze, burn*
     suscipiō, -ere, -cēpī, -ceptum - *to take up, receive*

Grammar and Comprehension Questions

1) Why does Homer tell us that Minerva and Mars were *aureī*? What might this literally indicate?
2) What noun does the phrase *amplectentem flentemque* modify?
3) What case is *cōnsiliō*? With what meaning?
4) Why are the arms described as *increpantia*?

In ūnā urbe erant nūptiae, diēs festī, iūdicia. Alteram autem urbem
duo exercitūs obsidēbant. Populus urbis armātus in moenibus stābat.
90 **Aureī** deī, Minerva et Mars, eōs adiuvābant. Tum Volcānus pinguēs agrōs,
aratra, bovēs descripsit, etiam vītēs, pastōrēs, et lātrantēs canēs. Dēnique
pavīmentum finxit in quō puerī puellaeque saltābant.

Omnibus hīs factīs, prīmā lūce Thetis ad nāvem Achillis revēnit
dōna Volcānī ferēns. Fīlium corpus Patroclī **amplectentem flentemque**
95 invēnit. Dea manum fīliī tenēns adlocūta est: "Mī fīlī, quamquam hunc
lūgēmus, tamen mortuus iacēns nōbīs relinquendus est. Nam **cōnsiliō**
deōrum interfectus est. Quīn māgnifica arma ā mē accipe; tālia nēmō
mortālium ante gessit." Tum dea **increpantia** arma dēposuit. Haec omnēs
aliī mīlitēs timēbant, sed Achillēs haec firmē spectāvit et, īrā crescente,
100 oculī flagrābant. Hīs dōnis susceptīs gaudēbat et proelium dēsīderābat.

Discussion Questions

1) Why has Homer chosen domestic scenes to decorate Achilles's
   shield?
2) What parts of Homer's description of Achilles's shield would be
   impossible for a static object? How are we to explain these?
3) What has happened to the wrath of Achilles, the theme of the epic?

Cultural Influences

The scene of Achilles mourning over Patroclus has been an inspiration to many artists such as paintings by Tiepolo "Achilles Mourning on the Seashore" (1757), Gavin Hamilton "Achilles Mourning Patroclus" (1765), Angelica Kauffmann "The Despair of Achilles on the Death of Patroclus" (1775), a marble relief by Thomas Banks "Thetis and the Nymphs Rising from the Sea to Console Achilles" (1778), and a bronze sculpture by Leonard Baskin "Achilles Mourning the Death of Patroclus" (1967).

Medusa (Glyptothek, Munich, Germany). Roman copy after
a 5th-century Greek original by Phidias, which was set on
the shield of Athena Parthenos. Shields often had the head
of Medusa in the center to frighten an opponent (this is
called an apotropaic use). What is on Achilles's shield?
(© Creative Commons 3.0/MatthiasKabel)

Chapter Fourteen

Reconciliation and Rage

After he received his new armor from his mother Thetis, Achilles wanted immediately to rush into battle and kill Hector to avenge Patroclus's death. Homer, however, delays Achilles's return by two practical considerations. First, Thetis advises Achilles that he must make a public reconciliation with Agamemnon. Second, Ulysses insists that the troops must not go into battle hungry. Achilles's impatience (and that of the audience) builds throughout this chapter.

Source

Homer, *Iliad* 19

1 **admoneō, -ēre, -uī, -itum** - *to advise, urge*

2 **pastor, -ōris, m.** - *shepherd, leader*

3 **retrahō, -ere, -trāxī, -tractum** - *to draw back, withdraw*

4 **avidus, -a, -um** - *eager*

5 **hoc**: describes the clause *nōs propter fēminam rixārī*

  rixor, -ārī, -ātus sum - *to quarrel violently, argue, clash*

  utinam: introduces an unfulfilled (contrary to fact) wish regarding the past

6 **antequam** (conj.) - *before*

  humus, -ī, f. - *the ground, earth, dirt*

  mordeō, -ēre, momordī, morsum - *to bite*

  humum momordissent: acts as the main clause of an understood past contrary to fact construction. This idiomatic expression originates in Homer.

7 **quod**: referring to the entire previous sentence

8 **praeteritus, -a, -um** - *past, gone by*

  mittāmus: *let go*

  dolet: impersonal, *it grieves (us)*

9 **fīniō, -īre, -īvī, -ītum** - *to end, stop, finish*

10 **agitō** (1) - *to drive, rouse, impel*

14 **culpa, -ae, f.** - *fault*

  Furiae, -ārum, f. - *Furies* (goddesses of vengeance; madness, frenzy)

15 **subitus, -a, -um** - *sudden*

16 **possem**: imperfect subjunctive in past potential or deliberative construction

18 **abstulerit**: from *auferō*

19 **herī** (adv.) - *yesterday*

GRAMMAR AND COMPREHENSION QUESTIONS

1) What mood and tense is *retrahās*? In what construction?
2) Who is the woman (*fēminam*) to whom Achilles refers?
3) What mood and tense are *mortua esset*?
4) What type of subjunctive is *mittāmus*?
5) What construction is *Achille dīcente*?
6) What gender, number, and case is *quae*? (Hint: look at the verb.) What is its antecedent?
7) How is *cum* to be understood in the context of *tamen* in the next clause?

Novīs armīs receptīs, Thetis Achillī admonuit: "Age, omnēs Danaōs
ad concilium convocā ut īram contrā Agamemnonem, pastōrem populī,
retrahās. Tum tē in hostēs armā." Statim Achillēs Danaōs convocāvit, quī
in concilium avidē ruērunt. Prīmum Achillēs stāns dīxit: "Fīlī Atreī, num
5   hoc optimum erat nōs propter **fēminam** rixārī? Utinam ista **mortua esset**
antequam eam cēpī; nam nōn tot Danaī humum momordissent, cum ego
īrāscēns ā proeliō abessem. Quod erat melius Trōiānīs Hectorīque. Sed
tamen haec praeterita **mittāmus**, quamquam dolet, et īram repellāmus.
Nunc īram meam fīniō, quia nōn oportet mē semper īrāscī. Iam age,
10   quam celerrimē Danaōs in proelium agitā ut contrā Trōiānōs pugnēmus."
Achille dīcente, omnēs Danaī gaudēbant.

Nunc Agamemnōn surrēxit responditque: "Mīlitēs amicīque, fīlium
Peleī adloquar. Sed vōs etiam audīte. Danaī contrā mē saepe dīcēbātis et
reprehendēbātis. At nōn mea culpa est, sed Iovis et fātī et Furiārum,
15   **quae** mē subitā dēmentiā cēpērunt ut praemium ab Achille abdūcerem.
Quid aliud facere possem? Etiam Iuppiter a Furiīs dēceptus est. Quōmodo
ego mortālis errōrem fugere possem? Sed **cum** dēceptus sim et Iuppiter
sānitātem abstulerit, tibi **tamen** satisfacere volō et dare omnia plūrima
dōna quae herī prōmīsī."

Discussion Questions

1) How does Achilles now treat Agamemnon? How does this compare
with his prior treatment?
2) Whom does Agamemnon initially address in his response? Does this
seem unusual?
3) Does Agamemnon seem to take responsibility for his actions?
4) Whom does Agamemnon address at the end?

21 **vīs**: from *volō, velle, voluī* (not to be confused with the noun *vīs, vis, f.*)

    est tuum (idiom) - *it is your concern, business, choice*

22 **terō, -ere, trīvī, trītum** - *to use up, waste*

23 **saeviō, -īre, -iī, -ītum** - *to rage, behave ferociously*

24 **interpellō** (1) - *to interrupt*

25 **ēsuriō, -īre, -ītum** - *to be hungry, suffer hunger*

    quīn (conj.) - *but rather*

26 **edō, ēsse, ēdī, ēsum** - *to eat*

    iubēre: dependent on *nōn decet*

    etiamsī (conj.) - *even if, even though*

    ardēns, -ntis - *eager, fierce*

    pōtiō, -ōnis, f. - *drink*

27 **dēficiō, -ere, -fēcī, -fectum** - *to fail*

    satur, -ura, -urum - *full, sated*

32 **cupidus, -a, -um** (+ gen.) - *desirous (of), wanting*

33 **obligō** (1) - *to pledge*

    mandātum, -ī, n. - *charge, order, instruction*

34 **legās**: in the sense *choose*

    hūc (adv.) - *to this place, to here*

36 **aliās** (adv.) - *at another time*

    quandōcumque (adv.) - *whenever*

37 **lacerō** (1) - *to tear, mangle, lacerate*

41 **refert** (impersonal + abl. of possessive adj.) - *it concerns, matters to*

Grammar and Comprehension Questions

1) What construction follows *videant*?
2) What tense is *dēficiet*?
3) What case is *omnem diem*? What does this case indicate here?
4) What is the antecedent of *quī*? In what construction?
5) What tense of the subjunctive is *sit*? What type of subjunctive is it?
6) What is the antecedent of *cuī*?

20   Achillēs **pedibus celer** respondit: "Fīlī Atreī, nōbilissime, rēx
hominum, sī dōna dare vīs, sī nōn vīs, est tuum. Sed nunc statim in
proeliō gaudeāmus; hīc manēre et tempus terere nōn decet. Omnēs
videant Achillem in prīmā aciē in Trōiānōs saevīre."

        Tum Ulixēs interpellāvit: "Minimē, dīvīne Achillēs. Nōn decet
25   ēsurientēs mīlitēs in longum proelium agere; quīn eōs prope nāvēs
ēsse bibereque iubēre. Nam mīles etiamsī ardēns sine cibō pōtiōneque
dēficiet, sed īdem satur contrā hostēs **omnem diem** pugnābit.
Age, prīmum mīlitēs ad castra redīre et cibum parāre iubē. Dēinde
Agamemnōn dōna in medium concilium ferat ut omnēs ea videant et tū
30   animō gaudeās."

        Agamemnōn, rēx hominum, respondit: "Omnia quae dīxistī mihi
placent. Quamquam cupidus proeliī, Achillēs et omnēs hīc maneant dum
dōna ferantur et fidem obligēmus. Et tibi, Ulixēs, hoc mandātum dō: ut
optimōs iuvenēs legās **quī** omnia dōna et fēminam ipsam hūc referant."

35   Nunc Achillēs pedibus celer: "Fīlī Atreī, nōbilissime, rēx hominum,
aliās haec cūrāre decet, quandōcumque intermissiō proeliī **sit** et nōn
tantum animus meus saeviat. Sed nunc hī mortuī iacent lacerātī, quōs
Hector interfēcit, **cui** Iuppiter glōriam dabat. Num nōs edere iubēs? Nunc
Danaōs in Trōiānōs incurrere iubeam; postquam sōl occidit tempus
40   erit ēsse. Ego nec edam nec bibam quoniam in castrīs meīs mortuus
Patroclus iacet lacerātus. Nam ēsse et bibere meā nōn refert, sed
occīdere."

DISCUSSION QUESTIONS

1) What poetic device is *pedibus celer*?
2) How does Achilles treat Agamemnon after his speech?
3) Do Achilles and the Greeks accept Agamemnon's explanation? Do you?
4) Does Achilles care about the gifts and the return of the woman?
5) Has Achilles really overcome his anger?

Briseis led from Achilles; she was a major cause of the rift between Achilles and
Agamemnon (Hieron painter, c. 480 BCE; Louvre, Paris, France)
(© Creative Commons 3.0/Marie-Lan Nguyen)

Chapter Fifteen

FURIOUS ACHILLES'S ENCOUNTERS
WITH AENEAS AND HECTOR

This chapter begins what many in Homer's audience have been waiting for: the return of Achilles to battle. Homer, however, still toys with us and increases our anticipation by descriptive scenes, divine interventions, prophecies, and delays. Agamemnon gives the splendid gifts and returns Briseis to Achilles. She mourns for kind Patroclus who had promised that Achilles would marry her. In the company of the Greek commanders, Achilles, mourning aloud for Patroclus, says he could suffer nothing worse than this loss, not even the death of his father or of his son, Neoptolemus, who is being raised on Scyros. This is the *Iliad*'s first mention of the son who will ultimately take Troy.

Although the rest of the commanders eat, Achilles will not. Therefore Minerva fills him with nectar and ambrosia to give him strength. Homer shows the fury of Achilles as he dons his new armor. He grinds his teeth and his eyes flash. With Automedon, his charioteer, he leaps into his chariot. As he departs for battle there is an extraordinary scene. Achilles addresses his four horses. The immortal horse Xanthus replies with a chilling prophecy.

SOURCE

Homer, *Iliad* 19, 20

2 **aliter** (adv.) - *in another way, otherwise, differently*

3 **incitō** (1) - *to stir up, inspire, rouse*

4 **iuba, -ae, f.** - *mane*

verrō, -ere, verrī, versum - *to sweep, brush*

5 **appropinquō** (1) (+ dat.) - *to come near, approach*

6 **tardus, -a, -um** - *slow*

7 **umerus, -ī, m.** - *shoulder*

exuō, -ere, -uī, -ūtum (+ abl. of person or source) - *to take off, strip*

immō (adv.) - *on the contrary, rather*

10 **praedīcō, -ere, -dīxī, -dictum** - *to foretell, predict, prophesy*

procul (adv. + abl.) - *far from*

11 **nimium, -iī, n.** - *too much, excess*

14 **contendō, -ere, -tendī, -tentum** - *to strive, exert oneself*

ulcīscor, -ī, ultus sum - *to take vengeance on*

15 **impellō, -ere, -pulī, -pulsum** - *to compel forward, drive, urge on*

simulō (1) - *to imitate, simulate*

aspectus, -ūs, m. - *appearance*

Lycāōn, -ōnis, m. - *Lycaon;* one of the many sons of Priam

16 **hērōs**: vocative s.

17 **peperit**: from *pariō, -ere*

18 **dīrigō, -ere, -rexī, -rectum** - *to direct, aim*

dēflectō, -ere, -flexī, -flexum - *to change the course of, divert, deflect*

19 **incendō, -ere, -cendī, -cēnsum** - *to inflame, inspire, excite*

GRAMMAR AND COMPREHENSION QUESTIONS

1) What case is *caput*? What is its grammatical function?
2) What construction is *ut . . . verreret*?
3) What case is *nōs*? What is its grammatical function?
4) Whom does Xanthus credit with killing Patroclus?
5) What tense and form is *moritūrum esse*? In what construction?
6) How do you translate *dum* with the subjunctive mood?
7) *Nē* plus the subjunctive in *dēflectat* creates what construction (more common in poetry)?

Achillēs castrīs relictīs splendidōs equōs terribilī vōce adlocūtus est: "Cūrāte ut mē ad Danaōs referātis aliter quam Patroclum quem mortuum relīquistis." Tum equus Xanthus ā Iūnōne incitātus **caput** dēmīsit **ut** omnis iuba humum **verreret** et respondit: "Salvum tē hodiē referēmus,

5   valide Achillēs, sed fātālis diēs tibi appropinquat. At **nōs** nōlī culpāre sed māgnum deum fātumque. Nam nec tardī nec neglegentēs erāmus ut Trōiānī arma umerīs Patroclī exuerint. Immō hunc Apollō occīdit ut glōriam Hectorī daret. Tē occīdī ā deō homineque fātum est."

Achillēs valdē sollicitus locūtus est: "Xanthe, cūr mortem meam

10   praedīcis? Ego ipse mē hīc procul patriā parentibusque **moritūrum esse** sciō. At tamen pugnāre nōn dēsinam **dum** Trōiānī nimium proeliī habeant." Hīs dictīs Achillēs in proelium incurrit. Omnēs Trōiānī autem genibus tremuērunt cum Achillem armīs splendidum vīdērent. Achillēs ipse Hectorem invenīre contendēbat ut eum ulciscerētur. Sed prīmum

15   Apollō Aenēan contrā Achillem impulit. Simulāns aspectum Lycāonis, fīliī Priamī, deus adlocūtus est: "Hērōs, deōs ōrā, quoniam Venus, fīlia Iovis, tē peperit, sed minor dea Thetis Achillem peperit. Adversus hastam in hunc dīrige. **Nē** hic tē verbīs terrōreque **dēflectat**." Hīs dictīs Aenēan incendit et māgnam vim in eō imposuit.

Discussion Questions

1) What is the effect of Xanthus's words? Why does Homer include this truly extraordinary scene?
2) Can you think of a modern talking horse?
3) Do you know who is the god, who the mortal destined to kill Achilles?
4) Did Achilles have to die at Troy? Did he have another choice?

20 **prōcēdō, -ere, -cessī, -cessum** - *to advance, proceed*

21 **prōsiliō, -īre, -siluī,** - *to leap forward, spring forward, rush*

23 **opīmus, -a, -um** - *rich, fertile*

24 **nōnne** (interrogative adv. introducing questions expecting the answer "yes") - *don't?*

quondam (adv.) - *formerly, once, in the past*

27 **haudquāquam** (adv.) - *by no means, not at all*

28 **antequam** (conj.) - *before*

30 **contumēlia, -ae, f.** - *insult*

31 **vituperō** (1) - *to find fault, disparage, vituperate*

32 **aliī . . . aliī:** datives of the pronoun *alius*

33 **nostrum:** partitive genitive

inānis, -e - *idle, useless*

compōnō, -ere, -posuī, -positum - *to settle, conclude*

37 **ōra, -ae, f.** - *rim, edge*

subsīdō, -ere, -sēdī - *to crouch down*

38 **mergō, -ere, mersī, mersum** - *to sink, bury*

stringō, -ere, strinxī, strictum - *to unsheathe, draw*

Grammar and Comprehension Questions

1) What case is *mē?*
2) What tense and voice is *rectūrum esse?* From what verb?
3) What tense is *occīdēs?*
4) What construction is *quōmodo . . . īnsecūtus sim?*
5) What noun is *meum* understood to modify?
6) What construction does *intellegēbat* introduce?
7) What did Achilles fail to understand about his new armor?
8) Identify precisely the form *penetrārī.*
9) What does the adjective *ingēns* modify?
10) Once Aeneas has thrown his spear, with what does he try to defend himself?

20   Duo hērōēs in pugnam prōcessērunt. Prīmum Achillēs pedibus celer "Aenēās," inquit, "cūr in **mē** ex aciē prōsiluistī? Spērāsne tē **rectūrum esse** Trōiānōs? Etiamsī mē **occīdēs**, tē Priamus nōn honōrābit. Nam huic multī fīliī sunt. Num Trōiānī tibi opīmōs agrōs prōmīsērunt sī mē occidās? Sed mē occīdere nōn facile erit. Nōnne meministī quondam tē

25   ab hastā meā fūgisse? Nōnne quoque meministī **quōmodo** tē sōlum in montibus **īnsecūtus sim**? Tum Iuppiter **tē celeriter currentem** servāvit. Nunc haudquāquam crēdō deōs tē servātūrōs esse. Ergō in medium aciem tē recipe antequam aliquod malum patiēris."

        Deinde Aenēās respondit: "Fīlī Peleī, numquam sperā tē mē velut

30   īnfantem verbīs territūrum esse, quoniam ego ipse contumēliās iacere et vituperāre possum. Ut genus tuum cognōvī, ita **meum** cognōvistī. Iuppiter autem vim modo aliī, modo aliī dat. Hodiē parentēs ūnum nostrum lūgēbunt. Pugnam nōn inānibus verbīs sed armīs compōnāmus." Dīxit et in ingēns scūtum Achillis gravem hastam iēcit. Sed timēns

35   Achillēs scūtum longē ā sē tenēbat. Stultus, quod nōn **intellegēbat** immortālia arma **penetrārī** nōn posse. Deinde Achillēs hastā ēmissā ōram scūtī Aenēae percussit. Aenēās subsīdēns scūtum super sē tenuit. Hasta in terram post Aenēan sē mersit. Achillēs gladiō strinctō in Aenēan ruit. Hic **ingēns** saxum manibus rapit quod adversum Achillem iaciat.

DISCUSSION QUESTIONS

1) What previous encounters with Aeneas does Achilles mention? How did Aeneas behave in these encounters?
2) What irony do you find in Achilles describing Aeneas as *tē celeriter currentem*?
3) Who strikes the first blow? How does this affect his characterization?
4) What surprising behavior of Achilles is described?

41   **audēns, -ntis** - *bold, courageous*

42   **Orcus, -ī, m.** - *Orcus*; the god of the underworld; *the underworld, death*

45   **supersum, -esse, -fuī, -futūrus** - *to survive*

46   **Dardanus, -ī, m.** - *Dardanus*; an ancestor of the Trojans, more associated with Aeneas's line than Priam's

     dēficiō, -ere, -fēcī, -fectum - *to fail, cease*

47   **posterī, -ōrum, m.** - *descendants, coming generations*

49   **ēvellō, -ere, -vellī, -vulsum** - *to pluck out, tear out*

50   **levō** (1) - *to lift up, raise up*

51   **volō** (1) - *to fly*

     extrēmum, -ī, n. - *furthest point, edge, limit*

54   **obviam** (adv. + *īre*) - *to meet*

55   **bonō animō** (idiom with *sum*) - *to be of good spirit, have courage*

     es: singular imperative of *sum*

58   **obstipēscō, -ere, -stipuī** - *to be struck dumb, dazed, to be astounded*

59   **vērē** (adv.) - *truly*

60   **refert** (impersonal idiom + abl. *meā*) - *it matters to me, it concerns me*

Grammar and Comprehension Questions

1) What tense and mood is *ēripuisset*? In what construction?
2) To whom does Neptune address the imperative *age*?
3) What tense and mood is *īrāscātur*? In what construction?
4) What surprising thing happens to the spear that Achilles threw at Aeneas?
5) What surprising thing happens to Aeneas himself?
6) What tense is *periit*?
7) What tense and mood is *vīdisset*? In what construction? Why is *posset* in a different tense?
8) What is the first principal part from which *nātum esse* comes?
9) What construction is *mihi excitandī sunt*?

40   Nunc Achillēs vītam ex Aeneā **ēripuisset** nisi Neptūnus ea vīdisset.
Deīs immortālibus "Heu" inquit "audentem Aenēan lūgeō, quī ab Achille
victus in Orcum mox dēscendet. Stultus! Nam verbīs Apollinis crēdidit,
quī mortem ab eō nōn āvertet. Sed cūr hic innocēns propter aliēna mala
frūstrā patitur? Semper autem dōna grāta deīs dat. **Age** nunc, hunc ā

45   morte ēripiam nē Iuppiter **īrāscātur**. Nam fātum est hunc superesse nē
genus Dardanī dēficiat. Genus Priamī autem dēficiet. Iam genus Aenēae
Trōiānōs et posterōs eius reget."

        Hīs dictīs, Neptūnus prīmum nebulam ante oculōs Achillis posuit,
deinde hastam ē terrā ēvellit quam prope pedēs Achillis posuit. Sed

50   Aenēan levāvit eumque iēcit ut hērōs super multōs mīlitēs, multōs equōs
volāret et ad extrēmum proeliī venīret. Ibi adstāns Neptūnus Aenēan
adlocūtus est: "Aenēās, quī deus hortābātur ut īnsānus cum Achille
pugnārēs, quī est validior quam tū et quem deī amant? Immō, cēde
quotiēns huic obviam īs, nē in Orcum dēscendās. Sed postquam Achillēs

55   **periit**, bonō animō es et cum optimīs pugnā quia nēmō Danaum tē
interficere poterit."

        Nunc discēdēns Neptūnus nebulam ab oculīs Achillis remōvit. Tum
Achillēs obstipuit cum hastam in terrā iacentem **vīdisset** et nusquam
hostem vidēre **posset**. Mīrāns Achillēs sēcum locūtus: "Vērē Aenēās

60   dīxit sē ā deā **nātum esse**. Sed nōn meā refert. Iste mē oppugnāre iterum
nōn audēbit. Nunc Danaī **mihi excitandī sunt** ut cēterōs Trōiānōs
oppugnent." Sīc Achillēs Danaōs hortātus est.

DISCUSSION QUESTIONS

1) Aeneas's epithet in Vergil's *Aeneid* is *pius*. How does this compare to
   the description of his character here?
2) For whose errors or crimes is Aeneas suffering? What were they?
3) During the Trojan War Neptune was usually on the side of the
   Greeks. Why now does he rescue Aeneas?
4) How important is Neptune's revelation of Aeneas's fate? What is he
   predicting?

64 **obstō, -stāre, -stitī, -stātum** (+ dat.) - *to meet face to face, make a stand against*

65 **ferrum, -ī, n.** - *iron; sword*

67 **crēber, -bra, -brum** - *crowded, tight-packed, dense*

aliter (adv.) - *otherwise*

71 **madeō, -ēre** (+ abl.) - *to be wet*

Polydōrus, -ī, m. - *Polydorus*

72 **trānsfīgō, -ere, -fīxī, -fictum** - *to pierce through, drive through*

mināx, -ācis - *menacing, threatening*

74 **irrītō** (1) - *to move to anger, provoke, vex*

75 **diūtius** (adv.) - *longer*

vītō (1) - *to avoid*

propius (adv.) - *nearer*

exitium, -iī, n. - *destruction, death*

80 **aura, -ae, f.** - *breeze*

dēflectō, -ere, -flexī, -flectum - *to change the course of, turn aside, deflect*

81 **saevus, -a, -um** - *savage, raging, fierce*

82 **crāssus, -a, -um** - *thick, dense*

involvō, -ere, -voluī, -volūtum - *to envelop, cover, wrap*

83 **impellō, -pelle, -pulī, -pulsum** - *to drive, thrust*

quartum (adv.) - *the fourth time*

84 **posthāc** (adv.) - *after this*

85 **quī**: shortened form of *aliquī* after *sī*

86 **dēprendō, -ere, -prendī, -prēnsum** - *to come suddenly upon and seize, to catch, overtake*

GRAMMAR AND COMPREHENSION QUESTIONS

1) What is the direct object of *efficiet*?
2) What literary device is *manūs eius flammīs similēs*?
3) What form must you understand to complete the meaning with *adlocūtus*?
4) What form is *iit*? From what verb?
5) Who is the *cārum amīcum* to whom Achilles refers?
6) What type of subjunctive is *vītēmus*?
7) Hector's words beginning *fīlī Peleī* to *possum* repeat those of Aeneas earlier. Do you know what to call this stylistic device that is an integral part of Homeric style?
8) What gender, number, and case is *omnia*? What is its grammatical function?
9) What does Minerva do to the spear Hector throws?
10) What does Achilles call Hector?
11) What mood is *adiuvet*? In what construction?

Tum adversus praeclārus Hector Trōiānīs clāmāvit: "Nē Achillem timeātis. Etiam iste omnia quae dīcit nōn **efficiet**. Ergō iam eī obstābō,

65   etsī **manūs eius flammīs similēs** sunt et cor simile ferrō." At nunc Apollō adstāns Hectorem **adlocūtus**: "Hector, sōlus contrā Achillem nōlī pugnāre, sed istum in crēbrīs mīlitibus exspectā. Aliter iste tē hastā gladiōque percutiet." Hīs verbīs audītīs, timēns Hector in multitūdinem sē recēpit.

70   Sed Achillēs furiōsus terribilī vōce contrā Trōiānōs ruit et permultōs occīdit ut humus sanguine mādēret. Tandem Achillēs Polydōrum, frātrem Hectoris, per abdōmen hastā trānsfīxit. Tum Hector īrātus obviam Achillī **iit**. Hunc vidēns Achillēs mīnāx clāmāvit: "Hīc est mīles quī plūs quam omnēs aliī mē irrītāvit, quoniam **cārum amīcum** meum occīdit. Nē

75   diūtius pugnam inter nōs **vītēmus**. Propius venī ut in exitium perveniās."

Sed Hector respondit: "**Fīlī Peleī**, numquam sperā tē mē velut īnfantem verbīs territūrum esse, quoniam ego ipse contumēliās iacere et vituperāre **possum**. Sciō tē validiōrem esse quam mē. **Omnia** tamen deī moderantur. Fortasse ego vītam ā tē hastā meā ēripiam." Hīs dictīs,

80   hastam ēmīsit, quam Minerva aurā dēflexit ut ad terram ante pedēs Achillis caderet. Tum saevus Achillēs terribilī clāmōre in Hectorem incurrit. At Apollō Hectorem facile levāns crāssā nebulā involuit. Achillēs ter incurrit, ter hastam in nebulam impulit, sed quartum oppugnāns clāmāvit: "Iterum mortem effūgistī, canis, quia Apollō tē servāvit. Posthāc

85   tamen tē vincam, sī quī deus mē **adiuvet**. At nunc aliī Trōiānī mihi īnsequendī sunt, quōs dēprendere possum." Tum Achillēs permultōs Trōiānōs multīs mōdīs furiōsē occīdit.

Discussion Questions

1) Does Apollo's advice to Hector to fight only from within a crowd conform to the heroic code of fighting?
2) What motivates Hector to ignore Apollo's advice?
3) What is the mental state of Achilles? What adjectives would you use in English to describe this?

Cultural Influences

A book that examines the mental state of Achilles is Jonathan Shay's *Achilles in Vietnam: Combat Trauma and the Undoing of Character* (Scribner, 1994). Chapter Three "Grief at the death of a Special Comrade" and Chapter Five "Berserk" are especially relevant. Shay compares the experiences of Vietnam soldiers who lost special friends and/or were betrayed by a commander to the situation of Achilles.

The Museum of Fine Arts, Boston showcases an amazing painting "Automedon with the Horses of Achilles" by Henri Regnault (oil, 1868). The painting is heroic in proportion at 124 by 129 1/2 inches. The horses rear up as Automedon tries to restrain them.

Aeneas and his son Ascanius land on the shores of Latium in Italy. Aeneas has been saved in battle by Neptune so that he can fulfill his fate and found a new civilization. The sow is an omen of where to found his new city (see *Aeneid*, Book 8). (Roman bas-relief, c. 140–150 CE; British Museum, London, England)
(© Creative Commons 2.5/Marie-Lan Nguyen)

Chapter Sixteen

Achilles's Battle Frenzy

In Book 21 of Homer's *Iliad* we see Achilles's full battle frenzy. The book is so focused on him that no other Greek hero is mentioned. As Achilles chases the panicked Trojans, they separate. Some manage to flee towards the city, but Achilles slaughters those who flee toward the river Scamander. He even kills suppliants who beg for mercy and captures twelve others for human sacrifice later at Patroclus's tomb. The carnage he creates is so extreme that the river, choked with bodies, begs the gods for help. This chapter begins with Achilles's encounter with the suppliant Lycaon, continues with Achilles's despair as he fights the river, and concludes with an encounter with the Trojan Agenor through which, by Apollo's intervention, all the surviving Trojans but Hector escape into Troy.

Source

Homer, *Iliad* 21

1   **Lycāōn, -āonis, m.** - *Lycaon*; son of
     King Priam and Laothoë

3   **genuit**: from *gignō*

4   **misericordia, -ae, f.** - *pity, mercy*

5   **antequam** (conj.) - *before*

     suprēmus, -a, -um - *final, last*

     obeō, -īre, -iī, -itum - *to meet, come
     up against*

7   **quīcumque, quaecumque,
     quodcumque** - *whoever, whatever*

8   **morere**: singular imperative of
     morior, morī, mortuus sum - *to die*

10   **collum, -ī, n.** - *neck*

     trānsfīgō, -ere, -fīxī, -fīxum - *to
     pierce, thrust through*

12   **lambō, -ere, -ī** - *to lick*

14   **cecidērunt**: from *cadō, -ere*

15   **Xanthus, -ī, m.** - *Xanthus*; a river
     near Troy

     altō: here as substantive, *the deep,
     the depths*

16   **saevus, -a, -um** - *harsh, savage,
     ferocious*

17   **saltem** (adv.) - *at least*

18   **exigō, -ere, -ēgī, -actum** - *to drive
     out*

     amoenus, -a, -um - *pleasing,
     beautiful, delightful*

19   **oppleō, -ēre, -ēvī, -ētum** - *to fill
     completely, fill up*

20   **audax, audācis** - *bold, daring, rash*

21   **inclūdō, -ere, -clūsī, -clūsum** - *to
     enclose, shut in, confine*

GRAMMAR AND COMPREHENSION QUESTIONS

1) What mood and tense is *occīdās*? In what construction?

2) What was Achilles's former custom regarding suppliants, before
   Patroclus's death?

3) What tense and mood is *mīserint*?

4) In what sense does Achilles call Lycaon *amīce*?

5) What case is *tē*? In what construction?

6) What form is *moritūrōs esse*? In what construction is it after *sperō*?

7) What construction is *ut . . . dent*?

8) What form of the adjective is *saeviora*?

9) What construction is *ut . . . possit*?

10) What case, number, and gender is *quae*? What is its grammatical
    function?

11) What construction follows *dum*? (What mood is the verb?)

Lycāōn, fīlius Priamī, genua Achillis amplectāns ōrābat: "Tibi
supplicō, Achillēs. Mē igitur pius miserēre. Nē mē **occīdās**; nōn enim
eadem māter mē cum Hectore genuit, quī amīcum tuum interfēcit." Sed
Achillēs furēns respondit: "Stulte, misericordiam nōlī exspectāre.
5   Antequam Patroclus diem suprēmum obiit, tum miserāns hostibus
parcere solēbam. At nunc nōn ūnus Trōiānōrum, praesertim fīlius Priamī,
mortem fugiet, quemcumque deī contrā mē **mīserint**. Ergō, **amīce**, etiam
morere. Cūr lāmentāris? Patroclus quoque mortuus est, quī **tē** multō
melior erat. Etiam ego mortem obībō, cum aliquis vītam ā mē hastā
10 sagittāve ēripiet." Hīs dictīs Achillēs glādiō collum Lycāonis trānsfīxit.
Tum Achillēs, cum mortuum Lycāonem in flūmen iēcisset, adlocūtus:
"Ibi cum piscibus iacē, quī vulnus lambent, nec māter tua tē tenēns
lāmentābitur. Sīc **sperō** omnēs Trōiānōs **moritūrōs esse ut** poenās prō
Patroclō et omnibus Danaīs **dent** quī mē absente cecidērunt."
15   Sed nunc flūmen Xanthus ex altō Achillī adlocūtus est: "Achillēs, tibi
māior vīs, facta **saeviōra** sunt quam omnibus, quoniam tē deī tuentur.
Sī Iuppiter tē omnēs Trōiānōs occīdere sinit, saltem eōs ex aquīs meīs
ad terram exactōs in terrā tum plūrimōs occīde. Nam amoenum flūmen
meum cadāveribus tam opplētur **ut** ad mare pervenīre nōn iam **possit**."
20   Cuī pedibus celer Achillēs respondit: "**Quae** iubēs faciam; at audācēs
Trōiānōs occīdere nōn dēsistam **dum** in urbe eōs inclūdam et cum
Hectore pugnem. Aut mē iste occīdet aut ego istum occīdam."

DISCUSSION QUESTIONS

1) Why did Lycaon think that Achilles might not be so angry with him?
2) What was the normally accepted ancient code of behavior toward
   suppliants? How do Achilles's actions compare to this code?
3) How does Achilles treat the corpse of Lycaon?
4) Whom does Achilles blame for the deaths of Patroclus and the other
   Greeks?
5) Does it make tactical sense for Achilles to want once again to trap
   the Trojans in their city?

23 rīpa, -ae, f. - *river-bank*

dēsiliō, -īre, -siluī, -sultum - *to jump down, leap down*

24 aestus, -ūs, m. - *current, swell*

25 attingō, -ere, -tigī, -tāctum - *to touch, reach*

26 surrēxit: from *surgō, -ere*

27 cōnstringō, -ere, -strinxī, -strictum - *to inhibit, restrict, check, obstruct*

27–28 questus est: from *queror, -ī*

30 praedīcō, -ere, -dīxī, -dictum - *to predict, foretell*

vellem: imperfect subjunctive of *volō* in unfulfilled wish construction, *I wish that...*

31 obruō, -ere, -uī, -utum - *to overwhelm, bury, swamp*

34 adsēnsus, -ūs, m. - *approval, assent*

adsum, -esse, -fuī, -futūrus - *to be present, near*

35 comprimō, -ere, -pressī, -pressum - *to constrict, hold back, curb*

36 inclūdō, -ere, -clūsī, -clūsum - *to shut in, enclose, confine*

Grammar and Comprehension Questions

1) What surprising epic struggle is described in the first paragraph?
2) What expectation does the word *num* indicate?
3) What tense and mood is *occīdisset*? What sense does this convey?
4) What construction is *illō querente*?
5) What is the antecedent of *quod*?
6) What tense is *effūgit*?

Hīs dictīs, dīvīnus Achillēs statim ē rīpā in flūmen dēsiluit et in
Trōiānōs incurrit. Sed flūmen tam māgnō aestū fluēbat ut hērōs stāre
25   nōn iam posset. Achillēs celeribus pedibus terram attingere temptābat;
māgnum flūmen autem super eum surrēxit ut labōrem Achillis
cōnstringeret et auxilium Trōiānīs ferret. Tum Achillēs gemēns questus
est, "Pater Iuppiter, **num** ūllus deus mē miserum servābit? Māter mea
quidem mē dēcepit cum mē sagittīs Apollinis sub mūrīs Trōiae cāsūrum
30   esse praedīxisset. Vellem ut fortis Hector mē fortem **occīdisset**. Nunc
autem misera mors mē quasi puerum in flūmine obrutum exspectat."

    Illō querente, Neptūnus Minervaque celeriter appropinquāvērunt.
Prīmum Neptūnus adlocūtus: "Nōlī timēre, fīlī Peleī, quoniam nōs duo
deī adsēnsū Iovis adsumus. Nōn est tibi fātum in flūmine morī, **quod**
35   mox comprimētur. Tibi etiam cōnsilium damus. Nē pugnāre dēsistās
dum fugientēs Trōiānōs in mūrīs Trōiae inclūdās. Tum, Hectore occīsō,
ad nāvēs redī. Tantam glōriam tibi Iuppiter dat." Tum Achillēs ē furentī
flūmine **effūgit** et plūrimōs Trōiānōs occīdit.

DISCUSSION QUESTIONS

    1) Do you know who myth tells us killed Achilles?
    2) What do you think of the divine interference of Minerva and
       Neptune?

40 **perturbātus, -a, -um** - *disorderly, confused, troubled*

41 **imperō** (1) (+ dat.) - *to order, command*

   aperiō, -īre, -uī, -tum - *to open*

42 **ēvādō, -ere, -vāsī, -vāsum** - *to get clear of, escape, evade*

   immittō, -ere, -mīsī, -missum - *to let in, admit*

43 **claudō, -ere, clausī, clausum** - *to shut, close*

   ineō, -īre, -iī, -itum - *to get in, enter*

44 **inruō, -ere, -uī** - *to rush in, dash in*

   Agēnor, -oris, m. - *Agenor;* son of the Trojan leader Antenor

45 **obvius, -a, -um** (+ dat.) - *opposite, in a position to confront*

   ocrea, -ae, f. - *greave*

   īciō, -ere, -ī, ictum - *to strike*

47 **saltus, -ūs, m.** - *leap, spring, bound*

48 **cālīgō, -inis, f.** - *mist, fog*

   simulō (1) - *to make oneself like, liken to*

49 **aufugiō, -ere, -fūgī** - *to run away, flee*

50 **tūtō** (adv.) - *safely*

GRAMMAR AND COMPREHENSION QUESTIONS

1) What form is *īnsequī*? In what construction?
2) What construction is *nē . . . ineat*?
3) What tense and mood are *interfectus esset* and *ēripuisset*? In what construction?

Intereā senex Priamus, rēx Trōiae, dē altā turre vīdit ingentem
40 Achillem **insequī** Trōiānōs mīlitēs perturbātōs. Gemēns dē turre
dēscendit et custōdibus portae imperāvit: "Portās aperīte ut mīlitēs
nostrī fugientēs Achillem ēvādere possint. Tum, mīlitibus immissīs,
portās statim claudite **nē** Achillēs ipse **ineat**." Rēge iubente, custōdēs
portās aperuērunt et multī Trōiānī inruēbant. Sed Agēnor, fīlius
45 Antēnoris, extrā Achillī obvius stetit. Hastā iactā ocream Achillis īcit,
sed immortālem ocream penetrāre nōn poterat. Deinde Achillēs māgnō
saltū in Agēnorem inruit; et eō tempore Agēnor **interfectus esset** nisi
Apollō eum in cālīgine tegēns ē proeliō **ēripuisset**. Tum Apollō simulāns
sē esse Agēnorem ā portā aufugiēbat, quem Achillēs celeriter
50 īnsequēbātur. Itaque aliī Trōiānī urbem intrāre tūtō poterant.

DISCUSSION QUESTION

1) How does Agenor behave in contrast to his fellow Trojans?

The Fight of Achilles against Scamander and Simois (two personified rivers)
(Auguste Couder, 1819; Louvre Museum, Paris, France)
(© Creative Commons 2.5/Marie-Lan Nguyen)

Chapter Seventeen

THE CLIMACTIC SLAYING OF HECTOR

Book 22 is the climax of the *Iliad* in which Achilles kills Hector. Surprisingly, it is one of the shorter books of the epic. This book chapter, however, is lengthy since the episode is the culmination of the epic in both action and imagery. Also, Vergil patterned the final battle between Aeneas and Turnus that closes the *Aeneid* (Book 12) upon this episode. In Homer the confrontation is beautifully framed by three speeches in which the speaker tries to dissuade Hector from fighting Achilles. After his death the Book closes with three corresponding speeches of grief. The actual battle is described at a fast pace and features some unexpected developments that evoke strong emotions from the audience.

SOURCE

Homer, *Iliad* 22

1   **inexōrābilis, -e** - *inexorable, relentless, that cannot be moved by entreaty*

4   **vānus, -a, -um** - *useless, vain, ineffectual*

5   **obstō, -āre, -stitī, -stātum** - *to hinder, block, obstruct*

    perniciōsus, -a, -um - *destructive, deadly, pernicious*

6   **cecidissent** - from *cadō*

    antequam (conj.) - *before*

    ēvādō, -ere, -vāsī, -vāsum - *to get clear, escape*

7   **properō** (1) - *to hurry, hasten*

    trāns (prep. + acc.) - *across, over*

9   **plangō, -ere, planxī, planctum** - *to beat, strike*

11   **obeō, -īre, -iī** or **-īvī, -itum** - *to meet face to face, meet with, come up against*

    asper, -era, -erum - *harsh, cruel, fierce*

12   **orbō** (1) (+ abl. of separation) - *to deprive of by death, to rob of*

13   **intrā** (prep. + acc.) - *within, inside*

14   **hinc** (adv.) - *from here*

15   **spoliō** (1) (+ abl. of the thing taken) - *to strip of*

    meī miserī - genitive with *miserāre*

16   **nurus, -ūs, f.** - *daughter-in-law*

17   **cōniciō, -ere, -iēcī, -iectum** - *to throw, hurl*

    postrēmō (adv.) - *after everything else, finally*

18   **dēvorō** (1) - *to gulp down, swallow, devour*

    acūtus, -a, -um - *sharp*

19   **decōrus, -a, -um** - *becoming, seemly, decent*

    vīsū - ablative supine from *videō*

20   **pudet** (impersonal with infinitive) - *it is shameful, it shames*

    for, fārī, fātus sum - *to speak, say*

    crīnis, -is, m. - *hair*

    scindō, -ere, scindī, scissum - *to tear, rend*

GRAMMAR AND COMPREHENSION QUESTIONS

1) How did Hector come to be alone in front of the gates?
2) What tense and mood is *cecidissent*? In what construction?
3) What is the force of *istum*? How does it differ from *hunc* or *eum*?
4) What tense and mood is *occīderit*? In what construction?
5) What tense and mood is *dēs*? From what verb? In what construction?
6) On what basis does Priam appeal to Hector? What has Priam experienced already?
7) What form is *mortuus sit*? From what verb?

Iam cēterī Trōiānī in urbem fūgerant. At inexōrābile fātum Hectorem
sōlum ante portam tenuit. Intereā Apollō Achillem adlocūtus est: "Cūr
tū mortālis mē immortālem īnsequeris? Nunc Trōiānī in urbem fūgērunt
dum hūc vānus curris. Nam mē deum numquam occīdēs." Achillēs multō
5   īrātus respondit: "Mē obstitistī, perniciōsissime omnium deum; aliter
multī Trōiānī in pulverem **cecidissent** antequam in Trōiam ēvāsērunt."
Hīs dictīs ad urbem properāvit velut equus trāns campum currit.

Prīmum Priamus dē mūrīs spectāns **istum** accēdentem vīdit. Senex
gemēns manibus caput suum planxit et fīlium suum ōrābat, quī prō portā
10   stābat. "Hector, nōlī, cāre fīlī, istum sōlus exspectāre nē ab Achille victus
mortem obeās. Iste asper enim multō validior est quam tū. Mē tam multīs
fortibus fīliīs orbāvit ut māgnopere dolērem. At sī tē Achillēs **occīderit**,
dolor multō māior mē mātremque tuam afflīget. Revenī intrā mūrōs, mī
fīlī, ut hinc Trōiānōs servēs et nē māgnam glōriam Achillī **dēs** cum iste
15   tē vītā spoliāverit. Meī miserī miserāre, quem senem dūrō fātō Iuppiter
dēlēbit postquam fīliōs meōs occīsōs, fīliās nurūsque captīvās, et
īnfantēs ad terram cōniectōs vīdī. Postrēmō canēs meī mē in domū meā
dēvorābunt et sanguinem bibent, postquam aliquī hostis mē acūtō gladiō
interfēcerit. Decōrus vīsū est iuvenis cum in proeliō **mortuus sit**, sed
20   senem in pulvere iacentem vidēre pudet." Nec plūra fātus crīnēs scindit,
sed animum Hectoris movēre nōn potuit.

Discussion Questions

1) What is Achilles's attitude towards the god Apollo?
2) How much confidence does Priam show in Hector's fighting?
3) Can Hector really save the Trojans from inside the walls?
4) What final indiginity of war does Priam imagine will happen to him?
5) Compare the fate of Priam's body with that of Pompey the Great.
    Vergil may have written Priam's death scene in *Aeneid* 4 as an
    allusion to Pompey's murder.
6) Priam's prediction of children thrown from the walls prefigures the
    fate of Astyanax which Andromache herself fearfully alluded to
    in *Iliad* 24.734–38. Why would the Greeks do such a thing? What
    threat does a young child represent?

22   **iūxtā** (prep. + acc.) - *close to, near to*

     mamma, -ae, f. - *breast*

     nūdō (1) - *to make naked, to bare*

24   **nūtriō, -īre, -īvī, -ītum** - *to suckle, feed at breast*

     arceō, -ēre, -uī - *to keep away, repulse*

25   **feretrum, -ī, n.** - *bier, funeral couch*

26   **vescor, -ī** (+ abl.) - *to feed on, eat*

29   **incendō, -ere, -cendī, -cēnsum** - *to kindle, excite*

     turbātus, -a, -um - *disturbed, troubled*

30   **Pōlydamās, -antos, m.** - *Polydamas;* Trojan hero who advised Hector to retreat within the walls

     culpō (1) - *to blame, censure*

32   **temeritās, -tātis, f.** - *rashness, recklessness*

34   **quis** = *aliquis* after *nē*

     fīdēns, -ntis (+ abl.) - *confident in, trusting in*

35   **obviam īre** (+ dat.): *to meet*

37   **inermis, -e** - *unarmed*

38   **gāza, -ae, f.** - *treasure*

     ablātum - from *auferō*

40   **dēlīberō** (1) - *to ponder, weigh, deliberate*

42   **uter, utra, utrum** (interrog. adj.) - *who? which (of two)?*

Grammar and Comprehension Questions

    1) To what does the demonstrative pronoun *eās* refer?

    2) What must you understand with *poterit* to complete the meaning?

    3) Do you know what the role of women was in burial?

    4) What construction follows *iubēbat*?

    5) What type of construction follows *nē*?

    6) What comparative form is *melius*?

    7) What type of subjunctive construction is *sit*?

    8) What type of use of the adjective is *bona*?

    9) What form is *ībō*? From what verb? What tense?

Iūxtā senem lacrimāns Hecuba stābat. Nunc mammās nūdāns rēgīna Hectorem ōrābat: "Hector, mī fīlī, **eās** aspiciēns pārē et meī miserāre, sī unquam tē nūtrīvī. Intrā mūrōs saevum Achillem arcē. Nam sī tē iste
25 occīderit, tē, dulcis fīlī, in feretrō lūgēre nōn poterō neque optima uxor **poterit.** Immō longē ā nōbīs canēs prope Graecās nāvēs tē vescentur."

Sīc pater māterque lacrimantēs cārum fīlium ōrābant, sed animum Hectoris movēre nōn potuērunt. Immō Achillem exspectāns Hector fortitūdinem in sē incendēbat. Turbātus sē adlocūtus est: "Heu, sī intrā
30 mūrōs recēdam, prīmus Pōlydamās mē culpābit. Nam ille **iubēbat** mē Trōiānōs in urbem dūcere antequam Achillēs in proelium redīvit. Sī eī pāruissem, hoc multō melius fuisset. At nunc populum meum temeritāte perdidī. Pudet mē apud Trōiānōs Trōiānāsque longīs cum vestibus **nē** quis dē mē dīcet: 'Hector vīribus suīs fīdēns populum perdidit.' **Melius**
35 itaque mihi **sit** ut obviam Achillī eam. Nam aut istō occīsō domum redībō aut ego ante urbem māgnā cum glōriā ab istō interficiar. Quodsī autem ingentī scūtō, galeā, hastāque dēpositīs inermis obviam Achillī eam et prōmittam Helenam et tōtam gāzam ā Paride ablātam reddere, et etiam omnia **bona** in urbe dare Graecīs et nihil cēlāre . . . At cūr tālia
40 dēlīberō? Sī inermis obviam istī **ībō**, iste mē nūdum nōn verēbitur sed velut fēminam occīdet. Ergō melius est quam celerrimē pugnāre. Mox vidēbimus utrī Iuppiter victōriam det." Ita Hector putābat.

Discussion Questions

1) On what basis does Hecuba appeal to her son?
2) What does her imagination prefigure will happen to Hector after his death?
3) Is it true that Hector has destroyed his people? Has he been reckless? If he is not responsible, who is?
4) What options does Hector consider before he engages in battle with Achilles?

43 **pār** (+ dat.) - *equal to*
    vibrō (1) - *to brandish, shake*

44 **aes, aeris, n.** - *bronze, armor*
    similiter (adv. + dat.) - *like, similar to*
    radius, -iī, m. - *ray*
    fulgeō, -ēre, fūlsī - *to shine, gleam*
    artus, -ūs, m. - *limb*

45 **occupō** (1) - *to seize, overcome*
    occupat . . . potest: these and the
    following present tenses are the
    historical present and are used to
    enhance the vividness of a passage.

46 **accipiter, -tris, m.** - *hawk*
    tremulus, -a, -um - *shaking,
    quaking, trembling*
    columba, -ae, f. - *dove*
    facile - neuter adjective as adverb

47 **involō** (1) - *to fly upon, attack*
    ēvolō (1) - *to fly away*
    identidem (adv.) - *again and again,
    repeatedly*

49 **praeter** (prep. + acc.) - *past, by*
    fōns, fontis, m. - *a natural spring,
    stream*

50 **lavō** (1) - *to wash*
    ob (prep. + acc.) - *on account of, for*

54 **agite**: idiom: *come!*

55 **permittāmus**: here governs clause
    with *ut* + subjunctive
    quamvīs (relative adverb) - *however
    much, although*

56 **saevus, -a, -um** - *brutal, cruel*

58 **damnō** (1) - *to condemn, doom*

59 **bonō animō** (idiom with *es*) - *Cheer
    up! Be of good spirit*
    es: singular imperative of *sum, esse*

60 **vīs**: from *volō, velle, voluī*

61 **etiamnum** (adv.) - *still*

62 **effūgissent**: plupft. subj. preceding
    nisi in a past contrary to fact
    condition

63 **celeritās, -tātis, f.** - *speed*

64 **aureus, -a, -um** - *golden*
    lībra, -ae, f. - *a balance, pair of scales*
    suspendō, -ere, -pendī, -pēnsum -
    to hang up, suspend

65 **sors, sortis, f.** - *lot;* here a physical
    representation of one's fate,
    perhaps a manikin or small
    statuette

66 **dēsīdō, -ere, -ēdī** - *to sink down, go
    down*

Grammar and Comprehension Questions

1) What bronze object is being referred to?
2) To what is Achilles compared? By implication to what is Hector
    compared?
3) What is the antecedent of *quibus*?
4) What tense is *lavāverant*?
5) What noun must be understood with *multō māior*?
6) Do you know the technical term for repeated phrases such as *pater
    hominum deumque*?
7) What case and number is *deum*?
8) What mood and tense are *ēripiāmus* and *permittāmus*? In what
    construction?

Intereā pār Martī Achillēs appropinquābat ingentem hastam vibrāns.
Huic aes similiter radiīs sōlis fulgēbat. Iam Hectorem per artūs tremor
45   occupat nec stāre potest, sed timēns currit. Fīlius Peleī celeribus pedibus
fīdēns īnsequitur velut celerrimus accipiter in tremulam columbam facile
involat, sed hanc ēvolantem iste acūtē clāmāns identidem oppugnat. Sīc
Achillēs īnsequitur Hectorem quī sub mūrōs Trōiae fugit. Ter currunt
circum mūrōs et praeter fontēs in **quibus** Trōiānae in pāce vestēs
50   **lavāverant**. Māgnus hērōs fugit, sed **multō māior** īnsequitur. Nōn ob
praedam sed vītam Hectoris currunt.

      Intereā dē monte Olympō deī observābant. Prīmum Iuppiter, **pater
hominum deumque**, adlocūtus: "Heu, cārum hominem fugientem videō.
Hectorem lūgeō quī plūrima sacrificia mihi fēcit. Agite, deī, dēlīberāte
55   utrum hunc ē morte **ēripiāmus** an **permittāmus** ut quamvīs bonus ā
saevō Achille occīdātur."

      Statim Minerva respondit: "Quāle verbum dīxistī? Cupis aliquem
mortālem ā morte redūcere? Diū enim fātō is damnātus est. Hoc faciās,
at aliī deī tē nōn approbābunt." Tum Iuppiter respondit: "Bonō animō es,
60   cāra fīlia. Age quōmodo vīs."

      Etiamnum celer Achillēs Hectorem īnsequēbatur, sed eum
capere nōn poterat. Nunc Hector mortem nōn effūgisset, nisi Apollō
fortitūdinem celeritātemque eī dedisset. Cum tamen quartum ad duōs
fontēs vēnissent, pater Iuppiter auream lībram suspendit in quā duās
65   sortēs, ūnam Hectoris, alteram Achillis posuit. Sōrs Hectoris gravior ad
mortem dēsēdit. Tum Apollō hērōem dēseruit.

Discussion Questions

1) What do you think of Hector fleeing? Does this affect his heroism?
2) Why do think Homer mentions the washing pools used by the
   women in former times?
3) Why especially does Jupiter mourn for Hector?
4) Have you read part of the paragraph giving Hector's response before?
   Do you know what this repetitive style is called?
5) In modern culture can you find a similar image of scales?

68 **lātūrōs esse**: from *ferō, ferre, tulī, lātum*

72 **adsequor, -quī, -cūtus sum** - *to overtake, catch up with*

Dēiphobus, -ī, m. - *Deiphobus; son of Priam and Hecuba and brother of Hector*

73 **simulō** (1) - *to put on the appearance of, assume the form of*

74 **abūtor, -ūtī, -ūsus sum** (+ abl.) - *to mistreat, abuse*

resistō, -ere, -stitī - *to stand still, halt, stop*

76 **ausus es**: from *audeō, -ēre* - *to dare*

77 **vērē** (adv.) - *truly*

80 **dolōsē** (adv.) - *treacherously, deceitfully*

82 **adversus** (prep. + acc.) - *opposite, facing, against*

83 **incitō** (1) - *to rouse, stimulate*

84 **testis, -is, m.** - *witness*

testor, -ārī, -ātus sum - *to call to witness, invoke as a witness*

85 **foedō** (1) - *to disfigure, mar, mistreat*

Grammar and Comprehension Questions

1) Why is the infinitive *lātūrōs esse* in the future tense?
2) What grammatical number does Minerva use to describe the upcoming action? What does this tell us?
3) What is the importance of the macron on *hīc*?
4) What case and number is *deae*? Why?
5) In what case is *omnibus cēterīs frātribus*? Why?
6) What governs the phrase *nē exīrem*?
7) What mood is *pugnēmus*? How then do you translate it?
8) What is the subject of *occīdātur*?
9) What form is *pugnandum*? With *ad* what is its construction? (See *Latin for the New Millennium*, Level 2, p. 344.)
10) What two alternatives does Hector consider as he faces Achilles?

At Minerva cum Achillem accessisset sīc adlocūta: "Nunc, dīvīne
Achillēs, spērō nōs māgnam glōriam Graecīs **lātūrōs esse**, postquam
ferōcem Hectorem occīderimus. Itaque **hīc** stā ut spīritum recipiās.

70 Ego autem Hectorī persuādēbō ut adversus pugnet." Hīs dictīs Achillēs
gaudēns **deae** paruit.

Tum Minerva splendidum Hectorem adsequēns Dēiphobum, frātrem
Hectoris, simulāvit. Dea "Cāre frāter," inquit, "Achillēs pedibus celer
circum Trōiam tē abūtitur. Sed age, resistentēs nōs dēfendāmus." Māgnus

75 Hector respondit, "Dēiphobe, ante multō cārissimus mihi erās **omnibus
cēterīs frātribus**. Sed nunc, quoniam sōlus ē mūrīs exīre ausus es ut mē
adiuvārēs, etiam māius tē honōrō." Tum Minerva, "Vērē pater māterque
mē **nē exīrem** ōrābant. Sed cor meum lūgēbat cum tē patī vidērem. Ergō
nunc adversum eum prōcēdāmus avidēque **pugnēmus** ut videāmus

80 utrum Achillēs spolia dē nōbīs referat an hastā tuā **occīdātur**." Sīc dolōsē
dea prōcessit, quam Hector secūtus est.

Adversus Achillem Hector "Nōn iam" inquit "tē timeō, quamvīs
ante tē fūgī. At nunc animus meus **ad pugnandum** mē incītat. Necesse
est aut mē vincere tē aut ā tē vincī. Sed deōs, optimōs testēs testāmur:

85 nam corpus tuum nōn foedābō, sī Iuppiter mihi victōriam dederit. Cum
splendida arma tua spoliāverim, Achillēs, corpus Graecīs reddam. Ita
etiam faciās."

DISCUSSION QUESTIONS

1) Does Minerva act fairly?
2) What is ironic in Minerva's explanation of how she came to help
   Hector?
3) With whom do you sympathize? Achilles or Hector?
4) How does the behavior of the warriors, who converse on the
   battlefield, compare to modern warfare?

88 **torvus, -a, -um** - *fierce, grim, savage*
in perpetuum: *into perpetuity, forever*
pactum, -ī, n. - *agreement, compact*

89 **lupus, -ī, m.** - *wolf*
ovis, -is, f. - *sheep*
ōdī, ōdisse, ōsum (defective verb occurring only in the perfect but translated as present) - *to hate*

91 **recordor, -ārī, -ātus sum** - *to call to mind, remember*
salūs, -ūtis, f. - *safety*

94 **infīgō, -ere, -fīxī, -fictum** - *to drive in, imbed*

95 **ēmendātus, -a, -um** - *perfect, faultless*

96 **compellō** (1) - *to address*

99 **aēneus, -a, -um** - *made of bronze, bronze*

100 **mergō, -ere, mersī, mersum** - *to plunge, sink*

profectō (adv.) - *undoubtedly, surely, certainly*

103 **perfodiō, -ere, -fōdī, -fossum** - *to make a hole through, pierce*

106 **ei** (interjection + dat.) - expresses anguish or distress - *ah me, woe is me*

107 **adsum, -esse, -fuī** - *to be present*

108 **intrā** (prep. + acc.) - *within*
prope: here adverbial, *near*

109 **placeō, -ēre, -uī, -itum** - (+ dat.) *to be pleasing to, to please*
benevolus, -a, -um - *kindly, friendly, benevolent*

110 **maneō, -ēre, mānsī, mānsum** - *to await*
contentiō, -ōnis, f. - *contest, fight*

111 **posterī, -ōrum, m.** - *descendants, coming generations*

Grammar and Comprehension Questions

1) What form is *recordāre*?
2) To what does *sē* refer?
3) What construction is *Hectore nōn vidente*?
4) What effect does Hector's use of the adjective *ēmendātum* create?
5) What mood and tense is *esset*? What does that mood imply in a condition?
6) What quality distinguishes Achilles's shield?
7) Why is Deiphobus not beside Hector? Where is he?
8) Why is *cognōscant* subjunctive?

Torvus Achillēs respondit: "Hector, in perpetuum inimīce, dē pactīs
nōlī dīcere. Nam nec lupī ovēsque pacta faciunt sed semper ōdērunt.
90 Itaque nūlla pacta inter nōs erint; immō alter alterum occīdet. Ergō
virtūtem **recordāre**! Tibi nūlla salūs est; nam Minerva hastā meā tē
superābit. Nunc poenās prō omnibus comitibus occīsīs dabis." Dīxit et
ingentem vibrantemque hastam iēcit. Sed illūstris Hector observāns eam
vītāvit, quae in terram post Hectorem **sē** infīxit. At Minerva hanc ēripuit
95 et Achillī reddidit, **Hectore nōn vidente**. Nunc Hector **ēmendātum**
Achillem compellāvit: "Male iēcistī, Achillēs dīvīne, nec ā Iove sortem
meam cōgnōvistī, sed hoc dīxistī ut virtūtis oblīviscerer. Sī deus
permittet, nōn in tergum meum hastam iaciēs sed in pectus cum in tē
incurram. Iam aēneam hastam meam cavē. Utinam in corpus tuum tōta
100 hasta mergat. Tē occīsō profectō hoc bellum Trōiānīs **esset** levius; nam
eīs tū es maximus dolor."

Hīs dictīs Hector longam hastam iēcit, quae medium scūtum
percussit. Tamen hasta scūtum ā deō factum perfodere nōn poterat.
Hector īrātus est, quia hastam frūstrā iēcerat. Tristis stetit nūllam aliam
105 hastam habēns. Tum Dēiphobum vocāvit ut ille longam hastam praebēret;
sed Dēiphobus aberat. Itaque Hector dolum intellegēns lūxit: "Ei mihi,
tandem deī ad mortem mē vocant. Cōgitābam Dēiphobum adesse, sed ille
intrā mūrōs est. Certē Minerva mē dēcipiēbat. Iam mala mors prope adest,
nec ūlla fuga est. Hoc Iovī Apollinīque diū placuit, quī mē ante benevolī
110 dēfendērunt. Nunc autem fātum mē manet. Sed sine contentiōne fāmāque
nōn moriar, quīn māgnum factum faciam quod posterī **cognōscant**."

DISCUSSION QUESTIONS

1) What do you think of Minerva's intervention? Can the action be
explained without divine involvement?
2) What is the importance of a wound to the chest rather than the
back?
3) Which god made Achilles's shield?
4) Whose arms originally were those that Hector is wearing?

112 **aquila, -ae, f.** - *eagle*
   volō (1) - *to fly*
114 **prōtegō, -ere, -texī, -tectum** - *to cover, protect*
   cornū, -ūs, n. - *horn (of helmet);* These were decorated with plumes.
   aciēs, -ēī, f. - *the cutting edge, point*
   fulgō, -ēre, fulsī - *to shine, gleam*
115 **candidus, -a, -um** - *shining, gleaming*
   stella, -ae, f. - *star*

116 **excōgitō** (1) - *to think up, devise*
117 **scrūtor, -ārī, -ātus sum** - *to examine, search*
119 **iugulum, -ī, n.** - *the throat*
120 **cervīx, -icis, f.** - *neck*
   artēria, -ae, f. - *windpipe*
   incīdō, -ere, -cīdī, -cīsum - *to cut open, slit, gash*
122 **fore** = *futūrum esse*
123 **ultor, -ōris, m.** - *avenger*
124 **avis, -is, f.** - *bird*

Grammar and Comprehension Questions

1) What case is *cornibus*? What is its grammatical function?
2) What case is *malum*? What is its grammatical function?
3) What construction is *ubi . . . prōtegerent*?
4) Why is *abessem* in the subjunctive?

Greek bronze helmet made in southern Italy 350–300 BCE (Getty Villa, California). Whose helmet is Hector wearing in this chapter? (© Creative Commons 2.0/Davide Ferro)

His dictīs Hector acūtō gladiō ēdūctō ut aquila altē volāns impetum
fēcit. Adversus Achillēs plēnus īrae prōcurrit. Pulchrum scūtum pectus eī
prōtegēbat, galea quattuor **cornibus** adnuēbat, aciēs hastae fulgēbat

115 similis candidae stellae, quam iam Achillēs dextrā vibrābat. **Malum**
illustrī Hectorī excōgitābat et sīc coepit omne splendidum corpus hostis
scrūtārī ut invenīret **ubi** arma hunc nōn **prōtegerent**. Nam Hector nōn
arma sua sed illa ā Patroclō spoliāta gerebat. Omne corpus prōtectum est
praeter iugulum, ubi mors celerrimē venit. Itaque, Hectore incurrente,

120 Achillēs hastam ēmīsit, quae cervicem perfōdit sed nōn artēriam incīdit.
Hector in pulverem cecidit super quem dīvīnus Achillēs glōriābātur:
"Hector, cum Patroclum occīdissēs, certē putābās tē fore salvum, quod
ego **abessem**. Stulte, nam ego ultor multō māior eō prope nāvēs
remanēbam et tē vīcī. Nunc canēs avēsque tē dēvorābunt, sed Graecī

125 Patroclum sepelient."

DISCUSSION QUESTIONS

1) What weak point does Achilles find in Hector's armor?
2) Compare the c. 500 BCE depiction on an Attic vase by the Berlin
   painter of the battle between Achilles and Hector with the
   description you read above.
3) How important was proper burial in the ancient world? Compare the
   myth of Antigone as told by Sophocles.
4) What was believed to happen to an unburied soul?
5) Is Achilles's fury against Hector justified in the context of war? Is
   what Hector has done properly termed *malum*?
6) What would Achilles like to do with Hector's body? What term do
   we have for this?

126   **īnfirmus, -a, -um** - *weak, feeble*
      obsecrō (1) - *to beg, implore*
      per (prep. + acc.) - *by*
127   **aes, aeris, n.** - *bronze*
128   **rīte** (adv.) - *with proper religious procedure, properly*
129   **truculentus, -a, -um** - *ferocious, aggressive, truculent*
      nē (conj. + imperative) - *don't*
131   **arceō, -ēre, -uī** (+ acc. of thing prevented, + dat. of thing protected) - *to keep off, prevent from approaching, fend off*
      deciēns (adv.) - *ten times*
      viciēns (adv.) - *twenty times*
132   **expendō, -ere, -pendī, -pēnsum** - *to weigh out, pay out*
      feretrum, -ī, n. - *funeral bier, couch*
134   **ferreus, -a, -um** - *made of iron, iron*
135   **pestis, -is, f.** - *plague, curse*
136   **Scaenus, -a, -um** - *Scaean*; applied to the main, western gates at Troy

137   **umbra, -ae, f.** - *shadow, shade, ghost*
141   **ēvellō, -ere, -vellī, -vulsum** - *to tear out, pull out*
      umerus, -ī, m. - *shoulder*
      sanguineus, -a, -um - *bloody, blood-stained*
142   **pulchritūdō, -inis, f.** - *beauty, handsomeness, excellence*
      intueor, -ērī, -itus sum - *to gaze upon, inspect*
      quīn (conj. + subj. after negative clauses) - *without it being the case that, who did not*
143   **fodiō, -ere, fōdī, fossum** - *to stab*
      mollis, -e - *soft*
144   **fax, facis, f.** - *torch*
      accendō, -ere, -censī, -censum - *to kindle, set on fire*
145   **paeān, -inis, m.** - *hymn of victory (usually to Apollo)*

GRAMMAR AND COMPREHENSION QUESTIONS

1) Why is *cognōveram* pluperfect? What is unusual about this verb?
2) What form of *morior* is *morere*?
3) Why is *foderet* in the subjunctive?
4) How do the other Greeks treat Hector's body?
5) What form is *eāmus*? From what verb?
6) Why is *hoc* neuter? To what does it refer? What impression does using the neuter convey?

Īnfirmus Hector obsecrābat: "Per vītam tuam et parentēs tē ōrō, nē cānēs mē dēvorent, quīn aes aurumque sūmās quae dōna māter paterque tibi dabunt. Corpus meum eīs redde ut Trōiānī mē rīte sepeliant." Sed truculentus Achillēs respondit: "Nē per genua nec parentēs mē ōrā.

130 Utinam possem tē dēvorāre prō malīs quae mihi ēgistī. Nēmō canēs tibi arcēbit, nōn sī deciēns aut viciēns plūra dōna praebēbunt et alia prōmittent, nōn sī Priamus pondus tuum aurō expendat. Nōn māter tua in feretrō lugēbit, sed canēs avēsque tē dēvorābunt." Tum Hector moriēns: "Bene **cognōveram** mē tibi persuadēre nōn posse, quia cor

135 tuum est ferreum. At nunc cavē nē pestis tibi fiam illō diē cum Paris Apollōque tē quamvīs fortem Scaenīs portīs dēleant." Hīs dictīs mōrs Hectorem oppressit et animus eius ē membrīs volāns ad umbrās fūgit vim iuventūtemque relinquēns.

Tum dīvīnus Achillēs Hectorem compellāvit: "**Morere**. Fātum meum

140 accipiam quandōcumque Iuppiter et aliī deī efficiant." Hīs dictīs hastam ē corpore ēvellit et dē umerīs sanguinea arma spoliāvit. Tum currentēs Graecī formam pulchritūdinemque Hectoris intuēbantur. Nēmō erat quīn corpus **foderet** loquēns, "Vidēte, Hector est multō mollior quam cum nāvēs facibus accenderet." Achillēs Graecōs adlocūtus: "**Eāmus** ad nāves

145 paeānem canentēs et **hoc** sūmāmus. Ingentem fāmam cōnsecūtī sumus; nam māgnum Hectorem occīdimus, quem ut deum Trōiānī celebrāvērunt."

DISCUSSION QUESTIONS

1) How valuable would Hector's weight in gold be? An ancient sort of pre-currency was a talent—about 26 kilograms or about 57 pounds. Approximate Hector's weight and multiply by the current value of gold per ounce. How much wealth is Achilles disdaining?
2) With what does Hector threaten Achilles? What role is he assuming?
3) Is Achilles disturbed by Hector's prediction?

147   **mutilō** (1) - *to maim, mutilate*

148   **nervus, -ī, m.** - *sinew, tendon*

      tālus, -ī, m. - *ankle*

      lōrum, -ī, n. - *strip of leather, thong*

      īnserō, -ere, -seruī, -sertum - *to insert, put in*

149   **ligō** (1) - *to bind, tie x* (acc.) *to y* (dat.)

      ascendō, -ere, -scendī, -scēnsum - *to ascend, mount*

150   **impōnō, -ere, -posuī, -positum** - *to place in, put in*

      stimulō (1) - *to goad, prick*

151   **pulverulentus, -a, -um** - *dusty*

152   **contaminō** (1) - *to defile*

154   **miserābiliter** (adv.) - *miserably, wretchedly*

157   **revereor, -verērī, -veritus sum** - *to respect, honor, revere*

163   **nēnia, -ae, f.** - *dirge, funeral, funeral song*

165   **sōlācium, -iī, n.** - *solace, comfort*

167   **nōndum** (adv.) - *not yet*

      subtīlis, -e - *fine, delicate*

168   **texō, -ere, texuī, tectum** - *to weave*

      ancilla, -ae, f. - *female servant, maidservant*

      imperō (1) (+ dat. + *ut*) - *to order, command*

      balneum, -ī, n. - *bath*

169   **calefaciō, -ere, -fēcī, -factum** - *to make warm or hot*

      Andromacha, -ae, f. - *Andromache; wife of Hector*

      ignōrō (1) - *to not know, be ignorant of*

GRAMMAR AND COMPREHENSION QUESTIONS

1) To what does *ea* refer?

2) What case is *sōlī*? With what word does it agree?

3) Why is *mihi* in the dative case?

4) What construction is *ōrandus est*?

5) What word correlates with *tantum*?

6) What construction is *tē mortuō* in the ablative?

7) What construction is *ut . . . honōrārent*?

Etiamnum Achillēs sīc furēbat ut corpus Hectoris mutilāre vellet. Ambōs nervōs tālōrum perforāvit per quōs lōra īnseruit. Tum **ea** curruī ligāvit ut caput Hectoris in terrā traherētur. Cum currum ascendisset et
150 splendida arma imposuisset Achillēs equōs stimulāvit ut rapidē currerent. Pulverulentus nūbēs surgēbat ubi caput māgnī Hectoris in pulvere trahēbātur. Nam iam Iuppiter permīsit hunc in patriā suā contāminārī.

Tālia vidēns Hecuba crīnēs scindit et lāmentāta est; Priamus miserābiliter gemuit. Omnis populus per urbem lāmentābātur quasi tōta
155 Trōia ārdēret. Priamus cīvēs ōrābat: "Cēdite, cārī. Permittite mihi **sōlī** ex urbe exīre et ad nāvēs Graecās accēdere. Iste asper **mihi ōrandus est**, sī fortasse senectūtem meam reverēns meī misereātur. Nam senex sum et pater eius Peleus etiam senex est, quī Achillem pestem nōbīs generāvit. Iste praeter aliōs nōbīs dolōrēs effēcit, quoniam plūrimōs fīliōs meōs
160 occīdit. Sed nunc quamquam dōlēns omnēs illōs nōn **tantum** lūgeō quantum Hectorem lūgeō, ut hic dolor mē ad mortem ferat." Sīc lacrimāns dīxit.

Deinde Hecuba Trōiānīs nēniam incēpit: "Fīlī, misera sum. **Tē mortuō** quālis vīta mihi miserae erit? Tū vīvēns glōriam mihi dabās;
165 omnibus Trōiānīs māgnum sōlācium praebuistī, **ut** omnēs tē ut deum **honōrārent**. Nunc mors fātumque tē adsecūta sunt." Sīc lacrimāns dīxit.

Sed uxor Hectoris clādem nōndum audīverat. Nam subtīlem vestem domī texēbat. Ancillīs imperāverat ut balneum Hectorī ē pugnā redeuntī calefacerētur. Misera Andromacha! quae ignōrābat Minervam manū
170 Achillis marītum suum occīdisse.

DISCUSSION QUESTIONS

1) What is the name of this tendon? Do you see any irony in this scene?
2) What would the ancient reader think about the treatment of Hector's body? What do you feel? Are there any modern comparisons?
3) Of what did a woman's fame consist? (You might want to compare Thucydides's report of Pericles funeral speech for the victims of war and plague in Athens [*Histories*, 1.48].)
4) Whom does Homer credit with Hector's death?

171 **strepitus, -ūs, m.** - *noise, din, roar*
    luctus, -ūs, m. - *grief*
    exorior, -īrī, -ortus sum - *to arise*
172 **conlābor, -lābī, -lapsus sum** - *to fall in a heap, collapse*
    radius, -iī, n. - *shuttle* (implement used in weaving)
    textōrius, -a, -um - *for weaving*
    recreō (1) - *to revive*
174 **palpitō** (1) - *to throb, palpitate*
    rigeō, -ēre - *to be stiff*
176 **sēiungō, -ere, -iūnxī, -iūnctum** - *to separate*
178 **āmēns, -mentis** - *out of one's mind, crazed*
180 **tenebrōsus, -a, -um** - *shadowy, dark, gloomy*
    operiō, -īre, -peruī, -pertum - *to cover*
181 **diadēma, -atis, n.** - *diadem, tiara*
183 **sustineō, -ēre, -tinuī, -tentum** - *to hold up, support*

184 **īnfēlīx, -icis** - *unfortunate, unhappy, miserable*
186 **vidua, -ae, f.** - *widow*
    modo (adv.) - *only*
188 **orbus, -a, -um** - *fatherless, orphaned*
    ēsuriō, -īre - *to be hungry, go hungry*
189 **Astyanax, -actis, m.** - *Astyanax; son of Hector and Andromache; a nickname that in Greek means "lord of the city"*
    opīmus, -a, -um - *rich, abundant, splendid*
    daps, dapis, f. - *feast, meal*
    sōlum (adv.) - *only*
    edō, ēsse, ēdī, esum - *to eat*
191 **appellō** (1) - *to call, address*
    vermis, -is, m. - *worm*
192 **satiō** (1) - *to satisfy, fill*
193 **adūrō, -ere, -ūssī, -ūstum** - *to burn*
194 **involvō, -ere, -volvī, -volūtum** - *to wrap up, envelop*

GRAMMAR AND COMPREHENSION QUESTIONS

1) What construction is *nē . . . sēiūnxerit*?
2) What tense is *remanēbat*? Why is the use of this tense significant?
3) What tense and mood is *dēdūxisset*? In what construction?
4) To whom does *hunc* refer?
5) What is unusual about the condition *vītet . . . erunt*?

Nunc Andromacha audīvit māgnum strepitum luctūs exorientem.
Membra conlapsa sunt et radius textōrius ad terram cecidit. Tum recreāta
vocāvit: "Venīte, ancillae, ut cognōscāmus quālis clādēs facta sit. Vōcem
mātris Hectoris audīvī. Cor meum palpitat, membra rigent. Certē aliquod
175 malum fīliīs Priamī fit. Vehementer timeō **nē** dīvīnus Achillēs fortem
Hectorem **sēiūnxerit** et ab urbe agat ut virtūtem fīniat, quae semper eī
erat. Numquam Hector in multitūdine **remanēbat**, sed semper in fronte
prōgrediēbātur." Hīs dictīs āmēns ē domū excurrēbat. Sed cum ad
portam vēnisset, stetit. Vīdit equōs trahere corpus Hectoris in pulvere.
180 Iam tenebrōsa nox oculōs Andromachae operuit et animus eam relīquit.
Procul ā capite splendidum diadēma cecidit, quod Venus eī dederat cum
Hector eam in matrimōnium **dēdūxisset**. Sed sorōrēs Hectoris nurūsque
Priamī Andromacham sustinēbant. Cum illa spīritum animumque
rēcepisset, lāmentābātur: "Hector, misera sum. Verē ūnum īnfēlix fātum
185 nōs coniunxit. Iam tū ad mortem sub terrā dēscendis, mē maestam
viduam hīc relīquistī. Puer noster est modo īnfāns. Nunc mortuus **hunc**
adiuvāre nōn poteris. Etiamsī ille Graecōs **vītet**, semper dolor laborque
eī **erunt**. Nam aliī terrās ab eō auferent. Orbī amīcīs cārentēs ēsuriunt.
Ante, Hectore vīvō, Astyanax opīmās dapēs sōlum ēdit; nunc, patre
190 mortuō, Astyanax plūrima patiētur, quem omnēs dominum urbis tum
appellābant. Et tē, Hector, nūdum, procul ā parentibus prope nāvēs
vermēs vescentur, cum cānēs satiātī sint. Tamen multa subtīlis vestis
domō adest; sed omnia haec adūram ut tē honōrem, quoniam in hīs tē
numquam involvam." Sīc lacrimāns dīxit et Trōiānī ūnā lāmentābantur.

DISCUSSION QUESTIONS

1) What is the significance of Andromache's diadem falling to the
   ground?
2) Does Andromache grieve for herself or her child?
3) Are Andromache's fears for Astyanax exaggerated?
4) What position did Astyanax hold in the royal line of inheritance?
5) For what would the finely woven clothing be used?

Achilles dragging the body of Hector (Diosphos painter [Athenian],
c. 500–475 BCE; the object was excavated in Eretria; now in
Louvre Museum, Paris, France) (Public Domain)

Chapter Eighteen

THE GHOST OF PATROCLUS; THE RANSOM OF HECTOR

Although Achilles has killed his nemesis, Hector, he is still inconsolable and vengeful. He continues to drag Hector's corpse and further abuse him by dropping him face-down in the dirt by Patroclus's bier. Finally, during an exhausted and fitful sleep, the ghost of Patroclus appears to Achilles with an appeal for burial. This appeal and Achilles's response is the first Latin passage here.

The next day Achilles buried Patroclus with all due ceremony but also sacrificed twelve Trojans together with some dogs.

The second part of Book 23 of the *Iliad* provides a respite from and contrast with the grimness of Book 22 and the start of 23. We see a different aspect of Achilles as he presents funeral games for Patroclus with extravagant prizes. (These games are the precursor of the Olympics. Vergil also used them as a model for the games for Anchises in *Aeneid* 5. Homer's account is also the first example of sports reporting!) In this Book we say goodbye to many of the familiar faces of the Greeks: Agamemnon, Menelaus, Ajax, and Odysseus. Achilles is the perfect host, resolving quarrels and giving special prizes, including one for Nestor.

Even after the funeral, however, Achilles cannot rest. His wrath, the thematic first word of the epic, is still raging as he futilely drags the corpse of Hector around Patroclus's tomb. On the divine plane all except the fanatically pro-Greek gods are offended by Achilles's abuse of Hector's body. (The immortal gods are not supposed to see mortal remains; these belong to Hades.) Finally on the twelfth day after Hector's death Apollo speaks on behalf of Hector, who was a righteous man beloved by the gods. Despite the protestations of Juno, Jupiter summons Thetis to his presence. Though sorrowful, Thetis comes and hears Jupiter's commands. These commands and their fulfillment comprise the second passage of this chapter.

SOURCE

Homer, *Iliad* 23, 24

1 **umbra, -ae, f.** - *shade; ghost*

superstō, -āre, -stetī, -statum - *to stand above, over*

3 **īnfernī, -ōrum, m.** - *the dead*

4 **arceō, -ēre, -uī** - *to prevent, hinder*

trānseō, -īre, -īvī, -itum - *to cross*

5 **misceō, -ēre, -uī, mixtum** - *to mix with, mingle with, associate with*

maereō, -ēre - *to mourn, grieve*

7 **subter** (prep. + acc.) - *below, underneath*

10 **propior, -ius** - *nearer, closer*

paululum (adv.) - *for a short time*

11 **bracchium, -iī, n.** - *arm*

12 **sonus, -ī, m.** - *sound, noise*

ēvānēscō, -ere, -vanuī - *to vanish*

13 **obstupefactus, -a, -um** - *stunned, astounded*

expergiscor, -ī, experrectus - *to become awake, wake up*

mīrābilis, -e - *amazing, marvelous*

vīsū: supine from *videō, -ēre*

14 **supersum, -esse, -fuī** - *to remain in existence, survive*

16 **īnfandus, -a, -um** - *unspeakable*

17 **arcessō, -ere, -īvī, -ītum** - *to summon*

nōvem (indecl. adj.) - *nine*

18 **concertō** (1) - *to contend in words, argue, dispute*

perspicax, -ācis - *keen-eyed*

19 **Mercurius, -ī, m.** - *Mercury;* the Greek Hermes, the messenger god but also the god who escorts souls to the underworld and the patron god of thieves

subripiō, -ere, -ipuī, -reptum - *to steal*

honestās, -ātis, f. - *honor, integrity*

20 **imperō** (1) (+ dat.) - *to give command to, order*

21 **renūntiō** (1) - *to bring back word, announce*

furiōsus, -a, -um - *out of one's wits, mad, out of control*

22 **iuxtā** (prep. + acc.) - *next to*

redimō, -ere, -ēmī, -emptum - *to ransom, give or get back for payment*

23 **Īris, -idis, f.** - *Iris,* the female messenger god who appears as the rainbow

24 **molliō, -īre, -īvī, -ītum** - *to soften, make less, placate*

GRAMMAR AND COMPREHENSION QUESTIONS

1) What construction is *ut . . . dēscendam*?
2) What river is meant?
3) To whom does *eīs* refer?
4) What tense is *consūmpserit*?
5) What happens to the image of Patroclus?
6) Why is *omnem noctem* in the accusative case?
7) What tense and mood is *arcessīverim*? In what construction?
8) To whom does *ipse* refer?
9) Why is *teneat* subjunctive in the *quod* clause?
10) What is the effect of *fortasse*?
11) Why is *hortētur* subjunctive?

Umbra Patroclī vīsa est superstāre et adloquī: "Dormīs immemor meī, Achillēs. Mē vīvum nōn neglegēbās, sed nunc mortuum neglegis. Sepelī mē quam celerrimē **ut** ad īnfernōs **dēscendam**. Nam umbrae, imāginēs mortuōrum, mē arcent nē flūmen trānseam et cum **eīs**

5   miscēam. Quīn adhūc errō. Manum mihi maerentī da. Nōn iterum enim ē morte veniam postquam ignis mē **consūmpserit**. Et tibi, dīvīne Achillēs, est fātum subter mūrōs Trōiae morīrī. Ergō ūnum rogō: ut ūna urna cinerēs nostrōs contineat."

Cuī Achillēs: "Quōmodo" inquit "hīc vēnistī, cāre, et haec iussistī?

10   Certē omnia haec faciam. Sed propius stā ut paululum amplectāmur et ūnā lāmentēmur." Hīs dictīs bracchia extendit sed Patroclum nōn tetigit. Nam umbra ut fūmus sonō acūtō sub terram ēvānescuit. Achillēs obstupefactus experrectus est et lāmentāns exclāmāvit: "Mīrābile vīsū! Animus et imāgō etiam in īnfernīs supersunt, etsī vīta abest. Nam

15   **omnem noctem** umbra Patroclī superstābat et iussit quae faciam."

Iuppiter: "Vēnistī quamvīs trīstis īnfandō dolōre, Thetis. Tamen dīcam **cūr** tē hūc **arcessīverim**. Nōvem diēs immortālēs dē corpore Hectoris et Achille concertāvērunt. Multī hortābantur ut perspicax Mercurius corpus subriperet. Sed ego hanc honestātem Achillī tribuō,

20   amīcitiam tuam tuēns. Statim igitur ī ad castra et fīliō tuō imperā. Renūntiā deōs et mē praecipuē īrāscī, **quod ipse** furiōsus corpus Hectoris iuxtā nāvēs **teneat** nec redimat. **Fortasse** mē tīmens Hectorem restituet. Ego autem Īridem ad Priamum mittam quae eum **hortētur** ut ad Graecās nāvēs eat splendida dōna ferēns quae īram Achillis molliant."

DISCUSSION QUESTIONS

1) How does the ghost of Patroclus ask Achilles to dispose of his body properly?
2) Does Achilles find any comfort in this vision of Patroclus?

27 **adsīdō, -ere, -ēdī** (+ dat.) - *to sit near (to)*

    mulceō, -ēre, mulsī - *to touch lightly, stroke, caress*

    quamdiū (interrogative adv.) - *for how long?*

28 **edō, ēsse, ēdī, ēsum** - *to eat, consume*

    edēs: future tense of this irregular verb

    meminisse: here takes the genitive of things

29 **inexōrābilis, -e** - *inexorable, relentless*

    immineō, -ēre - *to impend, threaten, be imminent*

32 **estō**: singular future imperative of *sum, esse*: *let it be, so be it*

33 **maeror, -ōris, m.** - *grief, sorrow, mourning*

34 **madeō, -ēre** - *to be wet or sodden*

35 **cervīx, -icis, f.** - *neck*

    operiō, -īre, -uī, -tum - *to cover*

    nuntia, -ae, f. - *female messenger*

    adstō, -stāre, -stitī - *to stand near, by*

36 **es**: singular present imperative of *sum, esse*

    nē + timueris: perfect subjunctive in a negative command

37 **benevolēns, -ntis** - *kind, friendly, benevolent*

40 **minister, -trī, m.** - *assistant, attendant*

    plaustrum, -ī, n. - *wagon, cart*

41 **revehō, -ere, -vexī, -vectum** - *to carry back*

42 **monstrō** (1) - *to point out, show*

44 **supplex, -icis** - *making humble entreaty, suppliant*

    benignē (adv.) - *kindly*

    thēsaurus, -ī, m. - *treasure chamber, vault, store-house*

45 **properō** (1) - *to hasten, hurry*

    opīmus, -a, -um - *rich, choice, sumptuous*

    ēligō, -ere, -lēgī, -lectum - *to select, choose, pick out*

46 **eundum est**: impersonal construction with dative and gerundive of *sum, esse*: *it must be gone by me, I must go*

Grammar and Comprehension Questions

    1) Why is *operta sunt* neuter plural?

    2) What kind of relative clause does *quae* introduce?

    3) What verb is to be understood with *redimendum*? In what construction?

25   Hīs dictīs Thetis pārēns ad terram et nāvēs Achillis celeriter
dēscendit. Ibi fīlius cum amīcīs lāmentābātur. Tum illūstris māter eī
adsēdit, manū mulsit, et adlocūta est: "Mī fīlī, quamdiū lāmentāns cor
edēs? Bonum est cibī et somnī meminisse. Nam nōn diū vīvēs; iam mōrs
et inexōrābile fātum tibi imminent. Sed dīligenter mē audī; nam nuntium
30   ā Iove ferō. Ipse dīcit deōs et sē praecipuē īrāscī quod furiōsus corpus
Hectoris iuxtā nāvēs teneās nec hoc redimās. Age nunc, corpus redde et
dōna accipe." Achillēs respondit: "Ita estō, sī Iuppiter ipse hoc iussit."
      Intereā Īris domum Priamī advēnit. Ibi maerōrem audīvit et
Priamum fīliōsque sedentēs vīdit quōrum vestēs lacrimīs madēbant.
35   Cervīx caputque rēgis pulvere **operta sunt**. Nuntia Iovis senem adstāns
parvā vōce adlocūta est: "Bonō animō es, Priame; nē timueris. Nōn malō
cōnsiliō sed benevolēns veniō. Nuntia Iovis sum, quī quamvīs longē tē
cūrat et tuī miserātur. Iuppiter imperat ut illūstrem Hectorem redimās
dōna ferēns **quae** īram Achillis molliant. Necesse est tē sōlum īre cum
40   ūnō seniore ministrō quī equōs plaustrumque moderētur. Ita corpus ad
urbem revehās. Nē mortem timueris; nam perspicax dux erit tibi quī viam
ad nāvēs Achillis mōnstret. Cum in castra vēneris, nec Achillēs nec sociī
tē occīdent. Nam ille nec stultus nec neglegēns nec improbus est. Tibi
supplicī **benignē** parcet." Īride discēdente, statim Priamus ad thēsaurum
45   properāvit ut optima opīmaque dōna ēligeret. Hecubam vocāns adlocūtus:
"Nuntia ad me ā Iove dēscendit. Mihi eundum est ad Graecās nāvēs et
corpus Hectoris opīmīs dōnīs **redimendum**. Age, cogitā quid faciam.
Nam animus meus mē ad Graecās nāvēs īre vehementer hortātur."

DISCUSSION QUESTIONS

1) Are you surprised at Achilles's quick agreement?
2) What outward signs of grief are apparent in Priam's palace?
3) Why is it significant that Priam must go almost alone?
4) How much courage does it take for Priam to go alone into the Greek
   camp?
5) Does the descriptor *benignē* seem to apply to Achilles's behavior so
   far in the epic?

49   vae (interjection + dat.) - *woe to, alas for*

50   abeō, -īre, -iī, -itum - *to go away, depart*

51   ferreus, -a, -um - *made of iron*

52   dēprehendō, -ere, -dī, -sum - *to catch, come upon suddenly*

     infīdus, -a, -um - *faithless, treacherous*

54   iecur, -oris, n. - *liver*

     ēsse: from *edō, ēsse, to eat, devour*

55   ulcīscor, -cī, ultus sum - *to take revenge upon*

56   retineō, -ēre, -uī, -tentum - *to hold back, keep, detain*

59   occīsūrum esse: from *occīdō, -ere*

     indulgeō, -ēre, -dulsī, -dultum (+ dat.) - *to give free course to, indulge in, devote oneself to*

60   duodecim (indecl. adj.) - *twelve*

     talentum, -ī, n. - *a unit of weight* (about 26 kilograms), *talent*

61   pōculum, -ī, n. - *cup*

62   expediō, -īre, -īvī, -ītum - *to make ready, prepare for use*

64   lībō (1) - *to pour a libation* (a drink offering), *to libate*

65   avis, -is, f. - *bird*

     dextrā (adverbial use of ablative) - *on the right hand side*

     volō (1) - *to fly*

66   suādeō, -ēre, suāsī, suāsum - *to recommend, urge, advise*

69   salūtem: the noun

     misericordia, -ae, f. - *pity, compassion, mercy*

70   iēns: present active nom. s. m. participle of *eō, īre*

71   fīdō, -ere, fīsus sum - *to have confidence*

72   aquila, -ae, f. - *eagle*

     trāns (prep. + acc.) - *across*

73   cōnscendō, -ere, -scendī, -scēnsum - *to mount, climb onto*

Grammar and Comprehension Questions

1) What mood is *lāmentēmur*?

2) What use of *quam* is this? (Note there is no feminine antecedent.)

3) Why is *possem* in the imperfect subjunctive?

4) What tense is *occīsūrum esse*?

5) What case is *vīnum*? What is its grammatical function?

6) What number is *lībārent*? Who is the subject?

7) What type of condition is *nisi . . . mittat . . . suādeam*?

8) Does the phrase *optime maxime* sound familiar? What case is this phrase?

9) How do the Trojans feel about Priam's departure?

50

Hīs dictīs uxor exclāmāvit: "Vae mihi, ubi illa sapientia tua abiit? Quōmodo cupis sōlus īre ad Graecās nāvēs et apud vīrum quī tot tantōsque fīliōs occīdit? Vērō cor tuum est ferreum. Nam iste, tē dēprehēnsō, saevus infīdusque tuī nōn miserābitur nec verēbitur. Nunc sēcrētō **lāmentēmur quam** fātum dēcrēverit ut Hector ā fortiore mīlite victus canēs aleret. Utinam iecur istius dentibus ēsse **possem**. Illō modō

55

istum ulcīscerem."

Senex Priamus respondit: "Nolī mē retinēre nec malum ōmen in aedibus fierī. Mihi nōn persuādēbis. Nam ipse deam audīvī vīdīque. Ergō ībō. Sī fātum meum est iuxtā nāvēs morī, tum volō Achillem mē fīlium meum tenentem **occīsūrum esse** postquam maerōrī indulserim."

60

Tum Priamus splendida dōna ēlēgit: vestēs, duodecim talenta aurī, pulcherrimum pōculum. Tantum cupiēbat fīlium suum redimere. Iussit plaustrum equōsque expedīrī. Omnibus parātīs, plūrima dōna in plaustrum posita sunt. Tum trīstis Hecuba revēnit **vīnum** in aureō pōculō ferēns ut Iovī **lībārent**. Hecuba rogāvit: "Potentem Iovem ōrā ut ōmen

65

mittat, celerem māgnumque avem dextrā volantem. Nam **nisi** Iuppiter tālem nuntium **mittat**, tē īre ad Graecās nāvēs nōn **suādeam**."

Priamus tum respondit: "Bonum est Iovem ōrāre ut meī miserētur." Sīc pōculum tollēns ōrāvit: "Pater Iuppiter, **optime maxime**, permitte ut salūtem misericordiamque apud Achillem inveniam. Ōmen mitte,

70

celerem māgnumque avem, tibi carissimum, dextrā volantem ut iēns ad Graecās nāvēs fīdam." Sīc illum ōrantem Iuppiter audīvit; statim ingentem aquilam mīsit, quae trāns urbem dextrā volāvit. Populus gaudēbat et Priamus properāns currum cōnscendit et minister plaustrum ēgit. Per urbem rapidē īvērunt, sed tōtus populus lāmentābātur quasi duo ad

75

mortem ruerent.

Discussion Questions

1) What do you think of Hecuba's wish?
2) Why would clothing be part of a ransom?
3) What is the bird of Jupiter?

78   **inermis, -e** - *unarmed, defenseless*

84   **comitor, -ārī, -ātus sum** - *to accompany, attend*

85   **recūsō** (1) - *to refuse, not accept, decline*

86   **invehō, -ere, -vexī, -vectum** - *to carry in, bring in*

88   **complectōr, -ctī, -plexus sum** - *to embrace, put one's arms round, clasp*

90   **tabernāculum, -ī, n.** - *tent, encampment*

92   **osculor, -ārī, -ātus sum** - *to kiss*

93   **mementō:** singular imperative of *meminī*

94   **aevum, -ī, n.** - *age, life*

      grandis, -e - *mature, advanced, elderly*

      vīcīnus, -ī, m. - *neighbor*

      quis for *aliquis* after *nec*

      perniciēs, -eī, f. - *destruction, ruin*

97   **generōsus, -a, -um** - *high-born, of noble birth*

      supersum, -esse, -fuī - *to survive, remain alive*

98   **nūper** (adv.) - *recently, lately*

99   **redimam** is present subjunctive in primary sequence, since *vēnī* is a present perfect

100   **recordor, -ārī, -ātus sum** - *to recall, call to mind*

      miserābilis, -e - *deserving pity, pitiable, pathetic*

GRAMMAR AND COMPREHENSION QUESTIONS

1) What tenses are *relīquissent* and *īrent*? Why are they two different tenses?

2) What case and number is *inermēs*?

3) Why is *cūrārent* subjunctive?

4) What gender, number, and case is *eī*? To whom does it refer?

5) How does Priam characterize his son Hector?

6) What construction is *deīs volentibus*?

7) What form is *comitāre* of this deponent verb?

8) What is the antecedent of *quae*?

9) What infinitive should you understand with *vīvum*?

10) What has Priam done that no other man has?

Cum duo urbem **relīquissent** et per campum **īrent**, miserāns
Iuppiter Mercurium dēmīsit. Similis iuvenī, mīlitī Achillis, Mercurius
duōs appropinquāvit, quī māgnopere timēbant. Nam **inermēs** māgnās
dīvitiās vehēbant. At Mercurius eōs benignē firmāvit et narrāvit corpus

80 Hectoris prope nāvēs Achillis etiamnum iacēre integrum, quod deī corpus
cūrārent. Priamus gaudēns respondit: "Certē bonum est dōna deīs dare.
Nam fīlius meus vīvus deōs numquam neglegēbat. Nunc **eī** igitur hunc
etiam mortuum cūrant. Age, hoc pōculum accipe et, **deīs volentibus**, mē
comitāre dum in castra Achillis adveniam." Sed deus, quamvīs pōculum

85 recūsāns, Priamum in castra dūxit. Postquam Mercurius ingentem
portam aperuit et dōna invexit, deus adlocūtus: "Senex, ego immortālis
deus vēnī, Mercurius. Nam pater mē dēmīsit ut tē dūcerem. At nunc
redībō. Tū intrāns genua Achillis complectere et eum per patrem,
immortālem mātrem, et fīlium suum obsecrā ut animum moveās."

90 Mercurius discēssit, sed Priamus statim in tabernāculum Achillis
intrāvit. Māgnus Priamus genua Achillis complexus saevās manūs
osculātus est, **quae** tot fīliōs occīderant. Achillēs illūstrem Priamum vīdens
mīrābātur. At Priamus ōrāvit: "Dīvīne Achillēs, patrem tuum mementō,
aevō grandem velut ego. Vīcīnī hunc vexant nec quis adest quī perniciem

95 arceat. Sed cum tē **vīvum** audiat, certē gaudet et sperat sē tē domum
revenientem salūtātūrum esse. Mihi tamen fātum est malum, quoniam
generōsōs fīliōs genuī quōrum nēmō superest. Ūnum, quī urbem percipuē
dēfendēbat, nōbilissimum Hectorem, nūper occīdistī. Prō hōc ad Graecās
nāvēs venī ut corpus redimam; splendida dōna ferō. Deōs observā, Achillēs,

100 et meī miserāre patrem tuum recordāns. Sed ego miserābilior sum, quod
fēcī quid nēmō alius: obsecrāvī vīrum quī fīliōs meōs occīderat."

DISCUSSION QUESTIONS

1) Do you know who Achilles's son is?
2) Do you think Priam's suggestion that Peleus is under threat from
    neighbors is realistic? Why does he say this?
3) Is it true that Priam has no sons left?

103 **āmoveō, -ēre, -mōvī, -mōtum** - *to cause to go away, to remove*

105 **surgō, -ere, -ēxī, -ectum** - *to rise, stand up*

106 **sublevō** (1) - *to raise, to lift*

ā (interjection) - *ah*, expressing pity, regret

profectō (adv.) - *surely, undoubtedly, certainly*

passus es: from *patior, patī, passus sum*

107 **ausus es**: from *audeō, -ēre, ausus sum*

108 **sella, -ae, f.** - *seat, chair*

109 **cōnsīdō, -ere, -sēdī, -sessum** - *to sit down, take a seat*

110 **commodum, -ī, n.** - *advantage, benefit*

111 **distribuō, -ere, -uī, -ūtum** - *to share out, allot, distribute*

vās, vāsis, n. - *vessel, vase*

112 **ātrium, -iī, n.** - *central hall, reception hall*

cuī: after *sī* = *alicuī*

113 **experior, -īrī, expertus sum** - *to experience*

114 **Tonāns, -antis** - *making thunder* (cult title of Jupiter)

famēs, -is, f. - *hunger, famine*

115 **ā nātū**: *from birth*

opulentus, -a, -um - *having many possessions, opulent, wealthy*

Myrmidonēs, -um, m. pl. - *the Myrmidons; people of Thessaly, followers of Achilles*

118 **ferunt** (idiomatic) - *they say, people say*

quondam (adv.) - *once, formerly*

120 **dūrō** (1) - *to hold out, endure*

Grammar and Comprehension Questions

1) From what does Achilles remove Priam?
2) To whom is *ā miser* addressed?
3) What use of *quam* is this?
4) Who else told Priam that his heart was *ferreum*?
5) What use of the subjunctive is *āmittāmus*?
6) What case is *sortēs*?
7) With what is *ambōbus* understood to agree?
8) Who is the *immortālem*?
9) What tense is *patiēris*?

Sīc Priamus locūtus est et animum Achillis mōvit ut patrem lūgēret.

Achillēs tum manum rēgis prehendēns eum ā sē āmōvit. Ūnā duo

lāmentābantur, alius fortem Hectorem, alius patrem Patroclumque.

105 Sed cum Achillēs satis lāmentātus erat, surrēxit et miserāns senem

sublevāvit. Tum adlocūtus: "**Ā miser**, profectō multa mala passus es.

Quam ausus es sōlus ad Graecās nāvēs venīre, ad vīrum quī multōs

nōbilēs fīliōs occīderat? Vērō cor tuum est **ferreum**. At age in hāc sellā

cōnside et, quamvīs sollicitī, lāmentātiōnem **āmittāmus**. Nūllum

110 commodum est in perpetuō maerōre. Sīc deī **sortēs** miserīs mortālibus

distribuērunt: maerentēs vīvimus sed deī ipsī sine cūrīs vīvunt. Duo vāsa

in ātriō Iovis stant, ūnum bonōrum, ūnum malōrum. Sī cuī Iuppiter

aliqua ex **ambōbus** dat, ille nunc bona, nunc mala experītur. Sed, cuī

Tonāns Iuppiter mala dat, illum contumēlia et famēs vexant. Deī plūrima

115 bona Peleō ā nātū dedērunt, quī opulentus Myrmidonēs regēbat et

immortālem in matrimōnium dūxit. Sed deus etiam huic mala nunc

dedit. Ego, sōlus fīlius, senem nōn cūrō quoniam longē ā patriā Troiae

sedeō, tē fīliōsque tuōs vexāns. Ferunt tē fēlīcem quondam fuisse. Nam

multās terrās regēbās et multōs fīliōs generāvistī. At tum deī hoc malum

120 effēcērunt: semper urbs tua proeliīs mortibusque vexātur. Dūrā tamen

nec semper lāmentāre. Nam lūgēns fīlium tuum nihil efficiēs nec hunc

redūcēs. Mox alium malum **patiēris**."

Discussion Questions

1) Do you find any irony in Achilles's words to Priam?
2) What role is Achilles playing?
3) What does Achilles now think of his accomplishments during the war? Do you remember what he called himself after the death of Patroclus?

124 **dīmittō, -ere, -mīsī, -missum** - *to release, let go*

126 **pepercistī**: from *parcō, -ere*

128 **ignōrō** (1) - *to be ignorant of, unaware*

131 **supplex, -icis** - *suppliant, begging*

133 **efferō, -erre, extulī, ēlātum** - *to carry out, take out, remove*

praeterquam (adv.) - *except*

amictus, -ūs, m. - *cloak, mantle*

134 **tunica, -ae, f.** - *tunic*

vestiō, -īre, -īvī, -ītum - *to dress, clothe*

ancilla, -ae, f. - *female servant, maidservant*

135 **lavō** (1) - *to wash, bathe*

unguō, -ere, ūnxī, ūnctum - *to smear with oil, anoint, rub*

136 **ferculum, -ī, n.** - *stretcher, litter*

sustulit: from *tollō, -ere*

137 **invocō** (1) - *to call upon*

139 **dignus, -a, -um** - *appropriate, suitable, worthy*

141 **quam**: *as*

142 **Nioba, -ae, f.** - *Niobe*; daughter of Tantalus. Her many children were killed by Apollo and Artemis since Niobe had boasted that she had more children than their mother Leto. Niobe metamorphosed into a stony cliff down which a stream like tears perpetually falls.

144 **multum**: here adverbial, *much*

145 **quisque, quaeque, quidque** (pronoun + adj.) - *each*

Grammar and Comprehension Questions

1) What tense of the subjunctive is *possēs*? Why?
2) What kind of relative clause is *quibus corpus vestiātur*?
3) How was the body prepared to give back to Priam?
4) What tense and mood is *audiās*? What type of condition is this?
5) How do you translate *meminerat* when the verb occurs only in the perfect system?

Apollo and Artemis slaying the fourteen children of Niobe. Achilles advises Priam to eat as even Niobe did after her children were slain. (Roman sarcophagus, 160–170 CE; Glyptothek, Munich, Germany) (Public Domain)

Senex Priamus respondit: "Nē in sellā mē ponās, dīvīne, dum Hector neglectus iacet. Quīn quam celerrimē fīlium meum dīmitte ut eum
125 videam. Splendida dōna accipe quae tulī. Domum redeās quoniam mihi pepercistī."

Tum saevus Achillēs: "Nōlī mē excitāre. Ipse Hectorem dīmittere in animō habeō. Māter mea, nuntia ā Iove, ad mē vēnit. Nec ignōrō aliquem deum tē ad Graecās nāvēs dūxisse; sōlus enim custōdēs effūgere et portās
130 aperīre nōn **possēs**. Nōlī igitur animum meum excitāre, senex, nē tē quamvīs supplicem occīdam et Iovem offendam."

Hīs dictīs senex timēns paruit. Achillēs ut leō ad portam properāvit, ē plaustrō splendida dōna extulit, praeterquam duōs amictūs et ūnam tunicam **quibus corpus vestiātur**. Tum Achillēs ancillās iussit corpus
135 lavāre et ungere. Hīs factīs, corpus amictibus et tunicā vestīvērunt. Achillēs ipse corpus in ferculum sustulit, quod sociī in plaustrum posuērunt. Tum gemēns Achillēs comitem Patroclum invocāvit: "Nōlī mihi īrāscī, sī, quamvīs in īnfernīs, **audiās** mē Hectorem Priamō redimere. Nam dōna sunt digna quōrum aptam partem tibi dabō."

140 Tum Achillēs in tabernāculum redīvit et Priamum adlocūtus: "Fīlius tuus, senex, redditur, quam iussistī; in ferculō iacet. Nunc age, cēnēmus. Nam etiam Nioba cibum **meminerat** postquam sex fīliōs et sex fīliās lūxit quōs Apollō Diānaque occīderant. Sīc nōs cēnāre necesse est. Posteā cārum fīlium in Trōiam referēns lūgeās. Illum populus multum lūgēbit."
145 Sīc duo ūnā cēnāvērunt, et quisque alterum mīrābātur.

DISCUSSION QUESTIONS

1) Has Achilles completely conquered his anger?
2) Why does Achilles call on Patroclus?
3) How can Achilles give Patroclus a portion of the ransom?
4) When Achilles and Priam eat together do the rules of *xenia* (guest-friendship) now apply between them?

146 **permittō, -ere, -mīsī, -missum** (+
dat. of person) - *to permit, allow*

147 **operiō, -īre, -uī, -pertum** - *to shut,
close*

148 **gustō** (1) - *to taste*
extrā (adv.) - *outside*

149 **quis = aliquis** after *nē*

151 **mora, -ae, f.** - *delay*

153 **incursus, -ūs, m.** - *attack, assault,
incursion*

154 **rīte** (adv.) - *with proper religious
procedure, with proper rights,
fittingly*

155 **rēgia, -ae, f.** - *palace*

156 **epulor, -ārī, -ātus sum** - *to feast*
undecimus, -a, -um - *eleventh*
tumulus, -ī, m. - *burial mound,
grave*
super (prep. + acc.) - *on top of, above*
ērigō, -ere, -rexī, -rectum - *to raise,
erect, set up*

157 **duodecimus, -a, -um** - *twelfth*

160 **lectus, -ī, m.** - *bed*
intrā: here adverbial, *inside*

161 **nīl = nihil**: here adverbial with
morāris

162 **moror, -ārī, -ātus sum** (with *nīl*
+ acc.) - *to pay no attention to, not
to care for*

163 **triplex, -icis** - *three times, triple,
threefold*

164 **agnōscō, -ere, -nōvī, -itum** - *to
recognize, identify*

166 **Aurōra, -ae, f.** - *Aurora*, the goddess
of the dawn, sunrise

167 **sōlum** (adv.) - *only*

Cassandra, -ae, f. - *Cassandra*;
beautiful daughter of Priam and
Hecuba, a prophet cursed with
never being believed

168 **gavīsī estis**: from *gaudeō, gaudēre*

172 **cantor, -ōris, m.** - *singer*

nēnia, -ae, f. - *song sung at a funeral,
dirge*

GRAMMAR AND COMPREHENSION QUESTIONS

1) What construction is *ad mē cōnsulendum*? Note the gerundive.
2) What form is *redimendō*?
3) What type of clause is *nē . . . timēret*?
4) What mood is *dent*? What does it indicate?
5) With what word does *obviam* go closely to complete the meaning?
6) What physical gesture does the mourning Andromache use?

Tum Priamus adlocūtus: "Dīvīne, mihi permitte dormīre, quoniam oculōs in somnō numquam operuī postquam fīlius meus ā tē occīsus est; semper enim lāmentābar. At nunc cibum vīnumque gustāvī. Anteā nihil gustāveram." Achillēs adlocūtus: "Extrā dormī, senex, nē quis Graecōrum

150 hīc tē inveniat. Nam semper **ad mē cōnsulendum** veniunt. Sī quis tē videat, Agamemnonī dīcat ut mora sit in corpore **redimendō**. At age, mihi verē dīc: quantōs diēs cupis ut illūstrem Hectorem sepeliās. Ego ipse intereā incursum Graecōrum prohibēbō."

Senex Priamus: "Sī vīs" inquit "nōs Hectorem rīte sepelīre, ita etiam

155 hoc faciās. Novem diēs Hectorem in rēgiā lūgeāmus, decimō diē eum sepeliāmus et epulēmur, undecimō diē tumulum super eum ērigāmus. Tum duodecimō diē pugnābimus, sī necesse est." Achillēs respondit: "Haec, ut iussistī, erunt. Tantum tempus proelium prohibēbō." Tum Achillēs dextram manum Priamī tenuit **nē** senex **timēret**. Deinde Priamus ad

160 lectum extrā īvit, sed Achillēs intrā dormīvit. Etiam deī dormiēbant, nisi sōlus Mercurius. Quīn stāns ad caput Priamī adlocūtus: "Nīl mala morāris, quoniam in hostibus dormīs, postquam Achillēs tibi pepercit. Fīlium splendidīs dōnīs redēmistī, sed cēterī fīliī triplicia dōna **dent** ut tē vīvum redimant, sī Agamemnōn aut alius tē agnōscat." Hīs dictīs rēx

165 māgnopere timēns ministrum excitāvit. Mercurius ipse plaustrum ē castrīs ēgit tum discessit. Aurōrā appārente, rēx ministerque lāmentantēs urbem appropinquābant. Sōlum Cassandra eōs advenīre Hectore in ferculō iacente vīdit. Clāmāvit: "Venīte, Trōiānī, sī umquam gāvīsī estis cum Hector ē pugnā revenīret. Nam ille urbī populōque māgnum

170 gaudium erat." Omnēs maerentēs **obviam** Priamō prope portās īvērunt. In prīmīs erant Andromacha et rēgīna. Cum ferculum in regiam tulissent et corpus in lectū posuissent, cantōrēs nēniam incepērunt.

DISCUSSION QUESTIONS

1) What kind of authority over the Greeks does Achilles assume he has?
2) What sort of gesture using the right hand is this?

173 **lāmentātiō, -ōnis, f.** - *lamentation, wailing*

174 **incohō** (1) - *to begin, commence*

175 **vidua, -ae, f.** - *widow*

    prius (adv.) - *before, sooner*

176 **dēfēnsor, -ōris, m.** - *defender, protector*

177 **serviō, -īre, -īvī, -ītum** (+ dat.) - *to serve, wait upon*

183 **identidem** (adv.) - *again and again, repeatedly*

187 **quotiēnscumque** (adv.) - *as often as, whenever*

    mītis, -is - *soft, gentle, mild*

188 **comprimō, -ere, -pressī, -pressum** - *to curb, check, repress, suppress*

    benignus, -a, -um - *kind*

191 **indūtiae, -ārum, f.** - *truce, cease-fire*

192 **inferō, -ferre, -tulī, -lātum** - *to bring or carry in*

193 **rogus, -ī, m.** - *funeral pyre*

    postrīdiē (adv.) - *on the next day, the day after*

194 **os, ossis, n.** - *bone*

    colligō, -ere, -lēgī, -lectum - *to gather up, collect*

    sepulchrum, -ī, n. - *grave, tomb*

195 **humō** (1) - *to bury, inter*

GRAMMAR AND COMPREHENSION QUESTIONS

1) What is the name of Hector and Andromache's son? What happens to him?

2) To whom does *hunc* refer?

3) How do you translate *cum* when followed in the main clause by *tamen*?

4) What form is *ferte*? From what verb?

5) Describe the funeral ritual with which the Trojans honor Hector.

6) What is the antecedent of *quod*?

Andromacha in bracchiīs caput Hectoris tenēns lāmentatiōnem
fēminārum incohābat: "Coniūnx, iuvenis mortuus es, relinquēns mē
175   viduam domō. Fīlius noster est īnfāns quī iuvenis numquam fīet; prius,
sine tē dēfēnsōre, urbs capiētur. Mox uxōrēs līberīque in celeribus nāvibus
discēdent, et ego ipsa et puer noster, ut hostibus serviāmus. Aut fortasse
aliquī Graecus plēnus īrā **hunc** dē altīs mūrīs iaciet quod frātrem, patrem
aut fīlium occīdistī. Omnēs tē lūgent, sed praecipuē ego quoniam moriēns
180   nūllum ultimum verbum mihi dīxistī." Sīc lacrimāns dīxit.

Nunc Hecuba nēniam ducēbat: "Hector, cārissime omnium fīliōrum,
tē vīvum omnēs deī amābant et nunc mortuum cūrant. **Cum** Achillēs
tē circā tumulum Patroclī identidem traheret, nunc **tamen** integer
pulcherque hīc iacēs."

185   Postrēmō Helena nēniam ducēbat: "Hector, cārissime omnium
frātrum coniugis, dūrum verbum mihi numquam dīxistī. Nōn,
sed quotiēnscumque alius mē reprehenderat, eum mītibus verbīs
compressistī. Semper benignus erās. Ergō tē lūgeō. Nēmō alius erat mihi
benignus amīcus; cēterī mē vītāvērunt." Sīc lacrimāns dīxit.

190   Deinde Priamus appellāvit: "Nunc, Trōiānī, ligna in urbem **ferte**.
Nōlīte Graecōs timēre; Achillēs duodecim diēs indūtiās prōmīsit ut
Hectorem rīte sepeliāmus." Itaque novem diēs ligna intulērunt, et decimō
diē corpus Hectoris in rogum posuērunt et incendērunt. Postrīdiē
lacrimantēs ossa collēgērunt et in auream urnam posuērunt. In sepulchrō
195   urnam humāvērunt, **quod** ingentibus saxīs tēxērunt. Postrēmō in rēgiā
Priamī epulātī sunt. Sīc illūstrem Hectorem sepelīvērunt.

DISCUSSION QUESTIONS

1) Does Andromache have any optimism for the future?
2) Why do you think Helen is the last speaker of the formal
    lamentation?
3) What does Helen's speech reveal about Hector's character? What
    does it reveal about the Trojan's attitude towards her?
4) Does the ending of the *Iliad* with its focus on Hector surprise you?

Achilles reclines over Hector's corpse (Attic, c. 490–480 BCE, attributed to Makron; Louvre Museum, Paris, France) (Public Domain)

Chapter Nineteen

ACHILLES'S LAST CONQUESTS AND DEATH: THE DEATH OF PENTHESILEA, THE DEATH OF MEMNON, THE THEFT OF THE PALLADIUM, THE DEATH OF ACHILLES

Homer ends his great epic, the *Iliad*, with the return and burial of Hector's body, but the war is not yet over. The end of the war was described in two epics of the Homeric cycle, *Ilias Parva (Little Iliad)* and *Iliou Persis (The Sack of Ilium)*, that no longer survive. There are, however, numerous incidents from the last year of the war that are famous and of which students should be aware. This chapter briefly details a number of key incidents before the fall of Troy: Achilles's killing of the Amazon Queen Penthesilea and of the Ethiopian King Memnon, son of Eos goddess of the dawn; Ulysses's theft of the Palladium, a sacred image of Minerva; the death of Achilles through an arrow guided by Apollo.

Since these episodes are for the most part separate from one another, each is preceded by a brief introduction and list of sources.

The Death of Penthesilea

After the death and ransom of Hector, Achilles continued to fight very successfully against the Trojans, although he knew he was destined to die at Troy. Penthesilea was queen of the Amazons, a tribe of warrior women from what is now northern Turkey near the Black Sea, and a daughter of Mars. Having accidentally killed a fellow Amazon, Penthesilea came to Priam to ask him for purification in return for which she promised military aid to the Trojans. In the *Aeneid* Vergil uses the Amazon queen as a model for his warrior Camilla who aids the Rutulians against the Trojans and Latins. Here we have a somewhat surprise ending to a military episode.

Sources

Diodorus Siculus, *Biblioteca* 2.46 • Apollodorus, *Epitome* 5.1–2 • Vergil, *Aeneid* 1.490–93 • Quintus of Smyrna (Quintus Smyrnaeus), *The Fall of Troy* 1.538–674

---

1   **Amazōn, -onis, f.** - *Amazon*; legendary warrior women from the east of Troy, allied to the Trojans

2   **Penthesilēa, -ae, f.** - *Penthesilea*; the Amazon queen

    comes, -itis, f. - *female companion*

4   **Volcānus, -ī, m.** - *Vulcan*; god of the forge

5   **perfringō, -ere, -frēgī, -fractum** - *to break, fracture*

6   **audacter** (adv.) - *boldly, daringly*

7   **invictus, -a, -um** - *unconquered, invincible*

    Mars, Martis, m. - *Mars*; the god of war, the Greek Ares

    genuit: from *gignō, -ere*

Grammar and Comprehension Questions

1) What construction does *ut* introduce?
2) What form is *fortior*?
3) What form is *sim*? From what verb?
4) To which two men does *duo* refer?
5) Who is the subject of *vulnerāret*?
6) What do you think of the heroes' reaction to Penthesilea?
7) What form is *occīsūrum esse*? From what verb?

In tumultū pugnae fīlius Pēleī et māgnus Aiax plūrimās Amāzonēs
occīdērunt. Penthesilēa cum comitēs suās interfectās vīdisset contrā
Achillem cucurrit. Prīmum illūstris Penthesilēa longam hastam iēcit quae
scūtum Achillis percussit. Sed scūtum ā Volcānō fabricātum tam dūrum
5   erat ut hastam rēgīnae perfringeret. Tum rēgīna secundam hastam contrā
Aiācem missūra audacter glōriāta est: "Ūnam hastam frūstrā ēmīsī, sed
nunc haec secunda vōs ambōs interficiet. Invictus Mars enim mē genuit
ut fortior quam ūllus vir **sim**." Hīs dictīs secundam hastam ēmīsit. Sed
duo eam contemnentēs rīsērunt. Hasta celeriter volāns ocream Aiācis
10   percussit. Aiax integer remanēbat; nam fātum ūllō hostī nōn permīsit
ut illum **vulnerāret**. Rēgīnā contemptā hērōs alium hostem oppugnāvit;
nam cōgnōvit Achillem rēgīnam facile **occīsūrum esse**. Sed Penthesilēa
īrāta gemuit quod hastam frūstrā ēmīserat.

DISCUSSION QUESTIONS

    1) Why was Penthesilea's spear ineffective against Achilles's shield?
    2) What did Penthesilea boast she was going to achieve with her second
        spear?
    3) Does Penthesilea behave like a typical Homeric warrior?
    4) Why does Penthesilea think she is exceptional?
    5) How is the name Amazon used today? How do these uses relate to
        the ancient group of warrior women?

14 **vānus, -a, -um** - *useless, foolish, vain*

16 **equidem** (adv.) - *indeed, truly, for my part*

17 **minor, -ārī, -ātus sum** (+ dat.) - *to threaten*

19 **dexter, -tra, -trum** - *right*

   mamma, -ae, f. - *breast*

20 **effundō, -ere, -fūdī, -fūsum** - *to pour forth*

   bipennis, -is, f. - *axe with two blades, two-edged axe*

   nebula, -ae, f. - *mist, fog, cloud*

23 **trānsfīgō, -ere, -fīxī, -fīxum** - *to pierce through*

   praeceps, -ipitis - *headlong*

25 **pulchritūdō, -inis, f.** - *beauty, handsomeness, excellence*

26 **admīror, -ārī, -ātus sum** - *to wonder at, marvel at, admire*

   Diāna, -ae, f. - *Diana*; goddess of the hunt; the Greek Artemis

27 **amīca, -ae, f.** - *lover, mistress*

   tantopere (adv.) - *so greatly*

   auxit: from *augeō, -ēre*

29 **dēdūcō, -ere, -dūxī, -ductum** - *to lead down, to escort*; used of escorting a bride to the groom's home, a central part of a Roman marriage ceremony

---

Grammar and Comprehension Questions

1) What use of *quam* is this?
2) What grammatical number is *quī*? To whom does it refer?
3) How is the queen characterized in the phrase *fortis rēgīnae*? What case is this?
4) What construction does *utrum* introduce? What word links to it?
5) What did Achilles begin to do before he saw the face of Penthesilea?
6) What type of ablative is *corde*?

Nunc Achillēs locūtus est: "Fēmina, **quam** vānīs verbīs glōriāns

15 contrā nōs pugnās **quī** multō māiōrēs sumus quam antiquī hērōēs.

Equidem māgnum Hectorem hastā meā nūper occīdī. At tū māgnopere

īnsānīs cum minārī mortem nōbīs audeās. Nunc ultimam lūcem aspice,

nec pater tuus tē servābit." Tum validā vī ingentem hastam ēmīsit. Hasta

celeriter volāns dextram mammam **fortis rēgīnae** percussit. Statim

20 sanguine effundente Penthesilēa bipennem dēiēcit et ātra nebula oculōs

operuit. Tamen rēgīna dēlīberābat **utrum** gladium ēdūcēns cum Achille

pugnāret an eī supplicāret. At Achillēs māgnā cum īrā incurrēns eam

hastā trānsfīxit. Illa praeceps in pulverem cecidit et ultimum spīritum

ēmīsit. Prōcurrēns Achillēs super corpus glōriārī incipiēns splendidam

25 galeam ā capite rēgīnae remōvit. Attonitus maximam pulchritūdinem

rēgīnae admīrātus est, quae dea Diāna dormiēns esse vidēbātur. Venus,

amīca Martis, pulchritūdinem tantopere auxit ut Achillēs amōre rēgīnae

superārētur. Sollicitus **corde** Achillēs mortem dolēbat quod eam nūptam

in Phthīam dēducere nōn poterat.

Discussion Questions

1) What do you think of glorying over a slain foe? Was this typical?
2) Why did Achilles grieve after he killed Penthesilea?
3) Is this grief consistent with Achilles's characterization?

Greeks fighting Amazons; Achilles and Penthesilea (Roman sarcophagus, 3rd century CE,
Vatican Museums, Rome, Italy) (© Creative Commons 3.0/Marie-Lan Nguyen)

THE DEATH OF MEMNON

Memnon was the son of the goddess of the dawn, Aurora (Eos, in Greek), and Tithonus, a Trojan prince and elder brother of Priam. As Aurora was crossing the sky
bringing in the day she saw the young Tithonus and fell madly in love. She begged
Jupiter to make him immortal, which he did. Unfortunately she also forgot to ask
for eternal youth so that eventually he got older and older and began to wither. In
pity for him Aurora put him in a wicker basket and ultimately changed him into a
cicada (a type of grasshopper). Aurora had abducted Tithonus to Ethiopia where
she gave birth to Memnon who became the Ethiopian king. As a member of Trojan
royalty and a hero he came with a huge mass of troops to the defense of Troy after
the death of Hector. The Trojans were greatly excited and relieved by his arrival.
After a night of welcome and rest Memnon entered the battle.

SOURCES

Pindar, *Pythian Ode* 6.28ff., *Nemean Ode* 6.48ff. • Ovid, *Metamorphoses*
13.576–622 • Quintus of Smyrna, *The Fall of Troy* 2.100–666

1 **Memnōn, -onis, m.** - *Memnon*; Ethiopean king

2 **Aethiops, -opis, m.** - *Ethiopean*

3 **confīdō, -ere, -fīsus sum** (+ dat.) - *to put one's trust in, have confidence in*

4 **Tītān, -ānis, m.** - *Titan*; one of the divine generation that preceded the Olympians; giant
   fulgeō, -ēre, fūlsī - *to shine, gleam*

5 **praestō, -āre, -stitī, -stitum** - *to prevail*

6 **gemitus, -ūs, m.** - *groan*
   generōsus, -a, -um - *high-born, noble*
   alibī (adv.) - *elsewhere*

8 **Antilochus, -ī, m.** - *Antilochus*; young son of Nestor; good friend of Achilles

9 **ēvītō** (1) - *to avoid, escape*

10 **vēlox, -ōcis** - *swift, speedy*

11 **solum, -ī, n.** - *ground*
   iaculor, -ārī, -ātus sum - *to throw, hurl*

12 **immōtus, -a, -um** - *unmoved*

13 **arceō, -ēre, -uī** (+ dat. of thing protected) - *to fend off, keep away, protect from*
   fodiō, -ere, fōdī, fossum - *to jab, stab*

14 **dēmergō, -ere, -mersī, -mersum** - *to submerge, sink*

GRAMMAR AND COMPREHENSION QUESTIONS

1) What case is *incurrentēs*? What word does it modify?
2) What case is *fulgentibus armis*? What is its function?
3) What case is *saxum*?

Diē veniente Memnōn surgēns arma cēpit. Celeriter Trōiānī
Aethiopēsque sē ē portīs effūdērunt. Graecī cum eōs **incurrentēs** procul
vīdissent statim arma sua cēpērunt. Nam vī Achillis confīdēbant. Ille
medius velut Tītān in pugnam **fulgentibus armīs** incurrit. Tum aciēbus

5   concurrentibus Aethiopēs prīmum praestābant. Undique erant clāmōrēs
gemitūsque. Sed Achillēs multōs **generōsōs** occīdit. Alibī acer Memnōn,
cum duōs mīlitēs Nestoris occīdisset, Nestorem ipsum oppugnābat.

Sed illūstris Antilochus, fīlius Nestoris, obviam Memnonī ruēns
longam hastam ēmīsit sed Memnōn hanc ēvītāvit quae alium Aethiopem

10   percussit. Īrātus hāc morte Memnōn vēlox ut leō contrā Antilochum
saluit. At Antilochus ingēns saxum ā solō sublātum iaculātus est. **Saxum**
Memnonem vī percussit, sed Memnōn immōtus stetit cuī firma galea
mortem arcuit. Ferōciter igitur īrātus pectus Antilochī hastā fōdit quae in
cor dēmersit, ubi mors celerrimē advenit.

Discussion Questions

1) Why is the adjective *generōsōs* significant when describing those
   whom Achilles killed?
2) Are you surprised to find Nestor actively fighting? Do you know how
   old he is?
3) What was Antilochus's specific motivation in trying to attack
   Memnon?

16 **praesēns, -ntis** - *present, in person*

17 **interfector, -ōris, m.** - *slayer, murderer*

18 **rītus, -ūs, m.** - (in pl.) *rites, ceremonies*
   rectē (adv.) - *correctly*

19 **adiūvāndum** - supine of purpose - *to help*

20 **Aurōra, -ae, f.** - *Aurora*; goddess of the dawn, mother of Memnon

24 **stitisset**: from *sistō*
   pudeō, -ēre, -uī, -itum est - *to fill with shame, make ashamed*

pudeat: here impersonal with acc. + inf. - *it would shame me*

29 **dēfēnsor, -ōris, m.** - *guardian, protector, defender*

30 **dēvorō** (1) - *to devour, consume*

31 **succurrō, -ere, -currī, -cursum** - *to run to help*

32 **trucīdō** (1) - *to slaughter, kill savagely*

35 **umerus, -ī, m.** - *shoulder, upper arm*
   suprā (prep. + acc.) - *above*

36 **titubō** (1) - *to totter, stagger*

Grammar and Comprehension Questions

1) What form is *celerrimē*? How do you construe it with *quam*?
2) Is Nestor's use of the word *interfectōrem* appropriate in the situation?
3) What does *currentēs* modify?
4) What mood and tense is *iacuisset*? In which construction?
5) What type of subjunctive is *pudeat*?
6) What case is *māgne dēfēnsor*?
7) What visual effect does the verb *titubāret* create? What poetic device is this?

Eos (Dawn) carries the body of her son, Memnon (cup potted by Calliades, painted by Douris, 490–480 BCE; Louvre Museum, Paris, France) (Public Domain)

15   Omnēs Graecī māgnopere dolēbant, sed maximē Nestor cum
praesēns fīlium suum mortuum esse vīdisset. Māgnā cum voce alium
fīlium clāmāvit: "**Quam celerrimē** venī. **Interfectōrem** ā corpore
Antilochī arceāmus ut fīlium omnibus rītibus rectē sepeliāmus." Fīlius et
comes adiūvāndum **currentēs** hastās contrā Memnonem mīsērunt,
20   sed dea Aurōra hās āvertit. Nunc Memnōn corpus Antilochī superstāns
arma spoliāre incipiēbat. At Nestor vehementer dolēns auxilium iterum
quaesīvit. Vērō ipse quamvīs senex Memnonī resistere cupiēbat. Mox
senex mortuus iuxtā fīlium **iacuisset**, nisi Memnōn illum incurrentem
māgnō cum clāmōre stitisset: "Senex, **pudeat** mē tēcum pugnāre, quī
25   tantopere senior es quam ego. Tālis victōria omnī honōre careat. Recēde
igitur nē invītus tē laedam." Dēsīderāns iuventūtem maestus Nestor
recessit. Tum Memnōn plūrimōs Danaōs occīdit.
         Nunc Nestor Achillem petīvit. Dolēns exclāmāvit: "Achillēs, **māgne
dēfēnsor** Danaum, fīlius meus mortuus est. Memnōn arma eius
30   spoliāvit. Nunc maximē timeō nē avēs canēsque corpus dēvorent. Sed
celeriter succurre!" Achillēs audiēns māgnopere dolēbat. Spectāns trāns
pugnam Memnonem multōs trucīdantem procul vīdit. Statim cucurrit ut
Memnonem oppugnāret. Memnōn ingēns saxum ā solō sublātum contrā
Achillem iaculātus est. Sed Achillēs nōn timuit quod scūtum sē prōtexit.
35   Nunc in Memnonem incurrēns dextrum umerum suprā scūtum percussit
ut Memnōn **titubāret**.

Discussion Questions

1) Why is Memnon unwilling to fight Nestor?
2) What does Nestor think will happen to Antilochus if he does not
   retrieve his body?

37 **lacertus, -ī, m.** - *upper arm*

39 **iactō** (1) - *to boast, brag*

40 **īnsuperābilis, -e** - *insuperable, unconquerable*

42 **quā** (adv.) - *where*

44 **Nēreus, -ī, m.** - *Nereus*; a sea-god and father of the Nereids, including Thetis

45 **beneficium, -iī, n.** - *kindness, good deed, benefit, favor*

48 **ictus, -ūs, m.** - *blow, thrust*

49 **āēr, āeris, m.** - *air*

impleō, -ēre, -plēvī, -plētum - *to fill, fill up*

50 **dōnec** (conj.) - *until*

51 **sanguineus, -a, -um** - *bloody*

crepō (1) - *to clatter, make a loud noise*

54 **aura, -ae, f.** - *breeze, light wind*

dēvolō (1) - *to fly to, swoop down*

55 **exanimis, -e** - *lifeless, dead*

attollō, -ere - *to lift up*

Aethiopia, -ae, f. - *Ethiopia*

GRAMMAR AND COMPREHENSION QUESTIONS

1) What mood does *ut* govern here? How do you translate it?
2) What clouds the sun and why?
3) What sound is there when Memnon falls?
4) What is Aurora's reaction? How does it affect the earth?
5) How is Memnon's body returned to his kingdom?

Tamen rēx magnīs cum animīs pugnāns fortī hastā lacertum Achillis percussit ut sanguis flueret. Tum Memnōn glōriāns: "Nunc moriēris manū meā vinctus. Stulte! Tū quī, multīs Trōiānīs occīsīs, iactābās tē, fīlium
40 deae, futūrum esse īnsuperābilem. At ego sum fīlius multō māiōris deae, Aurōrae, quae lūmen omnibus hominibus fert. Māter tua autem in altō marī habitat quā nēminem adiuvat."Achillēs respondit: "Quam stultē mē oppugnāre audēs, quoniam ego sum multō māior quam tū. Nam genus meum est ā māgnō Iove et fortī Nēreō, marīnō deō.
45   "Praetereā omnēs deī mātrem meam, Thetidem, prō multīs beneficiīs honōrant. Nunc autem, **ut** Hectore occīsō Patroclum ultus sum, sīc iam tē occīdendō Antilochum ulciscar." Tum gladium ēdūcēns in Memnonem incurrit. Ambō plūrimōs ictūs inter sē iēcērunt. Diū ācriter pugnantēs āerem pulvere implēvērunt ut sōl obscūrus fieret. Fērox pugna erat aequa
50 dōnec tandem Achillēs gladium in pectus illūstris Memnonis impulsit. Subitō Memnōn in sanguineum solum cecidit, armīs crepantibus, et animus lūcem vītamque relīquit. Aethiōpibus fugientibus Myrmidonēs splendida arma spoliāvērunt. At Aurōra gemēns in nūbibus sē cēlāvit ut tenebrae terram obscūrārent. Tum levēs aurae dēvolāvērunt ad campum
55 Trōiae et exanime corpus Memnonis attollentēs Aethiopiam rettulērunt.

DISCUSSION QUESTIONS

1) What does Memnon achieve against Achilles that no one else has done?
2) What does Memnon call Achilles? How does Achilles respond?
3) How was the body of Memnon rescued? Does this remind you of another rescue?

THE THEFT OF THE PALLADIUM

The Palladium was a sacred, wooden or stone statue of Minerva that was purported to have fallen from heaven, thus sent by the gods. It was housed in her temple on the Trojan citadel. Different sources provide different accounts, but it is agreed that Ulysses discovered from a prophet, either the Greek Calchas or the captured Trojan Helenus, that the city could not be taken while the Palladium remained within its walls. Sometimes this episode is conflated with another, which is recounted by Menelaus in *Odyssey* 4.242ff., in which Helen recognized the disguised Ulysses on a spy mission in Troy but did not alert anyone and allowed Ulysses to exit the city safely. Vergil elaborates upon the story of the theft of the Palladium in Sinon's deceptive explanation of the Trojan horse in *Aeneid* 2.

SOURCES

Apollodorus, *Epitome* 5.13 • Ovid, *Metamorphoses* 13.341–45 • Quintus of Smyrna, *The Fall of Troy* 10.350–60

---

1   **observō** (1) - to pay attention to, heed

     praedictum, -ī, n. - *prediction, prophecy*

     Diomēdēs, -is, m. - *Diomedes*; king of Argos and close friend of Ulysses

2   **verberō** (1) - *to beat, lash*

     pannus, -ī, m. - *rag*

     mendīcus, -ī, m. - *beggar*

3   **clam** (adv.) - *in secret, secretly*

4   **agnōscō, -ere, -nōvī, -nitum** - *to recognize*

5   **prōdō, -ere, -didī, -ditum** - *to betray, give over*

6   **statua, -ae, f.** - *statue*

7   **Palladium, -iī, n.** - *Palladium*; a statue of Athena/Minerva so named because another name for Athena was Pallas (in memory of a young girl she had accidentally killed)

9   **repetō, -ere, -īvī, -ītum** - *to seek again, direct course back to*

GRAMMAR AND COMPREHENSION QUESTIONS

1) Why did Ulysses beat himself?
2) How should you translate *cum*? Note that *tamen* follows in the next clause.
3) What can you infer was the size of the Palladium?
4) What is the antecedent of *quōs*?

Observāns praedictum Ulixēs cum Diomēde mediā nocte ā campīs discessit. Prīmum Ulixēs sē sevērē verberāverat et pannōs mendīcī induerat. Tum Ulixēs, Diomēde prope mūrōs Trōiae relictō, clam ascendēns urbem intrāvit. Nēmō in urbe eum agnōvit nisi Helena. **Cum**
5   illa eum prōdere posset, Ulixem **tamen** ad templum Minervae dūxit. Ibi postquam Ulixēs custōdem templī interfēcit, statuam Minervae, nōmine Palladium, fūrātus est. Tum, statuā sub pannīs cēlātā, ad mūrōs redīvit **quōs** iterum ascendit. Dēnique Ulixēs Diomēdēsque gaudentēs campōs Graecōs repetīvērunt.

Discussion Questions

1) Is Ulysses's disguise as a beggar in this episode unique? Do you know of any other instance when he assumes this disguise?
2) In *Iliad* 10 Diomedes and Ulixes go on another nighttime spying mission to find out the plans of the Trojans. Consult the passage (Chapter 7) and see what similarities and differences you can find.

The Death of Achilles

Many modern readers of the *Iliad* are disappointed that the epic does not include the death of Achilles, which was foreshadowed in Books 9 and 16 and indeed predicted when in Book 18 Achilles chose to return to battle to avenge Patroclus. His choice is reinforced several times subsequently. Readers seem to want his death to be the climactic episode, but the actual death of Achilles is in some ways anticlimactic and certainly not particularly heroic. Indeed one could call it ignominious.

It is important to note that Homer did not know anything about the story of Thetis trying to render the infant Achilles invulnerable by dipping him in the river Styx but forgetting about the heel by which she grasped him. This well-known myth is a subsequent addition, hinted at in Hyginus (64 BCE–17 CE) and expanded by the Roman epic poet Statius (c. 45–c. 96 CE), perhaps to explain the strange way in which he was killed. Earlier the Greek poet Apollonius of Rhodes (3rd c. BCE) in his *Argonautica* (4.869–72) tells how Thetis tried to make Achilles immortal by surrounding him with fire each night and anointing him with ambrosia during the day. Peleus, however, saw his son in the flames and reacted with horror. Thetis, furious at his intervention, immediately left, never to return to Peleus.

Sources

Apollodorus, *Epitome* 5.3–5 • Hyginus, *Fabulae* 107 • Ovid, *Metamorphoses* 12.580–611 • Quintus of Smyrna, *The Fall of Troy* 3.21–185

---

5 **ārsisset:** from *ardeō, -ēre*
ob (prep. + acc.) - *in front of, opposite*

7 **quis** after **nē** = *aliquis*
monitiō, -ōnis, f. - *warning*

8 **respiciō, -ere, -exī, -ectum** - *to heed, take notice of*
inexōrābilis, -e - *inexorable, relentless, that cannot be moved*

Parcae, -ārum, f. - *Parcae;* the Roman fates (Clotho, Lachesis, and Atropos)

9 **mīnor, -ārī, -ātus sum** (+ dat.) - *to threaten*
vetō, -āre, -tuī, -itum - *to forbid*

10 **superbus, -a, -um** - *proud, haughty*

12 **feriō, -īre** - *to strike, hit*

Grammar and Comprehension Questions

1) What case is *flūmina*?
2) What is the physical result of the carnage Achilles creates?
3) What tense and mood is *oppugnāvisset*? In what construction?

Postquam Antilochus sepultus est, Achillēs morte īrātus arma cēpit
ut amīcum suum ulciscerētur. In pugnā furēns hērōs tam plūrimōs hostēs
occīdit ut sanguis solum operīret et corpora **flūmina** implērent. Iam
Achillēs Trōiam ipsam **oppugnāvisset** et in urbem inruisset, nisi Apollō

5 vidēns tot Trōiānōs occīsōs īrā ārsisset. Dē Olympō deus dēscendit et ob
Achillem stetit; māgnā cum vōce clāmāvit: "Cēde, fīlī Pēleī. Nōlī hostēs ad
mortem mittere nē quis deōrum tē opprimat." Sed hērōs monitiōnem deī
nōn respexit; nam inexōrābilēs Parcae etiamnum appropinquābant. Fērox
Achillēs respondit: "Cūr mihi mīnāns vetās mē pugnāre cum

10 superbīs Trōiānīs? Paulō ante dēcipiēns mē ē proeliō ēdūxistī, cum
prīmum ā morte Hectorem servāvistī. Quīn recēde. Domum deōrum redī
nē tē quamvīs immortālem feriam." Hīs dictīs ā deō sē avertēns Trōiānōs
fugientēs ad urbem īnsecūtus est.

Discussion Questions

1) Does Apollo give Achilles fair warning? Is this usual for the gods?
2) How before did Apollo deceive Achilles?

Dying Achilles. The death of Achilles by an arrow in his heel. (sculpture by
Ernst Herter; 1884; Achilleion Gardens, Corfu, Greece) (Public Domain)

14 **impudēns, -ntis** - *shameless, impudent, brazen*

15 **prōvocō (1)** - *to call out to, challenge, provoke*

16 **Scaeus, -a, -um** - *Scaean,* referring to the westward gates of Troy

    venēnātus, -a, -um - *poisoned*

17 **tālus, -ī, m.** - *ankle*

    titubō (1) - *to totter, stagger*

18 **circumspiciō, -ere, -spexī, -spectum** - *to look all around*

19 **fūrtim** (adv.) - *stealthily, secretly*

    cōram (adv.) - *face to face, in person, openly*

20 **profundō, -ere, -fūdī, -fūsum** - *to pour forth*

    Orcus, -ī, m. - *Orcus*; Orcus, the Roman god of the underworld, equivalent to Hades

22 **stabilis, -e** - *firm, steady*

23 **languēscō, -ere, -uī** - *to grow physically weak, feeble*

    agnōscō, -ere, -nōvī, -nitum - *to recognize, acknowledge*

25 **oblītus est**: from *oblīvīscor* here with acc.

28 **frīgēscō, -ere, frixī** - *to become cold*

    innītor, -nītī, -nīxus sum (+ abl.) - *to lean on*

    minae, -ārum, f. pl. - *threats*

30 **fragor, -ōris, m.** - *crash*

31 **sonō, -āre, -uī, -itum** - *to make a noise, sound, to resound*

Grammar and Comprehension Questions

1) To whom does *iste* refer?
2) What does Achilles order Apollo do to?
3) Why is Achilles outraged when he is struck by an arrow?
4) What mood is *audeat*? What does the mood convey?
5) What is the subject of *mittet*?
6) How does Achilles react to the knowledge of his impending death?
7) How do the Trojans react to the wounding of Achilles?
8) How should *cum* be translated here?

At Apollō īrātus sē adlocūtus: "Ō impudēns! **Iste** furit quī deōs
15   prōvocat. At nunc nūllus deus hunc furentem servābit." Tum Apollō
Paridem simulāns prope Scaeās portās venēnātam sagittam in Achillem
ēmīsit, quae tālum hērōis percussit. Statim hērōs māgnō dolōre raptus
titubat et velut alta turris cecidit. Tamen circumspiciēns terribilī vōce
clāmāvit: "Quis fūrtim sagittam in mē ēmīsit? Iste **audeat** mē cōram
20   pugnāre! Tum hasta mea omnem sanguinem istius profundet et istum ad
Orcum **mittet**."

     Tum Achillēs sagittam ē vulnere stabilibus manibus ēdūxit, et,
sanguine profundente, languēscēbat fātum suum agnōscēns. Tum
īrāscēns sagittam ā sē iaculātus est. At tamen Achillēs virtūtem nōn
25   oblītus est. Etiamnum pugnāre cupiēbat, sed nēmō Trōiānōrum obviam
īre eī etsī sauciō audēbat. **Cum** vīs per vulnus lābēbātur, hērōs tamen
contrā hostēs oppugnāvit et multōs tum occīdit. At tandem membra
frīgēscēbant, vītā recēdente, ut hastā innīterētur. Sed etiamnum minās
contrā Trōiānōs clāmābat, quī appropinquāre nōndum ausī sunt. Tandem
30   hērōs fātō victus māgnō cum fragōre in terram cecidit et immortālia
arma super eum sonuērunt. Anima hērōis in īnfernōs recessit.

DISCUSSION QUESTIONS

     1) If Achilles had heeded the warning, would it have made any
         difference?
     2) Does it conform to the heroic code to shoot an enemy from afar?
     3) What feature of Apollo's arrow is particularly deadly? Is Apollo
         playing fair?
     4) What actually killed Achilles?
     5) Does Achilles's death seem appropriate for such a great hero? Might
         the author have some message here?

Chapter Twenty

The Quarrel over Achilles's Arms; The Suicide of Ajax; The Return of Philoctetes; The Death of Paris

Much like the last chapter, this final chapter includes episodes beyond the compass of the *Iliad* itself: the contest between Ulysses and Ajax over Achilles's immortally forged weapons; the subsequent madness and suicide of Ajax; finally the death of Paris by Philoctetes using the bow of Hercules.

After the shocking death of Achilles, at first the Trojans were still frightened to approach him. Then Paris urged them to bring his body into Troy to satisfy the vengeful feelings of the multitudes whose loved ones he had slain. Thus the Trojans approached the corpse, but Ajax quickly stood protectively over the body of his cousin. There ensued a ferocious battle over his corpse in which Ajax killed very many Trojans. This battle parallels earlier ones over the bodies of Sarpedon, Patroclus, and Hector. Eventually Ajax, with the help of other Greeks such as Ulysses, succeeded in bringing Achilles's body back into the Greek camp.

The Quarrel over Achilles's Arms

Ajax and the Greeks mourned Achilles bitterly and offered lavish funeral games in his honor. At the end of the games Thetis offered Achilles's arms to the bravest man, the one who had rescued her son's body. Ajax and Ulysses both came forward to claim that prize. There are several variant versions of how the decision was made, and this passage makes some reference to them. The majority of the passage, however, is based upon the Sophoclean version. Many of the points each of the heroes makes refer to episodes that have been described in earlier chapters of this book.

Sources

Sophocles, *Ajax* • Apollodorus, *Epitome* 5.6–7 • Hyginus, *Fabulae* 107 • Ovid, *Metamorphoses* 12.624–13.398 • Quintus of Smyrna, *The Fall of Troy* 5.121–486

---

2 **certāmen, -inis, n.** - *contest*

3 **quisque, quidque** (indef. pronoun) - *each (one), each (person)*

4 **mereō, -ēre, -uī, -itum** - *to earn, deserve, merit, claim*

5 **uter, utra, utrum** (pronoun) - *which of the two*

indignor, -ārī, -ātus sum - *to consider unworthy, be shamed, be indignant*

9 **ignāvus, -a, -um** - *lazy, cowardly*

pōne (adv.) - *in the rear, from behind*

10 **mementōte**: plural imperative of *meminī*

11 **prōvocō** (1) - *to challenge*

14 **coactus**: from *cogō, -ere*

15 **sagittārius, -ī, m.** - *archer, bowman*

Lemnus, -ī, f. - *Lemnos*; an island in the Aegean en route from Greece to Troy

16 **indicium, -iī, n.** - *evidence, proof*

prōditiō, -ōnis, f. - *betrayal, treachery*

17 **situs, -ūs, m.** - *site, position*

Grammar and Comprehension Questions

1) What construction follows *cūr*?
2) What mood is *ēligāmus*?
3) What does Ajax mean that Ulysses fought from the back? What was Ulysses's weapon?
4) What type of clause does *ut* introduce?
5) Do you see any irony in Ajax's use of *dolō* here?
6) What was Ulysses's motivation in seeking vengeance against Palamedes? (See Chapter Two.)

Nunc in conciliō Aiax, validissimus Danaum, rogat ut Agamemnōn
Nestorque certāmen iūdicent, quoniam facta ambōrum cognōvērunt.
Ulixēs cōnsentit. Tum certāmen verbōrum fit, in quō quisque dēclārat
cūr ipse arma Achillis mereat. (Aliquī dīcunt Nestorem iūdicāre nolle. Ille
5   quidem monuit: "Uter certāmen amīserit indignābitur. Aiax est in bellō
superior, Ulixēs in cōnsiliō. Trōiānōs captīvōs igitur iūdicēs **ēligāmus** ut
neuter hērōs nōbīscum īrāscātur.")

Prīmum Aiax incēpit: "Ego splendida arma Achillis meruī; iste nōn
meruit. Ulixēs ignāvus pōne pugnābat, sed ego semper in fronte prīmā
10   pugnābam. Mementōte mē sōlum contrā māgnum Hectorem tōtum
diem pugnāvisse, cum Hector omnēs Danaōs sēcum pugnāre prōvocāret.
Deinde sōlus Hectorem Trōiānōsque ante nāvēs pugnāvī **ut** hostēs nāvēs
nostrās nōn incenderent. Quid autem Ulixēs nōbīs fēcit? Prīmum iste
Trōiam advenīre nōlēbat; **dolō** coactus est. Tum vulnerātum Philoctētam,
15   māgnum sagittārium, in Lemnō dēseruit. Etiam ut Palamēdem
ulcisceretur, indicia prōditiōnis in tabernāculō eius falsē posuit; hōc dolō
mortem Palamēdis effēcit. Nunc autem Ulixēs nāvēs suās in mediō sitū
tenet quō tūtissimus erit. Nāvēs meās in extrēmō cornū posuī ut aliās
nāvēs dēfendere possem.

DISCUSSION QUESTIONS

1) Why did Nestor not want to judge the contest? Whom does he
suggest as judges?
2) To what prior fight with Hector does Ajax refer?
3) What are the essential points that Ajax makes in defense of his claim
on the arms?
4) What criticisms does Ajax make against Ulysses? Are these valid?

20 **fīdō, -ere, fīsus sum** (+ abl.) - *to trust (in), have confidence in, rely on*
    fallax, -ācis - *deceptive, deceitful*
    aequālis, -e - *equal*
21 **pusillus, -a, -um** - *puny, tiny*
22 **tractō** - *to wield, manage, handle*
    cōnsōbrīnus, -ī, m. - *cousin*
23 **māvīs:** second person s. present of *mālō, mālle, māluī*
26 **adrogō** (1) - *to lay claim to, claim as a right, adopt*
28 **aequō** (1) - *to equal, to match*
29 **mōmentum, -ī, n.** - *importance, influence*
    maximī momentī: genitive of valuation, *of greatest importance*
    acūmen, -inis, n. - *sharpness, acuteness*
    ingenium, -iī, n. - *intellect*
    praestō, -āre, -stitī, -stitum (+ dat.) - *to excel*
30 **quisque, quidque** (indef. pronoun) - *each one*
31 **incertus, -a, -um** - *uncertain, unclear*
32 **dēligō, -ere, -lēgī, -lectum** - *to choose, select*
33 **obstupefactus, -a, -um** - *stunned, struck dumb*

pudor, -ōris, m. - *a feeling of shame, shame*
obruō, -ere, -uī, -utum - *to overwhelm, overpower*
34 **prōsequor, -ī, -secūtus sum** - *to escort, accompany*
35 **occidō, -ere, -cidī, -casum** - *to set*
    dīrus, -a, -um - *awful, dire, dreadful*
36 **meditor, -ārī, -ātus sum** - *to contemplate, ponder*
36–37 **ab eīs . . . ab Ulixe . . . ulciscī:** *to avenge himself on, to take vengeance from*
36 **dēdecorō** (1) - *to bring discredit on, dishonor, disgrace*
39 **iniciō, -ere, -iēcī, -iectum** - *to throw in, instill, inflict*
    grex, gregis, m. - *flock, herd*
    ovis, -is, f. - *sheep*
    ariēs, -etis, m. - *ram*
40 **maledīcō, -ere, -dīxī, -dictum** (+ dat.) - *to abuse verbally, insult*
41 **cālīgō, -inis, f.** - *mist, darkness, obscurity*
42 **sōlum** (adv.) - *only*
    trucīdō (1) - *to slaughter*

Grammar and Comprehension Questions

1) What does Ajax suggest as the way to decide who should get the arms?
2) What form is *aestimanda*? In what construction with *sunt*?
3) What case is *istī*?
4) What tense and mood is *dēlēgerint*? In what construction?
5) What construction does *ut* introduce here?
6) Do you know of other instances in which Minerva protects Ulysses?
7) What construction does *crēdēns* introduce?
8) How does Minerva deceive Ajax?

20   Nunc fīdēns fallācī linguā exspectat ut ipse aequālis cum magnīs
mīlitibus habeātur. Postrēmō pusillus Ulixēs nec ingentia arma Achillis
gerere potest nec māgnam hastam tractāre. Ego, cōnsōbrīnus Achillis,
haec arma aptē geram. Aut, sī māvīs, prō armīs pugnēmus."

      Contrā Ulixēs respondit: "Vīs nōn omnia aufert. Alia beneficia

25 etiam **aestimanda sunt**. Prīmum ego Achillem ad hoc bellum dūxī ut
omnia māgna facta eius adrogāre possem. Deinde Trōiam clam intrāvī
ut Palladium in castra nostra referrem. Ego etiam prō corpore Achillis
fortiter pugnāvī. Postrēmō istum Aiācem vīribus aequō atque, quod est
maximī momentī, **istī** in acūmine ingeniī multō praestō."

30   Cum quisque hērōs causam suam dīxisset, Ulixēs victor iūdicātus
est. (Incertum est utrum Agamemnōn et Nestor an Trōiānī captīvī
victōrem **dēlēgerint**.) Tum Ulixēs in victōriā māgnopere gaudēbat, sed
Aiax stābat obstupefactus. Statim pudor māgnum hērōem obruit **ut** nec
dīcere nec movēre posset. Tandem comitēs eum ad nāvem prōsecūtī sunt.

35 Iam sōle occidente cēterī Danaī dormiēbant, nisi Aiax quī dīra cōnsilia
meditābātur. Nam ab eīs quī sē dēdecorāverant et praesertim ab Ulixe sē
ulcīscī cupiēbat. Arma induēns ē tabernāculō excurrit ut dūcēs Danaum
oppugnāret. Sed Minerva Ulixem dīligēns īnsaniam in mentem Aiācis
iniēcit ut Aiax gregem ovium oppugnāret et occīderet. **Crēdēns** arietem

40 esse Ulixem illī vehementer maledīxit antequam occīdit. Triumphāns ad
tabernāculum redīvit, sed mox Minerva cālīginem īnsaniae remōvit ut
Aiax sōlum ovēs trucidātōs nōn hominēs vidēret.

DISCUSSION QUESTIONS

    1) What does Ajax think about Odysseus's stature?
    2) Examine the family relationship between Achilles and Ajax. How are
        they related?
    3) What do you think of Ulysses claiming Achilles's deeds as essentially
        his own?
    4) Can Ulysses really claim to be Ajax's equal in strength?
    5) Has Ajax really suffered disgrace by the loss of Achilles's arms?
    6) Is Ajax's concern with honor reminiscent of another hero's concern?

The Suicide of Ajax

After Minerva removed the cloud of insanity in which she had cloaked him, Ajax was overcome with shame. Now he realized that, having killed a flock of sheep instead of the Greek leaders, he would be a laughing-stock. The proud warrior cannot tolerate such ignominy and takes action.

Sources

Sophocles, *Ajax* • Apollodorus, *Epitome* 5.6–7 • Hyginus, *Fabulae* 107 • Ovid, *Metamorphoses* 12.624–13.398 • Quintus of Smyrna, *The Fall of Troy* 5.121–486

1	**obruō, -ere, -uī, -utum** - *to overwhelm, overpower*	7	**eundem** (+ dat.) - gerundive of *eō, īre* - *he must go*
	comprehendō, -ere, -hendī, -hēnsum - *to comprehend, understand*	9	**īnfīgō, -ere, -fīxī, -fīxum** - *to drive in, imbed, fix*
2	**fallō, -ere, fefellī, falsum** - *to trick, mislead, deceive*		**Mercurius, -iī, m.** - *Mercury;* the Greek Hermes; leader of souls to the underworld
3	**cōnscīscō, -ere, -scīvī, -scitum** (+ dat.) *to decree for oneself, decide*	10	**Furiae, -ārum, f.** - *the Furies;* dread goddesses who take vengeance for great crimes, avenging spirits
	Tecmessa, -ae, f. - *Tecmessa;* daughter of King Teuthras and mistress of Ajax		**Atrīdae, -ārum, m.** - *the Atreidae;* the two sons of Atreus, Agamemnon and Menelaus
4	**amīca, -ae, f.** - *mistress, lover*	11	**aiai** (exclamation) - a Greek exclamation of distress - *alas, alas,* which replicates the sound of Ajax's name in Greek
5	**nothus, -a, -um** - *illegitimate, bastard*		
	cōnsōlor, -ārī, -ātus sum - *to console, comfort, reassure*		

Grammar and Comprehension Questions

1) What tense and mood is *fēcisset*? In what construction?
2) What word must you take with *falsum* to complete the meaning and construction?
3) What tense is *occīderis*? In what type of condition?
4) Where did Ajax get the sword he uses? Do you see irony here?
5) What verb do you understand to govern *Furiās*? What does he ask of the Furies?

Nunc māior pudor Aiācem obruit cum comprehenderet quid
fēcisset. Hērōs cōgnōvit sē ā deīs **falsum** dēceptumque esse et nūllum
hominem adesse. Ergō Aiax mortem sibi cōnscīvit. Sed Tecmessa, captīva
amīca Aiācis et ab hōc māter fīliī, hērōem obsecrābat: "Nōlī nōs dēserere.

5   Nam sī tē **occīderis**, Danaī nōs contemnent. Fīlius noster nothus
habēbitur et multam contumēliam patiētur." Tum Aiax eam cōnsōlābātur,
sed mox dīcēbat sibi eundem esse ad lītus ut vēniam ā Minervā peteret.
Sōlus in lītore gladium, quod Hector post certāmen sibi honōris causā
dederat, in humō īnfīxit. Tum prīmum hērōs Mercurium precātus ut

10   sē ad īnfernōs celeriter dūceret et deinde **Furiās** ut Atrīdās pūnīrent.
Precibus factīs clāmāns "aiai" in gladium incurrit.

DISCUSSION QUESTION

1) Is Ajax's relationship with Tecmessa similar to another master-slave
relationship?

13 **Teucer, Teucrī, m.** - *Teucer;* half-
    brother of Ajax by Telamon

    nātus: from *nāscor, nāscī*

    arcessō, -ere, -īvī, -ītum - *to send
    for, fetch*

15 **recūsō** (1) - *to refuse*

    iussum, -ī, n. - *command, order*

    spondeō, -ēre, spopondī, spōnsum -
    to pledge, solemnly promise

16 **fās** (indecl. noun + inf.) - *it is morally
    right, proper, ordained by the gods*

18 **secundum** (prep. + acc.) - *after,
    second to*

    cēnseō, -ēre, cēnsuī, cēnsum - *to
    value, deem*

19 **rīte** (adv.) - *with correct religious
    procedure, properly*

GRAMMAR AND COMPREHENSION QUESTIONS

1) What tense is *sepultūrum esse*?
2) What tense, mood, and voice are *factī essent*?

Tecmessa covers the body of Ajax, who committed suicide by impaling himself on
his own sword. (Brygos painter, c. 490 BCE; Getty Museum, California)
(© Creative Commons 3.0/Remi Mathis)

Brevī tempore anxia Tecmessa properāns corpus invēnit.

Quamquam lāmentāns Teucrum, eōdem patre nātum, statim arcessīvit.

At Agamemnōn Menelāusque celeriter advenientēs corpus sepelīre

15   recūsāvērunt. Tum Teucer autem contrā iussa eōrum sē corpus

sepultūrum esse spopondit. Tandem Ulixēs affirmāvit fās esse Aiācem

sepelīre. Nam, quamquam ipse Aiaxque inimīcī **factī essent**, Ulixēs

hērōem honorāvit et eum maximum mīlitem secundum Achillem cēnsuit.

Itaque Aiax rīte sepultus est.

DISCUSSION QUESTIONS

1) Why would Agamemnon and Menelaus want to deny Ajax burial?
   How important was proper burial?
2) Why does Ulysses intervene on Ajax's behalf?
3) Ajax's feud with Ulysses continues in *Odyssey* 11 where Ajax refuses
   to speak to Ulysses even in death. Does this rejection seem
   excessive? (Vergil used this scene as a model for his underworld
   scene between Dido and Aeneas in Book 4 of the *Aeneid*.)

The Return of Philoctetes

In Chapter Two of this volume the story of Philoctetes was recounted. Briefly, en route to Troy during a stop-over on the island of Lemnos, Philoctetes was bitten by a poisonous snake. His wound became badly infected and stank so dreadfully that, at the advice of Ulysses, the Greeks abandoned him on the island to fend for himself with the great bow and arrows of Hercules. Now in the tenth year of the war the prophet Calchas (or the captured Trojan prophet Helenus) revealed that Troy could not be taken without Philoctetes and the bow of Hercules. By now the son of Achilles, Neoptolemus, had come to Troy to fight. (He is also called Pyrrhus. See Chapter One for his birth on Scyros while Achilles was in hiding.) As a result of the prophecy the Greeks send Ulysses and Neoptolemus with a band of soldiers to Lemnos.

There are several versions of this story. The details vary regarding: 1) how Philoctetes was wounded, 2) who accompanied Ulysses: Neoptolemus or Diomedes, and 3) which physician cured Philoctetes. This description primarily follows the Sophoclean version.

Sources

Homer, *Iliad* 2.721–25 • Sophocles, *Philoctetes* • Apollodorus, *Epitome* 5.8 • Vergil, *Aeneid* 3.401 • Quintus Smyrnaeus, *The Fall of Troy* 10.179–363 • Ovid, *Metamorphoses* 13.45–55

---

1   **ignōscō, -ere, -nōvī, -nōtum** (+ dat. of person, acc. of offense) - *to forgive*

4   **caverna, -ae, f.** - *cave, cavern*

8   **misericordia, -ae, f.** - *pity, compassion*

     ergā (prep. + acc.) - *towards, for*

11   **patientia, -ae, f.** - *suffering*

13   **sopor, -ōris, m.** - *overpowering sleep, stupor, coma*

14   **fīdēns, -ntis** (+ abl.) - *confident in, trusting*

Grammar and Comprehension Questions

1) Why is *dēseruisset* subjunctive?
2) What construction is *nunc sē Scȳrum redīre*? On what word does it depend?
3) Which noun is the subject of the indirect statement? *sopōrem* or *sē*?
4) Who is the subject of *tueātur*?

Ulixēs intellegit Philoctētam sibi nōn ignōtūrum esse quod illum
graviter patientem **dēseruisset**. Ulixēs igitur Neoptolemum monet:
"Philoctētēs fallendus est ut Trōiam cum arcū veniat." Neoptolemus
invītus cōnsentit. Philoctētēs in parvā cavernā habitābat et parva
5   animālia māgnō arcū occīdēbat ut vescerētur.

Cum Ulixēs Neoptolemusque Lemnum advēnissent, Ulixēs sē
cēlāvit. Tum Philoctētēs dolōre afflīctus Neoptolemum mīlitēsque invēnit.
Prīmum Neoptolemus māgnam misericordiam ergā Philoctētam ostendit.
Tum iuvenis simulat sē īrātum Trōiam relīquisse quod Danaī arma patris
10   suī Ulixī dedissent; **nunc sē Scȳrum redīre**. Statim Philoctētēs miseram
vītam māgnamque patientiam dēscrībit. Tum rogat ut Neoptolemus sē
Scȳrum etiam dūcat. Neoptolemus libenter cōnsentit. At nunc saevus
dolor Philoctētam occupat et cognōvit **sopōrem sē** mox superātūrum
esse. Fīdēns iuvene māgnum arcum dat ut **tueātur**; nam Philoctētēs
15   hostēs timēbat.

DISCUSSION QUESTION

1) What is the pretense Neoptolemus presents to Philoctetes to gain his
trust?

The recall of Philoctetes from Lemnos. Odysseus/Ulysses on the left; Diomedes (not
featured in this chapter) on the right. (marble slab before mid-2nd century BCE, from
Brauron in Attica, Greece; Archaeological Museum of Brauron) (Public Domain)

16   suādeō, -ēre, suāsī, suāsum - *to*
     urge, recommend

17   rēiciō, -ere, -iēcī, -iectum - *to reject,*
     refuse

     expergiscor, -ī, experrectus sum -
     to wake up, become awake

19   dēspiciō, -ere, -spexī, -spectum - *to*
     despise

     coniūrātiō, -ōnis, f. - *conspiracy,*
     plot

20   patefaciō, -ere, -fēcī, -factum - *to*
     reveal, uncover, disclose

     scīlicet (adv.) - *naturally, obviously*

     repetō, -ere, -īvī, -ītum - *to demand*
     back, claim back

21   latebra, -ae, f. - *hiding place*

26   dēsperō (1) - *to despair*

27   sepulcrum, -ī, n. - *burial, tomb*

     famēs, -is, f. - *starvation, hunger*

     conficiō, -ere, -fēcī, -fectum - *to*
     overwhelm, kill

28   atrōciter (adv.) - *terribly, dreadfully,*
     cruelly

30   medicus, -ī, m. - *doctor*

33   vīsū: supine from *videō, -ēre*

36   speciēs, -ēī, f. - *appearance, sight*

     laetus, -a, -um (+ abl.) - *happy in/at*

37   Machāōn, -onos, m. - *Machaon;,*
     a Greek physician at Troy (See
     Chapter Eight.)

Grammar and Comprehension Questions

1) What construction is *quid faciat*?
2) To whom does *sibi* refer?
3) What use of *quam* is this?
4) Why is *adiuvem* subjunctive?
5) At his moment of deepest despair what does Philoctetes think will
   be his fate?
6) What case is *fame*? With what function?
7) What arguments does Neoptolemus use to persuade Philoctetes to
   come to Troy?
8) What case is *arcū*? What governs it?

Philoctētā dormiente, mīlitēs suādent Neoptolemum cum arcū iam discēdere, sed iuvenis hoc cōnsilium rēiēcit. Mox Philoctētēs expergiscēns gaudet quod Neoptolemus sē nōn dēseruerat. Neoptolemus patientis Philoctētae miserāns dolum suum dēspicit. Ergō tōtam coniūrātiōnem

20   patefacit. Philoctētēs scīlicet īrātus arcum repetit sine quō vīvere nōn potest. Neoptolemus tamen **quid faciat** nescit. Sed statim Ulixēs ē latebrā exiēns imperat ut iuvenis arcum **sibi** det. Etiam nuntiat sē Philoctētem Trōiam navigāre coactūrum esse. Philoctētēs autem respondit, "Mē occīdam potius **quam** Atrīdās tēque, inimīcōs meōs, **adiuvem**." Tum

25   obsecrat ut Neoptolemus sē adiuvet. At Neoptolemus Ulixēsque cum arcū discēdunt. Iam hērōs dēspērat crēdēns cavernam sibi obscūrum sepulcrum futūram esse; nam sine arcū **fame** cōnficiētur. At nunc subitō cum arcū Neoptolemus revēnit! Iuvenis nōn poterat hērōem tam atrōciter dēcipere. Nunc temptat Philoctētae persuādēre ut Trōiam sēcum nāviget.

30   Nam ibi medicī vulnus sānāre poterint et tum hērōs ipse fortia facta efficiet. Sed Philoctētēs tantās iniūriās ignōscere nōn potest. Nunc Neoptolemus intellegit hērōem persuadērī nōn posse. Prōmittit igitur hērōem sēcum Scȳrum dūcere. Dum discēdere parant, mīrābile vīsū dīvīnus Herculēs appāret! Deus iubet Philoctētem Trōiam nāvigāre; nam ibi **arcū** Herculis

35   ūtēns hērōs Paridem occīdet et tandem Trōia cadet. Statim Philoctētēs speciē vōceque deī laetus dēnique discēdere Trōiam vult.

Omnēs navigantēs celeriter Trōiam adveniunt. Ibi Machāōn medicāmentīs Philoctētam sānat. Nunc integer hērōs plūrimōs hostēs māgnō arcū Herculis occīdit.

DISCUSSION QUESTIONS

1) Why does Neoptolemus change his mind about deceiving Philoctetes?
2) Does Neoptolemus's behavior seem at all similar to his father's?
3) Compare Ulysses here to his characterization in the *Odyssey*.
4) Compare this characterization of Neoptolemus/Pyrrhus to Vergil's account of the fall of Troy in *Aeneid* 2.
5) Examine the appearance of Hercules as a *deus ex machina*, a plot device in Greek tragedy.

THE DEATH OF PARIS

As in the passage above, there are several variations on the involvement of Philoctetes in the death of Paris. Was it just the bow of Hercules that Philoctetes brought that killed Achilles? Or did Philoctetes himself using the bow kill Paris, and with how many shots? The passage below depicts one version of the shooting of Paris as well as his lingering death and a surprising new character.

SOURCES

Apollodorus, *Epitome* 5.8 • Quintus Smyrnaeus, *The Fall of Troy* 10.179–489

---

3   **dēclinō** (1) - *to swerve, turn aside*

5   **sōlum** (adv.) - *only, merely*

     stringō, -ere, strinxī, strictum - *to graze, scratch*

     frustrōr, -ārī, -ātus sum - *to deceive with false hope, frustrate, disappoint*

6   **venēnātus, -a, -um** - *poisoned*

     pharetra, -ae, f. - *quiver*

     nervus, -ī, m. - *string (of bow)*

     aptō (1) (+ dat.) - *to fit on, fasten*

7   **aberrō** (1) - *to stray, miss, go wide of the mark*

     latus, -eris, n. - *side, flank*

9   **nympha, -ae, f.** - *nymph*, a semi-divine spirit of nature

   Oenōnē, -ēs, f. - *Oenone;* a nymph who lived on Mt. Ida

   rēiciō, -ere, -iēcī, -iectum - *to reject, refuse*

10   **abripiō, -ere, -ripuī, -reptum** - *to remove, carry away, abduct*

     ad Helenam abripiendam: *ad* + gerundive is another way to create a purpose construction

11   **pūtidus, -a, -um** - *festering, rotting*

     cruciō (1) - *to torture, torment*

     Īda, -ae, f. - *Mt. Ida*; a large mountain near Troy

13   **ignōscō, -ere, -nōvī, -nōtum** (+ dat. of person) - *to forgive*

GRAMMAR AND COMPREHENSION QUESTIONS

1) What happened to Paris's first arrow?
2) What case and construction is *multum tempus*?
3) Whom does *adveniēns* modify?
4) What case is *meī*? Why?
5) What form is *miserāre*?

Cum Paris Philoctētam tot Trōiānōs occīdisse vīdisset, eī obviam
īvit. Prīmum Paris sagittam in Philoctētam mīsit, sed Graecus celeriter
dēclīnāns sagittam vītāvit. Sed sagitta alium Graecum percussit
occīditque. Tum Philoctētēs comitem ulciscēns māgnō arcū Herculis
5   sagittam in Paridem mīsit, sed haec mānum sōlum strinxit. Frustrātus
nunc venēnātam sagittam ē pharetrā ēductam nervō aptāvit et in Paridem
iterum mīsit. Haec sagitta nōn aberrāvit sed latus Paridis percussit. Paris
graviter saucius fūgit. **Multum tempus** maximum dolōrem patiēbātur.
   Tum dē nymphā Oenōne cōgitābat, quam prius amāverat et rēiēcerat cum
10   Spartam ad Helenam abripiendam nāvigāvisset. Paris igitur, quamquam
pūtidō vulnere cruciātus, montem Īdam ascendit ut Oenōnem obsecrāret.
Nam sciēbat nympham sē medicāmentīs sānāre posse. **Adveniēns**
statim Oenōnī supplicābat: "Ōrō ut mihi ignoscās. Utinam tē numquam
relīquissem et Helenam numquam vīdissem! Heu, fāta mē ad istam īre
15   coēgērunt. **Meī** graviter patientis **miserāre**! Mē sānā, quoniam potes."

DISCUSSION QUESTIONS

1) Does Paris's aggressive move seem consistent with his character?
2) Does using a poisoned arrow seem fair? Do you know of anyone else
   who used poisoned arrows?
3) Does Paris take responsibility for his own actions?

16 **commoveō, -ēre, -mōvī, -mōtum** -
   to move emotionally, touch
18 **abeō, -īre, -īvī, -itum** - *to go away*
20 **dūritia, -ae, f.** - *hardness, sternness,
   severity, harshness*
21 **lūcus, -ī, m.** - *grove, woodland clearing*
22 **flagrō (1)** - *to blaze, burn*

rogus, -ī, m. - *funeral pyre*
exstruō, -ere, -struxī, -structum -
   *to construct, make by heaping or
   piling material*
23 **īnsiliō, -īre, -uī** - *to leap or jump on*
24 **ārsit:** from *ārdeō, -ēre*

GRAMMAR AND COMPREHENSION QUESTIONS

1) What form is *abī*?
2) What do you think of Oenone's response to Paris?
3) What is the antecedent of *quae*? *Nymphae* or *Oenōnī*? How do you tell?
4) What is the antecedent of *quem*?

The Judgment of Paris. From left to right: Minerva (with helmet), Hermes (with caduceus), Venus surrounded by drapery, Oenone with panpipes, Paris, Eros/Cupid. Paris rejected Oenone after Venus offered him Helen when he declared her victor in the beauty contest. (front panel of Roman sarcophagus, c. 117–138 CE; Museo Nationale Romano in the Ludovisi collection, Rome, Italy) (Public Domain)

At Oenōnē, quondam rēiecta, nunc nōn commōta est. Illa respondit: "Rogā Helenam ut tē sānat, aut Venerem quae tē tantum amat. Tē nōn iuvābō. **Abī!**" Tum Paris rēiectus discessit, et īnfirmus dēscendere montem temptābat. Tandem venēnō victus in Īdā mortuus est. **Nymphae**
20   mortem **Oenōnī** nuntiāvērunt, **quae** iam dūritiam suam acerbē dolēbat. Domō cucurrit ut corpus Paridis invenīret. Cum ad lūcum vēnisset, corpus in flagrantī rogō vīdit, **quem** nymphae pastōrēsque exstrūxerant. Statim nūllō verbō dictō in rogum īnsiluit. Itaque Oenōnē cum cārō Paride ārsit.

DISCUSSION QUESTIONS

1) Are you surprised that Oenone did not relent from her anger?
2) Have you heard of behavior similar to Oenone's drastic reaction to Paris's death?

Epilogue

THE AFTERMATH OF THE TROJAN WAR

O ne might think that after the death of Paris the Trojan War would have ended and that Helen would have been returned to Menelaus. This, however, was not the case. It seems that too much time and too many lives had been invested in the war to give up now. The Greeks wanted not only Helen but also the treasure that Paris had taken from Sparta. Moreover, they would surely demand war reparations for all the lives lost during the ten-year war. Yet all this is irrelevant, since with the death of Paris Helen then married Deiphobus, a Trojan prince who was the brother of Hector and Paris. The prophet Helenus apparently had also contended for her but lost. Myth tells us that Helenus then left Troy and was possibly captured by the Greeks to whom he gave critical prophecies regarding the fall of Troy.

A reader might well ask why this volume does not continue to tell the entire story of the fall of Troy and its aftermath. The simple answer to that question is that it has been done masterfully by classical authors in both Greek and Latin, particularly by Vergil in his great epic, the *Aeneid*. As mentioned in the Introduction, one of the purposes of this volume is to provide a sound mythical description of certain episodes in the Trojan War that Vergil used in crafting his epic. I cannot hope to rival Vergil's powerful account of the fall of Troy as told by Aeneas in *Aeneid* 2. Nonetheless I can here provide a few dramatic incidents that are, for the most part, beyond the sphere of Vergil. As in the body of this book, however, the reader should be advised that these myths have many variants. This epilogue follows the most common version of any particular myth.

Virtually all students know about the Trojan horse, the device designed by Ulysses and built by Epeius. What they are curious about is why the Trojans were so gullible. Vergil in *Aeneid* 2.13–249 provides a very credible explanation. Homer's *Odyssey* also contains two episodes (4.267–89, 11.523–33) that feature the Trojan horse from the perspective of the men hidden within it. As Vergil describes it, the sack of the city was rapid and brutal. The symbolic end of the city came with the murder and beheading of King Priam at his own altar by Neoptolemus (also called Pyrrhus), the son of Achilles (see Chapter One above). This was witnessed by Aeneas, who was destined to be the survivor of the Trojan royal line and to found a new settlement in Italy that would ultimately become Rome. This destiny is of course the material of the *Aeneid*.

Neoptolemus kills Priam on the altar of Jupiter while Hecuba begs for mercy.
(Group of Würzburg vase, c. 510 BCE; Staatliche Antikensammlungen,
Munich, Germany) (Public Domain)

After the capture of the city the Greeks sacked it in accordance with ancient practice: any surviving men were killed; the women and children were enslaved. Euripides's tragedy *Trojan Women* describes the distribution of the female slaves and the return of Helen to Menelaus. Initially Menelaus claimed that he planned to kill her for her infidelity, but we see from *Odyssey* 4 that she suffered no consequences. There is a short palinode (a poem retracting a former statement) by the Greek lyric poet Stesichorus in which he claims that Helen never went to Troy. It was in fact a divinely created image of Helen that caused all the trouble, while the real Helen was spirited away to Egypt for the duration of the war. In his play *Helen* Euripides somewhat comically depicts the reunion of the phantom Helen with the real Helen while Menelaus was marooned in Egypt on his way home from the war.

The distribution of the other Trojan women involves great tragedy. The great queen Hecuba (the Greek Hekabe) was chosen by Ulysses or, in some versions, Agamemnon. Early on the Greek journey home Hecuba met the king Polymestor to whom Priam had entrusted both their son Polydorus and some Trojan treasure. When the king heard of Troy's fall, he murdered Polydorus and absconded with the treasure. After she learned of the death of this son, her last hope, she avenged her child by murdering Polymestor's children and blinding him. Hecuba then went mad and metamorphosed into a barking dog, a truly tragic end for the noble queen.

Andromache, the wife of Hector, was given as a slave to Neoptolemus, son of the man who had slain her entire family as well as her husband, the great Hector. Readers may recall the touching domestic scene in *Iliad* 6 (Chapter Five of this volume) in which Hector worried most not about his own death but about the enslavement of Andromache. His fears were fulfilled in a most dreadful way. As a slave Andromache bore three sons to Neoptolemus. Neoptolemus, however, was then murdered by Orestes, the son of Agamemnon, because Neoptolemus's wife Hesione had originally been promised to Orestes. Upon the murder of Neoptolemus Andromache then married the Trojan prophet Helenus, who had become the slave of Neoptolemus, and they established a rather pathetic mini-Troy in western Greece. Aeneas visits this settlement on his voyage to Italy and receives important prophecies from Helenus (*Aeneid* 3).

At the fall of Troy Neoptolemus also insisted that acknowledgment be given to the spirit of Achilles. Specifically he claimed that the ghost of Achilles demanded the sacrifice of Polyxena, the youngest daughter of Priam and Hecuba, at Achilles's tomb. Her sacrifice is a major plot element in Euripides's play *Hecuba* and the Roman Seneca's play *Trojan Women.*

Polyxena sacrificed at the tomb of Achilles (Tyrrhenian amphora by the Timiades painter, c. 570–530 BCE; British Museum, London, England)
(© Creative Commons 2.5/Marie-Lan Nguyen)

Another daughter of Priam and Hecuba was Cassandra, prophetess and priestess of Apollo. The god had been in love with her and had given her the gift of prophecy if she would yield to him. Initially Cassandra agreed but then reneged. Apollo could not take back his gift; instead he ensured that no one would ever believe her prophecies. So, throughout the ten years of the war Cassandra knew the future and warned what would happen, but the Trojans thought she was crazy. What a dreadful torment this must have been! At the city's fall Agamemnon claimed Cassandra, which caused amazement among the Greeks, since he could have claimed many women considered more suitable. We will see more about Cassandra shortly.

Finally, one of the most poignant episodes of the fall of Troy and of the savagery of war involves Astyanax, the infant son of Hector and Andromache (see Chapter Five above). In *Iliad* 6 Astyanax was terrified by his father in his helmet; then Hector, having removed the helmet, picked up his son and prayed to Jupiter that he be greater than his father. At the close of the *Iliad* Andromache actually foreshadows what will happen to her son: that the Greeks will hurl him from the tower in vengeance for all those whom Hector slew (24.734–39). The Greek motive is also to eradicate the royal line of Priam. The killing of the innocent child is a central scene of both Euripides's and Seneca's *Trojan Women*.

One might think that the triumphant Greeks reaped the benefits of the war, but few returned unscathed. Their tales of return (Greek *nostos, nostoi* in the plural) were popular material for epics, but only Homer's *Odyssey* survives as a representative of this genre. Much of the material below is derived from Nestor's account in *Odyssey* 3.130–92. (The aged Nestor is a true survivor; he is still alive and thriving as king of Pylos ten years after the conclusion of the war.)

First, the Greek leaders themselves, eager to return home, quarreled over how much sacrifice should be given to the gods in gratitude for their victory. Menelaus wanted to return home immediately, whereas Agamemnon believed they should stay at Troy to complete great sacrifices to the gods. One group of ships quickly left with Menelaus. This group included Nestor (see Chapters Three, Four, Six, Eight) who, once at sea, decided to take the riskier route straight across the Aegean Sea to Greece. Taking this route enabled him to get home to Pylos quickly with a following wind. Menelaus, however, took the more traditional land-hugging route and, caught in a great storm sent by the gods, was blown off course to Egypt; it took him seven years to get home. Odysseus, who had initially returned to Troy to support Agamemnon's position, was later hit by the storm as he rounded the Peloponnesus. This was the beginning of his wide-ranging odyssey.

Diomedes (see Chapters One, Four, Five, Sixteen) had also taken the riskier route and arrived safely in Argos. His wife, however, had been unfaithful and had been plotting to kill him on his return. Diomedes eluded the trap but had to escape his land and flee to southern Italy where he also found troubles but ultimately founded a number of cities.

The return of the leader of the expedition, Agamemnon, is chillingly recorded in Aeschylus's great play *Agamemnon*, the first play of his *Oresteia* trilogy. His wife Clytemnestra, horrified by Agamemnon's sacrifice of their daughter Iphigenia demanded by the goddess Diana (a post-Homeric story; see *Latina Mythica*, Chapter Twenty), had been plotting vengeance for the duration of the war. She had allied herself with Aegisthus, Agamemnon's cousin, whose siblings had been slaughtered and fed to their unwitting father Thyestes, who then placed a curse on the house of Atreus. Aegisthus secretly in the palace and Clytemnestra openly had been ruling Mycenae. Clytemnestra had cleverly set up a series of fire beacons to alert her the moment that Troy fell so that she could be ready for Agamemnon's return. She welcomes him with overblown praise and tales of her own suffering in his absence. Then she insists that he walk into the palace on a crimson carpet of extremely expensive and fine cloth. Though reluctant to draw such attention to himself, Agamemnon seems to be bullied into submission and enters. Once inside Clytemnestra traps him in the bath in a robe that acts like a straitjacket and stabs him fatally three times. She also kills the captive Cassandra together with Agamemnon apparently in vengeance that he brought a lover home. So, instead of returning home to reap the rewards of a triumphant military campaign over a great enemy, Agamemnon is murdered and his kingdom is turned over to his sworn enemy. The awful end of Agamemnon is referred to multiple times in the *Odyssey*. In *Odyssey* 11 Agamemnon's ghost warns Odysseus to avoid his fate by returning in secret. Though it took Odysseus ten years to return home, we know that he heeded Agamemnon's warning and returned disguised as a beggar. Thus he was able to rescue his wife Penelope from obnoxious and dangerous suitors who had invaded his home and to reestablish his kingship.

Of course the stories of the characters involved in the Trojan War do not stop with these few individuals. Greek warriors such as the Lesser Ajax (Oilean Ajax) had their own, usually unfortunate, tales of return, and the children of the heroes, such as Orestes, contribute a great deal more to the rich complexity of Greek mythology. This book, however, must end somewhere, and it seems appropriate to conclude now that the Greek and Trojan heroes featured in this volume have finished their sagas. The saga of Aeneas of course continues in Vergil's *Aeneid*. Thus I would urge readers to continue *in linguā Latīnā!*

Vocabulary

A

ā *or* ab (prep. + abl.) - *from, away from; by* (agent)

abdōmen, -inis, n. - *belly, abdomen*

abdūcō, -ere, -dūxī, -ductum - *to lead away, abduct, remove*

absēns, absentis - *away, absent*

absum, -esse, -fuī, -futūrus - *to be away, absent*

accēdō, -ere, -cessī, -cessum - *to come near, approach*

accidō, -ere, accidī - *to fall upon, happen*

accipiō, -ere, -cēpī, -ceptum - *to take, receive, accept*

ācer, ācris, ācre - *sharp, keen, eager, fierce*

acerbus, -a, -um - *harsh, bitter*

Achillēs, -is, m. - *Achilles;* son of Peleus and the goddess Thetis, from Phthia in Greece; leader of the Myrmidons

aciēs, -ēī, f. - *line of battle, battle line*

acūtus, -a, -um - *sharp*

ad (prep. + acc.) - *to, up to, near; with regards to*

addō, -ere, -didī, -ditum - *to add*

addūcō, -ere, -dūxī, -ductum - *to lead forward, bring forward*

adhūc (adv.) - *still, up to this time*

adiuvō, -āre, -iūvī, -iūtum - *to help, aid, assist*

adloquor, -loquī, -locūtus sum - *to address, speak to*

adnuō, -ere, -nuī, -nūtum - *to nod*

adsequor, -sequī, -secūtus sum - *to overtake, catch up with*

adstō, -stāre, -stitī - *to stand by, near*

adsum, -esse, -fuī - *to be present*

adulēscēns, -ntis, m. - *young man*

adveniō, -īre, -vēnī, -ventum - *to come to, arrive at*

adversus, -a, -um - *facing, opposite*

adversum (prep. + acc.) - *against*

aedēs, -is, f. - *house*

Aenēās, -ae, m. (acc. *Aenēan*) - *Aeneas,* son of Venus and Anchises, Trojan warrior, future founder of the Roman people

aequālis, -e - *equal*

aequus, -a, -um - *level, even; fair, equal*

aes, aeris, n. - *bronze*

aestimō (1) - *to regard, consider, esteem*

aeternus, -a, -um - *eternal*

affirmō (1) - *to assert, maintain*

afflīgō, -ere, -flīxī, -flīctum - *to strike, distress, afflict*

Agamemnōn, -onis, m. - *Agamemnon;* king of Mycenae and leader of the expedition against Troy

age/agite (idiomatic) - *come!, go on!*

ager, agrī, m. - *field*

agnōscō, -ere, -nōvī, -nitum - *to recognize, acknowledge*

agō, -ere, ēgī, āctum - *to lead, drive, do, act, conduct; to pass, spend time;* age/agite: *come, go on!*

Aiax, -ācis, m. - *Ajax,* the Greek Aias, one of the major Greek warriors, cousin of Achilles

aliēnus, -a, -um - *foreign to, inconsistent with, belonging to another*

aliquī, aliqua, aliquod (indef. adj.) - *some*

aliquis, aliqua, aliquid (indef. pronoun) - *some one, some thing*

aliter (adv.) - *otherwise*

alius, alia, aliud (adj. and pronoun) - *other, another*

  alius . . . alius: *the one . . . the other*

alō, -ere, aluī, altum - *to nourish, feed*

alter, -era, -erum - *the other* (of two), *second;*

  alter . . . alter: *the one . . . the other*

altus, -a, -um - *tall, deep*

ambō, -ae, -ō (pl. adj. + pronoun) (dat. + abl. m.
  ambōbus) - *both*

amīcitia, -ae, f. - *friendship*

amīcus, -a, -um - *friendly, kindly*

amīcus, -ī, m. - *friend*

āmittō, -ere, -mīsī, -missum - *to lose, let go*

amō (1) - *to love*

amor, -ōris, m. - *love*

āmoveō, -ēre, -mōvī, -mōtum - *to move away, withdraw*

an (conj.) - *or*

Andromacha, -ae, f. - *Andromache;* wife of Hector

anima, -ae, f. - *soul, spirit*

animal, -ālis, n. - *animal, living thing*

animus, -ī, m. - *spirit, soul, mind*

annus, -ī, m. - *year*

ante (adv.; prep. + acc.) - *before, in front of*

anteā (adv.) - *before, formerly*

antepōnō, -ere, -posuī, -positum (+ dat.) - *to put before, prefer*

antequam (conj.) - *before*

Antilochus, -ī, m. - *Antilochus;* son of Nestor, friend of Achilles

antiquus, -a, -um - *ancient, of old*

anxius, -a, -um - *anxious, worried, nervous*

aperiō, -īre, -uī, -pertum - *to open*

appareō, -ēre, -uī - *to appear*

appellō (1) - *to call, address*

Apollō, -inis, m. - *Apollo;* god of prophecy, music and poetry, archery, medicine and disease

approbō (1) - *to approve*

appropinquō (1) - *to approach, near*

aptus, -a, -um - *fitted (with), fitting, appropriate*

apud (prep. + acc.) - *among, in the presence of, at the house of, at*

aqua, -ae, f. - *water*

āra, -ae, f. - *altar*

arbor, -oris, f. - *tree*

arceō, -ēre, -uī - *to prevent from approaching, keep away, repulse*

arcus, -ūs, m. - *bow*

ārdeō, -ēre, ārsī - *to burn, be on fire*

argentum, -ī, n. - *silver*

arma, -ōrum, n. pl. - *arms, weapons*

armātus, -a, -um - *armed*

armō (1) - *to arm*

arō (1) - *to plow*

ascendō, -ere, -dī, -cēnsum - *to go up, climb, ascend*

asper, -era, -erum - *rough, harsh, cruel, fierce*

aspiciō, -ere, aspexī, aspectum - *to look at*

Astyanax, -actis, m. - *Astyanax;* son of Hector and Andromache

at (conj.) - *but* (stronger than *sed*)

ater, atra, atrum - *black, grim, dreadful*

atque (conj.) - *and, and also, and even*

atquī (conj.) - *but, and yet, nevertheless*

Atrīdae, -ārum, m. - *the Atreidae;* the two sons of Atreus, Agamemnon and Menelaus

attonitus, -a, -um - *astonished, stunned, stupefied*

audax, -ācis - *bold, confident, daring*

audeō, -ēre, ausus sum - *to dare*

audiō, -īre, -īvī, -ītum - *to hear, listen to*

auferō, -ferre, abstulī, ablātum - *to bear away, gain; to steal*

augeō, -ēre, auxī, auctum - *to increase*

Aulis, -idis, f. - *Aulis;* port on the east coast of Greece from which the Greeks sailed for Troy

aurīga, -ae, m. - *charioteer*

aureus, -a, -um - *made of gold, golden*

Aurōra, -ae, f. - *Aurora;* goddess of the dawn, the Greek Eos

aurum, -ī, n. - *gold*

aut (conj.) - *or*

  aut . . . aut - *either . . . or*

autem (postpositive conj.) - *however; moreover*

Automedōn, -ontis, m. - *Automedon,* the charioteer of Achilles

auxilium, -iī, n. - *help, aid*

avārus, -a, -um - *greedy*

āvertō, -ere, -vertī, -versum - *to turn away, aside; keep off, avert*

avidus, -a, -um - *eager*

B

bellātor, -ōris, m. - *warrior, fighter*

bellum, -ī, n. - *war*

bene (adv.) - *well*

beneficium, -iī, n. - *good deed, benefit, favor*

bibō, -ere, bibī - *to drink*

bōs, bovis, m. - *bull, ox*

brācchium, -iī, n. - *arm*

brevis, -e - *short, small, brief*

Brīsēis, -idos, f. (Greek acc. *Brīsēida*) - *Briseis; prize of Achilles*

C

cadāver, -eris, n. - *dead body, corpse, cadaver*

cadō, -ere, cecidī, cāsum - *to fall*

caelum, -ī, n. - *sky, heaven*

campus, -ī, m. - *plain, field, open space*

canis, -is, m./f. - *dog*

canō, -ere, cecinī, cantum - *to sing*

capillus, -ī, m. - *hair*

capiō, -ere, cēpī, captum - *to take, capture, seize*

captīvus, -a, -um - *captured in war, taken prisoner, captive*

caput, -itis, n. - *head*

careō, -ēre, -uī, -itūrus (+ abl.) - *to lack, be without*

carō, carnis, f. - *meat, flesh*

cārus, -a, -um - *dear, beloved*

casa, -ae, f. - *house*

castra, -ōrum, n. pl. - *camp, encampment*

causa, -ae, f. - *cause, reason*

  causā (+ preceding gen.) - *for the sake of, on account of*

caveō, -ēre, cāvī, cautum - *to beware*

cēdō, -ere, cessī, cessum - *to go, withdraw; yield, grant*

celer, -eris, -ere - *swift*

cēlō (1) - *to hide, conceal*

cēnō (1) - *to dine, eat*

certāmen, -inis, n. - *contest*

certus, -a, -um - *certain, sure, definite*

cēterus, -a, -um - *other, remaining; in pl., the rest*

cibus, -ī, m. - *food*

cinis, -eris, m. - *ash*

circā/circum (prep. + acc.) - *around*

circumeō, -īre, -īvī, -itum - *to go around, surround*

circumstō, -stāre, -stetī - *to stand around, surround*

clādēs, -is, f. - *disaster*

clam (adv.) - *secretly*

clāmō (1) - *to scream, shout*

clāmor, -ōris, m. - *shout, cry*

clārus, -a, -um - *clear, distinguished, famous*

classis, -is, f. - *fleet*

coepī, coepisse, coeptum (defective verb; in perfect only: + inf.) - *to begin to*

cōgitō (1) - *to think, consider, plan, devise*

cōgnōscō, -ere, -nōvī, -nitum - (present) - *to get to know*; (perfect) - *to know*

cōgō, -ere, coēgī, coāctum - *to force, compel*

collum, -ī, n. - *neck*

comes, -itis, m./f. - *companion, associate*

compellō (1) - *to address*

concēdō, -ere, -cessī, -cessum - *to allow, grant*

concurrō, -ere, -currī, -cursum - *to run together, clash*

concilium, -iī, n. - *council*

coniungō, -ere, -iūnxī, -iūnctum - *to join together, connect, yoke*

coniūnx, -ugis, m./f. - *partner in marriage, consort, husband, wife*

cōnsentiō, -īre, -sēnsī, -sēnsum - *to consent, agree*

cōnsequor, -sequī, -secūtus sum - *to acquire, gain*

cōnservō (1) - *to preserve, maintain, conserve*

cōnsilium, -iī, n. - *counsel, advice, plan*

cōnsōlor, -ārī, -ātus sum - *to comfort, console*

cōnspiciō, -icere, -exī, -ectum - *to catch sight of, see*

cōnstituō, -ere, -tuī, -tūtum - *to establish, set up, decide*

cōnsulō, -ere, -suluī, -sultum - *to consult*

cōnsūmō, -ere, -sūmpsī, -sūmptum - *to consume*

contemnō, -ere, -tempsī, -temptum - *to despise, regard with contempt*

contendō, -ere, -tendī, -tentum - *to struggle, contend*

contineō, -ēre, -tinuī, -tentum - *to hold, keep together, contain*

contrā (prep. + acc.) - *against*

contumēlia, -ae, f. - *insult, indignity, affront*

conveniō, -īre, -vēnī, -ventum - *to assemble, meet, convene*

convocō (1) - *to call together, convene*

cor, cordis, n. - *heart*

cornū, -ūs, n. - *horn*

corpus, -oris, n. - *body*

crēdō, -ere, -idī, -itum (+ dat.) - *to believe, trust*

crēscō, -ere, crēvī - *to grow*

crīmen, -inis, n. - *charge, crime, illegal action*

crīnis, -is, m. - *hair*

culpō (1) - *to blame, censure*

cum (conj. with subj.) - *when, since, although;* (with indic.) - *when*

cum (prep. + abl.) - *with*

cupiō, -ere, -īvī, -ītum - *to desire, wish, long for*

cūr (adv.) - *why*

cūra, -ae, f. - *care, concern, anxiety*

cūrō (1) - *to care for, attend to; heal, cure*

currō, -ere, cucurrī, cursum - *to run*

currus, -ūs, m. - *chariot*

custōs, -ōdis, m. - *guard*

D

Danaī, -um, m. pl.- *Danaans;* the Greeks

Danaus, -a, -um - *Greek*

dē (prep. + abl.) - *down from, from; concerning, about, of*

dea, -ae, f. - *goddess*

dēcēdō, -ere, -cessī, -cessum - *to go away, withdraw*

decem (indecl. adj.) - *ten*

dēcernō, -ere, -crēvī, -crētum - *to decide, determine*

decet (impersonal verb + acc. + inf.) - *it is becoming, fitting that*

decimus, -a, -um - *tenth*

dēcipiō, -ere, -cēpī, -ceptum - *to deceive*

dēclārō (1) - *to demonstrate, indicate, show*

dēclīnō (1) - *to swerve aside, turn aside*

dēdūcō, -ere, -dūxī, -ductum - *to lead away*

dēfendō, -ere, -fendī, -fēnsum - *to ward off, defend, protect*

dēiciō, -ere, -iēcī, -iectum - *to throw down, cause to fall*

deinde (adv.) - *thereupon, next, then*

Dēiphobus, -ī, m. - *Deiphobus;* brother of Hector

dēleō, -ēre, -ēvī, -ētum - *to destroy*

dēlīberō (1) - *to ponder, weigh, deliberate*

dēmentia, -ae, f. - *madness*

dēmittō, -ere, -mīsī -missum - *to send down, let down, lower, let go*

dēmōnstrō (1) - *to point out, show, demonstrate*

dēnique (adv.) - *at last, finally*

dēpōnō, -ere, -posuī, -positum - *to place down, put down*

dēscendō, -ere, -scendī, -scēnsum - *to descend*

dēserō, -ere, -uī, -itum - *to desert, abandon*

dēsīderō (1) - *to long for, desire*

dēsignō (1) - *to mark out, destine, designate*

dēsiliō, -īre, -uī - *to leap down, jump down, dismount*

dēsinō, -ere, -sivī, -situm (+ gen.) - *to cease, leave off*

dēsistō, -ere, -stitī - *to cease, desist from*

dēspērō (1) - *to despair*

dētrahō, -ere, -trāxī, -trāctum - *to take away, drag away*

deus, -ī, m. - *god*

dēvastō (1) - *to devastate, ruin*

dēveniō, -īre, -vēnī, -ventum - *to come down*

dēvorō (1) - *to gulp down, swallow, devour*

dexter, -tra, -trum - *right*

dextra, -ae, f. - *right hand*

dīcō, -ere, dīxī, dictum - *to say, tell*

diēs, -ēī, m./f. - *day*

digitus, -ī, m. - *finger*

dignus, -a, -um (+ abl.) - *worthy, worthy of*

dīligēns, -ntis - *diligent, attentive*

dīligō, -ere, -lēxī, -lēctum - *to esteem highly, love*

discēdō, -ere, -cessī, -cessum - *to go away, depart*

discō, -ere, didicī - *to learn*

discordia, -ae, f. - *discord, strife*

distribuō, -ere, -uī, -ūtum - *to divide up, distribute*

diū (adv.) - *for a long time*

    diūtius - *longer*

dīvīnus, -a, -um - *divine, godlike*

dīvitiae, -ārum, f. - *riches, wealth*

dō, dare, dedī, datum - *to give*

doceō, -ēre, docuī, doctum - *to teach*

doleō, -ēre, -uī, -itūrus - *to grieve, suffer, feel pain;* (+ acc.) - *to feel grief at*

dolor, -ōris, m. - *pain, grief*

dolus, -ī, m. - *trick, deceit, deception*

domī (adv.) - *at home*

dominus, -ī, m. - *master, lord*

domus, -ūs, f. - *house, home;* **domī** - *at home;* **domō** - *from home;* **domum** - *(to) home*

dōnō (1) - (+ acc. of person, abl. of thing) - *to give, gift*

dōnum, -ī, n. - *gift*

dormiō, -īre, -īvī, -ītum - *to sleep*

dubitō (1) - *to doubt, hesitate*

dūcō, -ere, dūxī, ductum - *to lead*

dulcis, -e - *sweet, pleasant, agreeable*

dum (conj. + indic. present) - *while;* (+ subj.) - *until*

dummodo (conj. + subj.) - *provided that, so long as, on condition that*

duo, duae, duo - *two*

duodecim (indecl. adj.) - *twelve*

dūrus, -a, -um - *harsh, hard*

dux, ducis, m. - *leader, general*

E

ē or ex (prep. + abl.) - *out of, from*

ēdūcō, -ere, -dūxī, -ductum - *to lead out, draw out*

efficiō, -ere, -fēcī, -fectum - *to bring about, cause, accomplish;* (often + ut) - *to cause to happen, bring about that*

effugiō, -ere, -fūgī - *to flee, escape*

effundō, -ere, -fūdī, -fūsum - *to pour forth, shed*

ego, meī, mihi, mē, mē - *I, me*

ēgredior, -ī, -gressus sum - *to go out, depart, disembark*

ēlegans, -antis - *elegant, attractive*

ēligō, -ere, -lēgī, -lectum - *to select, choose, pick out*

ēloquēns, -entis - *eloquent*

ēmittō, -ere, -mīsī, -missum - *to send out, dispatch; let fly*

enim (postpositive conj.) - *for, in fact, truly*

eō, īre, īvī or iī, itum - *to go*

epistula, -ae, f. - *letter*

epulor, -ārī, -ātus sum - *to feast*

equus, -ī, m. - *horse*

ergō (adv.) - *therefore*

ēripiō, -ere, -ripuī, -reptum - *to snatch away*

errō (1) - *to wander, err; to make a mistake*

error, -ōris, m. - *error, mistake*

et (conj.) - *and; even*

    et . . . et - *both . . . and*

etiam (adv.) - *also, even*

etiamnum (adv.) - *even now, still*

etiamsī (conj.) - *even if, although*

etsī (conj.) - *even if, although*

ēvellō, -ere, -vellī, -vulsum - *to tear out, pull out*

ex: see ē

exactus, -a, -um - *exact, precise*

excitō (1) - *to awaken, rouse, stir up*

exclāmō (1) - *to cry out, exclaim*

excōgitō (1) - *to think up, devise*

excurrō, -ere, -currī, -cursum - *to run or rush out*

exeō, -īre, -īvī, -itum - *to go out, exit*

exercitus, -ūs, m. - *army*

expellō, -ere, -pulī, -pulsum - *to drive out, expel*

experior, -īrī, expertus sum - *to test, try, experience*

expers, -ertis (+ gen.) - *having no share in, free from*

expōnō, -ere, -posuī, -positum - *to set forth, explain; to expose, leave behind*

exspectō (1) (+ *ut* clause) - *to wait for, await, expect*

exstinguō, -ere, -stinxī, -stinctum - *to extinguish, put out*

extendō, -ere, -dī, -tentum - *to stretch out, extend*

extrā (prep. + acc.; adv.) - *outside*

extrēmus, -a, -um - *situated at the end, last*

F

fabricō (1) - *to fashion, forge, shape*

faciēs, -ēī, f. - *face, appearance*

facile (adv.) - *easily*

facilis, -e - *easy*

faciō, -ere, fēcī, factum - *to do, make*

fallō, -ere, fefellī, falsum - *to trick, mislead, deceive*

falsus, -a, -um - *false, deceptive*

fātālis, -e - *fatal, deadly*

fatīgō (1) - *to fatigue, exhaust*

fātum, -ī, n. - *fate, destiny*

fēlīx, -īcis - *fortunate, happy*

fēmina, -ae, f. - *woman*

fēmineus, -a, -um - *belonging to a woman, female, womanly*

ferculum -ī, n. - *stretcher, litter*

feretrum, -ī, n. - *bier, funeral couch*

ferreus, -a, -um - *iron, made of iron*

ferō, ferre, tulī, lātum - *to bear, carry; endure*

ferōx, -ōcis - *fierce, savage*

ferreus, -a, -um - *made of iron*

ferrum, -ī, n. - *iron; sword*

fīdēns, -ntis (+ abl.) - *confident in, trusting in*

fidēs, -eī, f. - *faith, loyalty*

fīdō, -ere, fīsus sum (+ abl.) - *to trust (in), have confidence in, rely on*

fīlia, -ae, f. - *daughter*

fīlius, -iī, m. - *son*

fingō, -ere, fīnxī, fictum - *to imagine, form in the mind*

fīniō, -īre, -īvī, -ītum - *to end, put an end to*

fīō, fierī, factus sum - *to become, occur, happen*

firmō (1) - *to strengthen*

firmus, -a, -um - *strong, durable*

flamma, -ae, f. - *flame*

fleō, -ēre, flēvī, flētum - *to cry, weep*

flūmen, -inis, n. - *river*

fluō, -ere, flūxī, flūxum - *to flow*

for, fārī, fātus sum - *to speak, say*

forma, -ae, f. - *form, appearance*

fortasse (adv.) - *perhaps*

fortis, -e - *strong, brave*

fortiter (adv.) - *bravely, strongly*

fortitūdō, -inis, f. - *courage*

frangō, -ere, frēgī, frāctum - *to break, shatter*

frāter, -tris, m. - *brother*

frequēns, -ntis -*crowded, numerous*

frōns, frontis, f. - *brow, forehead; front*

in fronte prīmā (idiom) - *in the first rank*

fruor, fruī, frūctus sum (+ abl.) - *to enjoy*

frūstrā (adv.) - *in vain, to no avail*

fuga, -ae, f. - *flight, escape*

fugiō, -ere, fūgī, fugitūrus - *to flee, hurry away; avoid, escape*

fulgeō, -ēre, fūlsī - *to shine, gleam*

fūmus, -ī, m. - *smoke*

fundō, -ere, fūdī, fūsum - *to pour*

furiōsus, -a, -um - *furious, enraged*

furō, -ere, furuī - *to rage, be insane*

fūror, -ārī, -ātus sum - *to steal*

G

galea, -ae, f. - *helmet*

gaudeō, -ēre, gāvīsus sum - *to be glad, rejoice*

gemō, -ere, -uī, -itum - *to groan, moan*

generō (1) - *to generate, produce, give birth to*

generōsus, -a, -um - *high-born, noble*

genū, -ūs, n. - *knee*

genus, -eris, n. - *type, kind; birth*

gerō, -ere, gessī, gestum - *to carry, carry on, manage, conduct, wage; to wear*

   sē gerere: *to conduct oneself, behave*

gignō, -ere, genuī, genitum - *to produce, give birth (to)*

gladius, -iī, m. - *sword*

glōria, -ae, f. - *glory, fame*

glōrior, -ārī, -ātus sum - *to boast, glory*

Graecus, -a, -um - *Greek*

   Graecī, -ōrum, m. pl. - *the Greeks*

grātia, -ae, f. - *favor, grace; influence*

   grātiās agere (idiom + dat.) - *to thank*

grātus, -a, -um - *thankful, pleasing, gratifying*

gravis, -e - *heavy, serious, severe*

H

habeō, -ēre, -uī, -itum - *to have, hold; consider, regard*

habitō (1) - *to live*

haesitō (1) - *to hesitate*

hasta, -ae, f. - *spear*

Hector, -oris, m. - *Hector*; eldest son of King Priam and Queen Hecuba, chief Trojan warrior

Helena, -ae, f. - *Helen*; queen of Sparta, wife of Menelaus, but who nevertheless went to Troy with Paris

Herculēs, -is, m. - *Hercules*; the great Greek hero Heracles

hērōs, -ōis, m. - *hero*

heu (interj.) - *alas*

hīc (adv.) - *here*

hic, haec, hoc (demonstrative pronoun or adj.) - *this; he, she, it, they*

historia, -ae, f. - *history, story, narrative*

hodiē (adv.) - *today*

homō, hominis, m. - *man* (human being)

honor, -ōris, m. - *honor, respect, esteem*

honōrō (1) - *to honor, celebrate, respect*

hōra, -ae, f. - *hour, time*

horrendus, -a, -um - *horrendous, dreadful*

horreō, -ēre, -uī - *to shudder at, tremble at*

horribilis, -e - *horrible, frightful, dreadful*

hortor, -ārī, -ātus sum - *to urge, encourage*

hostis, -is, m. - *enemy;* **hostēs, -ium** - *the enemy*

humus, -ī, f. - *ground, earth, soil*

I

iaceō, -ēre, iacuī - *to lie down*

iaciō, -ere, iēcī, iactum - *to throw, hurl*

iactō (1) - *to throw, cast; to boast, brag*

iaculor, -ārī, -ātus sum - *to throw, hurl*

iam (adv.) - *now, already*

ibi (adv.) - *there*

īdem, eadem, idem (demonstrative pronoun or adj.) - *the same*

igitur (postpositive conj.) - *therefore, consequently*

ignāvus, -a, -um - *cowardly*

ignis, -is, m. - *fire*

ignōscō, -ere, -nōvī, -nōtum (+ dat. of person, acc. of thing) - *to forgive*

ille, illa, illud (demon. pronoun or adj.) - *that*

illūstris, -e - *distinguished, illustrious*

imāgō, -inis, f. - *image, likeness*

immemor, -oris (+ gen.) - *unmindful of, forgetful of*

immō (conj.) - *on the contrary, rather*

immōbilis, -e - *unmoving, immovable*

immortālis, -e - *immortal, ageless*

imperātor, -ōris, m. - *general, commander*

imperō (1) (+ dat.) - *to give command to, order that*

impetus, -ūs, m. - *attack*

impleō, -ēre, -plēvī, -plētum - *to fill up*

impōnō, -ere, -posuī, -positum - *to place in, bestow*

improbus, -a, -um - *bad, wicked*

impudēns, -ntis - *impudent, shameless*

in (prep. + abl.) - *in, on*; (+ acc.) - *into, toward, against*

incendō, -ere, -cendī, -cēnsum - *to set fire to, burn, incinerate*

incipiō, -ere, -cēpī, -ceptum - *to begin, commence*

incurrō, -ere, -currī, -cursum - *to rush, charge (at), attack*

indigeō, -ēre, -uī (+ abl.) - *to need, want, lack*

indūcō, -ere, -dūxī, -ductum - *to lead on/in, entice*

induō, -ere, -uī, -ūtum - *to put on, don*

inermis, -e - *unarmed, defenseless*

īnfāns, -fantis, m. (also adj.) - *infant, young child*

īnfēlix, -icis - *unhappy, miserable*

īnfernī, -ōrum, m. - *the dead, those below*

īnfirmus, -a, -um - *weak, feeble*

ingenium, -iī, n. - *intellect, intelligence*

ingēns, -ntis - *huge*

inimīcus, -ī, m. - *enemy, opponent*

iniūria, -ae, f. - *unjust treatment, injury*

innocēns, -ntis - *innocent, blameless*

innumerābilis, -e - *numberless, innumerable*

inquam, inquis, inquit (defective verb occurring after one or two words of direct quote) - *to say*

īnsānia, -ae, f. - *insanity, madness*

īnsāniō, -īre, -īvī, -ītum - *to be out of one's mind, insane, mad*

īnsānus, -a, -um - *unsound of mind, mad, insane*

īnsequor, -sequī, -secūtus sum - *to pursue (with hostile intent)*

īnsolenter (adv.) - *haughtily, arrogantly, insolently*

īnsolentia, -ae, f. - *arrogance, insolence*

īnspīrō (1) (+ dat./acc.) - *to breathe in, inspire*

īnsula, -ae, f. - *island*

integer, -gra, -grum - *untouched, unhurt, whole*

intellegō, -ere, -lēxī, -lēctum - *to understand*

inter (prep. + acc.) - *between, among*

interdum (adv.) - *sometimes*

intereā (adv.) - *meanwhile*

interficio, -ere, -fēcī, -fectum - *to kill, murder*

intermissiō, -ōnis, f. - *break, intermission*

intrō (1) - *to enter*

inveniō, -īre, -vēnī, -ventum - *to come upon, find, discover*

invītus, -a, -um - *unwilling, against one's will*

Iovis, Iovem, Iove: see *Iuppiter*

ipse, ipsa, ipsum (demonstrative + intensive pronoun or adj.) - *myself, yourself, himself, herself, itself, themselves*

īra, -ae, f. - *anger, wrath, ire*

īrāscor, -ī, īrātus sum (+ dat. of person) - *to be angry*

īrātus, -a, -um - *angered, angry*

irrītō (1) - *to exasperate, irritate*

is, ea, id (personal + demonstrative pronoun + adj.) - *he, she, it; this* or *that person* or *thing*

iste, ista, istud (demonstrative pronoun + adj.) - *that* (of yours), *that* (with pejorative associations)

ita (adv.) - *so, thus*

itaque (adv.) - *and so, therefore*

iter, itineris, n. - *road, trip, journey*

iterum (adv.) - *again, a second time*

iubeō, -ēre, iūssī, iūssum - *to order, command*

iūcundus, -a, -um - *pleasant, agreeable, delightful*

iūdicō (1) - *to judge*

iungō, -ere, iūnxī, iūnctum - *to join, yoke*

Iūnō, -ōnis, f. - *Juno; wife of Jupiter, the Greek Hera*

Iuppiter, Iovis, m. - *Jupiter, Jove; king of the gods, the Greek Zeus*

iūrō (1) - *to swear*

iuvenis, -is, m. - *youth*

iuventūs, -tūtis, f. - *youth* (time of life)

iuvō, -āre, iūvī, iūtum - *to help, aid, assist*

iuxtā (prep. + acc.) - *next to*

L

labor, -ōris, m. - *labor, toil*

lābor, lābī, lāpsus sum - *to slip, slide, slip away*

lacrima, -ae, f. - *tear*

lacrimō (1) - *to weep*

laedō, -ere, laesī, laesum - *to injure, harm*

laetus, -a, -um - *happy, glad, joyful*

lāmentor, -ārī, -ātus sum - *to wail, lament*

latus: see *ferō, ferre*

lēgātus, -ī, m. - *ambassador, delegate*

legō, -ere, lēgī, lectum - *to read, choose*

Lemnus, -ī, f. - *Lemnos;* an island in the north Aegean sea

leō, -ōnis, m. - *lion*

levis, -e - *light*

libenter (adv.) - *gladly, willingly*

līberī, -ōrum, m. - *children*

līberō (1) - *to free*

lītus, -oris, n. - *shore, coast*

locus, -ī, m. - *place, battle position*

　loca, -ōrum, n. - *places; region*

longē (adv.) - *far, far off*

longus, -a, -um - *long*

loquor, loquī, locūtus sum - *to speak*

lōrīca, -ae, f. - *corselet, breast-plate*

lūcrum, -ī, n. - *profit, gain*

lūgeō, -ēre, lūxī, luctum - *to mourn, grieve over, lament*

lūmen, -inis, n. - *light*

lūx, lūcis, f. - *light*

　prīmā lūce: *at dawn*

Lyciī, -ōrum, m. pl. - *the Lycians;* allies of the Trojans from what is now southern Turkey

M

maereō, -ēre - *to mourn, grieve, be sad*

maestus, -a, -um - *unhappy, sad, mournful*

māgnificus, -a, -um - *magnificent*

māgnopere (adv.) - *greatly, exceedingly*

māgnus, -a, -um - *great*

māior, māius - *greater*

malus, -a, -um - *bad, evil*

mandātum, -ī, n. - *order, command, instruction*

maneō, -ēre, mānsī, mānsum - *to remain, stay; to wait for*

manus, -ūs, f. - *hand*

mare, -is, n. - *sea*

marīnus, -a, -um - *of the sea, marine*

marītus, -ī, m. - *husband*

Mars, Martis, m. - *Mars;* god of war, the Greek Ares

māter, -tris, f. - *mother*

mātrimōnium, -iī, n. - *marriage*

maximus, -a, -um - *greatest, very great*

medicāmentum, -ī, n. - *drug, medicine*

medius, -a, -um - *middle, the middle (of)*

melior, -ius - *better*

membrum, -ī, n. - *limb*

meminī, meminisse (defective verb only occurring in the perfect tense system) - *to remember*

　mementō (s. imperative), **mementōte** (pl. imperative)

Menelāus, -ī, m. - *Menelaus;* king of Sparta, husband of Helen

mēns, mentis, f. - *mind, spirit*

Mercurius, -iī, m. - *Mercury;* the Greek Hermes; messenger god and leader of souls to the underworld

meus, -a, -um - *my, mine*

mīles, mīlitis, m. - *soldier*

mille (indecl. adj. in s.) - *thousand*

　mīlia, -ium, n. pl. - *thousands*

Minerva, -ae, f. - *Minerva;* the Greek Athena

minimē (adv., super.) - *least, very little; no*

minister, -trī, m. - *attendant, servant*

minor, -ārī, -ātus sum (+ dat.) - *to threaten*

minor, minus (comp. adj.) - *smaller*

mīrābilis, -e - *amazing, wondrous, remarkable*

mīror, -ārī, -ātus sum - *to marvel, wonder at, be surprised*

miser, -era, -erum - *wretched, miserable, unfortunate*

miseror, -ārī, -ātus sum (+ acc. or gen.) - *to pity, feel sorry for*

mittō, -ere, mīsī, missum - *to send, let go*

moderor, -ārī, -ātus sum - *to manage, direct, guide*

modo . . . modo (adv.) - *at one time . . . at another time, now . . . now*

modus, -ī, m. - *way, method, manner*

moenia, -ium, n. pl. - *walls of a city*

molliō, -īre, -īvī, -ītum - *to soften, make less, placate*

mollis, -e - *soft*

moneō, -ēre, -uī, -itum - *to warn, advise, remind*

mōns, montis, m. - *mountain*

monumentum, -ī, n. - *monument*

morbus, -ī, m. - *disease, sickness*

morior, -ī, mortuus sum (fut. passive participle *moritūrus*) - *to die*

mors, mortis, f. - *death*

mortālis, -e - *mortal*

mortuus, -a, -um - *dead*

moveō, -ēre, mōvī, mōtum - *to move; arouse, affect*

mox (adv.) - *soon*

multitūdō, -dinis, f. - *crowd, throng, multitude*

multō (adv.) - *by much, much*

multum (adv.) - *much*

multus, -a, -um - *much, many*

murmurō (1) - *to murmur, mutter*

mūrus, -ī, m. - *wall, wall-fence*

mutō (1) - *to change, alter*

Mycēnae, -ārum, f. - *Mycenae*; the Greek city over which Agamemnon ruled

Myrmidonēs, -um, m. pl. - *Myrmidons*; the people of Achilles, named for their descent from ants

N

nam (conj.) - *for, in fact*

narrō (1) - *to tell, narrate, report*

nāscor, nāscī, nātus sum - *to be born*

nāvigātiō, -ōnis, f. - *voyage*

nāvigō (1) - *to sail, navigate*

nāvis, -is, f. - *ship*

nē (conj. + subj.) - *that . . . not, in order that . . . not*; (with clauses of fearing) - *that, lest*

nē (adv.) . . . **quidem** - *not even*

nebula, -ae, f. - *mist, fog, cloud*

nec or **neque** (conj.) - *and not, nor*

 nec . . . nec or **neque . . . neque** - *neither . . . nor*

necesse est (+ inf.) - *it is necessary*

necō (1) - *to murder, kill*

neglegō, -ere, -ēxī, -ēctum - *to neglect*

negō (1) - *to deny; refuse*

nēmō, (nullīus), nēminī, nēminem, (nūllō, -ā) - *no one, nobody*

nēnia, -ae, f. - *funeral song, dirge*

Neoptolemus, -ī, m. - *Neoptolemus*; "new warrior," the son of Achilles, also called Pyrrhus

Neptūnus, -ī, m. - *Neptune*; god of the sea; the Greek Poseidon

Nestor, -oris, m. - *Nestor*; aged Greek king of Pylos; excellent speaker and advisor

neque: see **nec**

neuter, -tra, -trum - *neither (of two)*

niger, -gra, -grum - *dark, black*

nihil (indecl.) - *nothing*

nisi (conj.) - *if not, unless, except*

nōbilis, -e - *renowned, famous, noble, distinguished*

nōmen, -inis, n. - *name*

nōlō, nōlle, nōluī - *to not wish, to be unwilling*

nōn (adv.) - *not*

nōndum (adv.) - *not yet*

nōnne (interrogative adverb introducing questions expecting the answer yes) - *don't . . . ?*

nōs, nostrum, nōbīs, nōs, nōbīs - *we, us*

noster, -tra, -trum - *our, ours*

novem (indecl. adj.) - *nine*

novus, -a, -um - *new, strange*

nox, noctis, f. - *night*

nūbēs, -is, f. - *cloud*

nūdus, -a, -um - *naked, nude*

nūllus, -a, -um - *no, none, not any*

num (interrog. adverb introducing questions expecting the answer "no") - *surely not?*

numquam (adv.) - *never*

nunc (adv.) - *now, at present*

nuntiō (1) - *to announce, report*

nuntius, -iī, m. - *messenger, message*

nūper (adv.) - *recently*

nūpta, -ae, f. - *bride*

nūptiae, -ārum, f. pl. - *wedding, marriage*

nurus, -ūs, f. - *daughter-in-law*

nusquam (adv.) - *nowhere*

O

ob (prep. + acc.) - *on account of, because of, for; before, in front of*

oblīvīscor, -cī, oblītus sum (+ gen. or acc.) - *to forget*

obscūrō (1) - *to cover, hide, obscure*

obscūrus, -a, -um - *dark, hidden, indistinct*

obsecrō (1) - *to beg, implore*

observō (1) - *to watch, observe, respect*

obviam (adv.) (with *īre* or other verb of motion + dat.) - *to meet*

occidō, -ere, -cidī, -cāsum - *to fall, fall down; to set* (of the sun)

occīdō, -ere, -cīdī, -cīsum - *to kill*

occupō (1) - *to occupy, seize, invade*

occurrō, -ere, -currī, -cursum (+ dat.) - *to hurry to meet, meet*

ocrea, -ae, f. - *greave* (protection for lower leg)

octō (indecl. adj.) - *eight*

oculus, -ī, m. - *eye*

odium, -iī, n. - *hatred*

odor, -ōris, m. - *odor, smell, stench*

offendō, -ere, -fendī, -fēnsum - *to happen upon, offend*

Olympus, -ī, m. - *Olympus;* the mountain abode of the gods

ōmen, -inis, n. - *omen, portent, sign*

omnipotēns, -entis - *almighty, all-powerful, omnipotent*

omnīnō (adv.) - *wholly, altogether, entirely, at all*

omnis, -e - *all, every, each*

onus, -eris, n. - *weight, burden*

operiō, -īre, -uī, -tum - *to cover over, conceal*

oportet, -ere, oportuit (impersonal; + acc. + inf.) - *it is fitting, right*

opprimō, -ere, -pressī, -pressum - *to overwhelm, suppress*

oppugnō (1) - *to fight against, attack, assail*

optimus, -a, -um - *best;* in vocative: *sir*

opus, -eris, n. - *work, task; deed*

ōrāculum, -ī, n. - *oracle, prophecy*

ōrō (1) - *to plead, beg, beseech; pray to*

ostendō, -ere, -tendī, -tentum - *to show*

P

Palamēdēs, -is, m. - *Palamedes;* king of Euboea in Greece

palla, -ae, f. - *palla,* a woman's mantle, cloak, robe, usually rectangular in shape

Palladium, -iī, n. - *Palladium;* statue of Athena/Minerva

pār, paris - *equal*

parēns, -ntis, m./f. - *parent*

parcō, -ere, pepercī (+ dat.) - *to spare someone or somebody*

parēns, -ntis, m./f. - *parent*

pāreō, -ēre, -uī (+ dat.) - *to obey*

pariō, -ere, peperī, partum - *to give birth to*

Paris, -ridis, m. - *Paris;* prince of Troy; also called Alexander

parō (1) - *to prepare, provide*

pars, partis, f. - *part, portion*

parvus, -a, -um - *small, little*

patefaciō, -ere, -fēcī, -factum - *to make open, disclose, reveal*

pater, patris, m. - *father*

patientia, -ae, f. - *endurance*

patior, -ī, passus sum - *to suffer, endure*

patria, -ae, f. - *fatherland*

Patroclus, -ī, m. - *Patroclus;* son of Menoetius, best friend of Achilles

paulō (adv.) - *a little bit, to a small extent*

pāx, pācis, f. - *peace*

pectus, -oris, n. - *chest*

Pēleus, -ī, m. - *Peleus;* king of Phthia, father of Achilles

pellis, -is, f. - *skin, hide*

pellō, -ere, pepulī, pulsum - *to push, drive*

Pēnelopa, -ae, f. - *Penelope;* wife of Ulysses and mother of Telemachus

penetrō (1) - *to penetrate, pierce*

per (prep. + acc.) - *through;* with people and things sworn by, *by*

percutiō, -ere, -cussī, -cussum - *to strike*

perdō, -ere, -didī, -ditum - *to destroy, ruin, lose*

pereō, -īre, -iī, -itum - *to be destroyed, perish*

perfectus, -a, -um - *complete, perfect*

perficiō, -ere, -fēcī, -fectum - *to complete, accomplish*

perfodiō, -ere, -fōdī, -fossum - *to make a hole through, pierce*

perforō (1) - *to bore through, pierce, perforate*

perīclitor, -ārī, -ātus sum - *to be in danger, run a risk*

perīculum, -ī, n. - *danger, risk*

permittō, -ere, -mīsī, -missum - *to permit, allow*

permultus, -a, -um - *very many, a great many*

perpetuus, -a, -um - *continuous, permanent, perpetual*

perspicax, -ācis - *keen-eyed, perspicacious*

persuadeō, -ēre, -suāsī, -suāsum (+ dat.) - *to persuade*

perturbō (1) - *to upset, confound, perturb*

perveniō, -īre, -vēnī, -ventum - *to arrive, arrive at, reach*

pes, pedis, m. - *foot*

pestis, -is, f. - *plague, ruin*

petō, -ere, -īvī, -ītum - *to seek*

Philoctētēs, -ae, m. - *Philoctetes;* warrior king from near Phthia, the kingdom of Achilles

Phthīa, -ae, f. - *Phthia;* home of Achilles in Thessaly, Greece

piscis, -is, m. - *fish*

pius, -a, -um - *pious, faithful*

placeō, -ēre, -uī, -itum (+ dat.) - *to please*

plaustrum, -ī, n. - *wagon, cart*

plēnus, -a, -um (+ gen. or abl.) - *full, full (of), abundant*

plūrimus, -a, -um - *very much, the most, very many*

plūs (adv.) - *more*

plūs, plūris, n. (+ partitive gen.; also adj.) - *more*

pōculum, -ī, n. - *cup*

poena, -ae, f. - *penalty, punishment*

　　poenās dare: (idiom) - *to pay the penalty*

pondus, -eris, n. - *weight*

pōnō, -ere, posuī, positum - *to put, place*

populus, -ī, m. - *people; nation*

porta, -ae, f. - *gate, entrance*

portō (1) - *to carry, transport*

possum, posse, potuī - *to be able, can*

post (prep. + acc.) - *after, behind*

posteā (adv.) - *afterwards*

postquam (conj.) - *after*

postrēmō (adv.) - *finally, at last*

potēns, -ntis - *powerful, mighty*

potestās, -tātis, f. - *power, ability*

potius (adv.) - *rather*

praebeō, -ēre, -uī, -itum - *to offer, provide*

praecipuus, -a, -um - *special, exceptional*

praeclārus, -a, -um - *brilliant, outstanding, glorious*

praedīcō, -ere, -dīxī, -dictum - *to predict, foretell*

praemium, -iī, n. - *reward, prize*

praesertim (adv.) - *especially*

praesidium, -iī, n. - *garrison; protection*

praestāns, -antis - *exceptional, outstanding, superior*

praestō, -āre, -stitī, -stitum - *to make available, supply, fulfill; to surpass, exceed, excel*

praesum, -esse, -fuī - *to be in charge of; to be present*

praeter (prep. + acc.) - *besides, except, in addition to, beyond*

praetereā (adv.) - *in addition to that, besides, moreover*

precor, -ārī, -ātus sum - *to ask for, pray for/to*

prehendō, -ere, -dī, -sum - *to take hold of, grasp*

pretium, -iī, n. - *prize, ransom*

prex, precis, f. - *prayer*

Priamus, -ī, m. - *Priam;* king of Troy

prīmō (adv.) - *at first, first*

prīmum (adv.) - *first, in the first place*

prīmus, -a, -um - *first*

　　prīma lūce: *at dawn*

prō (prep. + abl.) - *before, on behalf of, in return for, for; in front of*

prōcēdō, -ere, -cessī, -cessum - *to proceed, advance*

procul (adv.) - *far, far away*

prōcurrō, -ere, -currī, -cursum - *to run forward, run to the attack*

prōdūcō, -ere, -dūxī, -ductum - *to produce, bring forth*

proelium, -iī, n. - *battle*

profectō (adv.) - *surely, undoubtedly, certainly*

profundō, -ere, -fūdī, -fūsum - *to pour forth*

prōgredior, -ī, -gressus sum - *to go forward, proceed*

prohibeō, -ēre, -uī, -itum - *to prevent, hinder*

prōmittō, -ere, -mīsī, -missum - *to promise*

prōnuntiō (1) - *to proclaim, announce*

prope (prep. + acc.) - *near, by*

propellō, -ere, -pulī, -pulsum - *to drive forward, propel*

properō (1) - *to hasten, rush*

propter (prep. + acc.) - *on account of, because of*

prōtegō, -ere, -texī, -tectum - *to cover, protect*

prōvocō (1) - *to call out to, challenge, provoke*

pudor, -ōris, m. - *a feeling of shame, shame*

puella, -ae, f. - *girl*

puer, puerī, m. - *boy*

pugna, -ae, f. - *fight, battle*

pugnō (1) - *to fight*

pulcher, -chra, -chrum - *beautiful, handsome, nice*

pulchritūdō, -inis, f. - *beauty, handsomeness, excellence*

pulvis, -eris, m. - *dust*

puniō, -īre, -īvī, -itum - *to punish*

putō (1) - *to think, imagine*

Q

quaerō, -ere, quaesīvī, -sītum - *to look for, search for, seek*

quālis, -e (interrog. + relative adj.) - *what sort of, such as*

quam (interrog. adv. + exclamatory particle) - *how*

quam (conj. with comparative) - *than;* with superlative, *as . . . as possible*

quamquam (conj.) - *although*

quamvīs (conj.) - *although*

quandōcumque (adv.) - *at whatever time, whenever*

quantus, -a, -um - *how large, how great, how much, how many, as much*

quartum (adv.) - *for the fourth time*

quattuor (indecl. adj.) - *four*

-que (conj. added to second of two words to be joined) - *and*

queror, -ī, questus sum - *to complain*

quī, quae, quod (relative + interrog. pronoun) - *who, which, what, that*

quia (conj.) - *because*

quid (interrog. adv.) - *why?*

quīdam, quaedam, quiddam (indef. pronoun), quīdam, quaedam, quoddam (indef. adj.) - *a certain, some*

quidem (adv.) - *indeed*

quīn (conj.) - *but rather, instead*

quis, quid (interrog. pronoun) - *who?, what?*

quisquam, quidquam (indef. pronoun) - *any, anyone, anything*

quisque, quidque (indef. pronoun) - *each one*

quisquis, quidquid (indef. pronoun) - *whoever, whatever*

quō (adv.) - *to which place, whither, where*

quod (conj.) - *because*

quodsī (conj.) - *but if*

quōmodo (conj.) - *how, in what way*

quoniam (conj.) - *since*

quoque (adv.) - *also*

quotiēns (conj.) - *as often as, whenever*

R

rapidus, -a, -um - *swift, rapid*

rapiō, -ere, rapuī, raptum - *to seize, carry away, steal*

recēdō, -ere, -cessī, -cessum - *to go back, withdraw, retire*

recipiō, -ere, -cēpī, -ceptum - *to receive, take back, recover*

   sē recipere: *to retreat*

recurrō, -ere, -currī, -cursum - *to run, hurry back*

reddō, -ere, -didī, -ditum - *to give back, return*

redeō, -īre, -īvī, -itum - *to go back, return*

redimō, -ere, -ēmī, -emptum - *to buy back, ransom*

redūcō, -ere, -dūxī, -ductum - *to lead back*

referō, -ferre, -ttulī, -lātum - *to bring back, carry back; report* refugiō, -ere, -fūgī - *to turn back and flee*

rēgia, -ae, f. - *palace*

rēgīna, -ae, f. - *queen*

regō, -ere, rēxī, rēctum - *to rule, guide, direct*

rēiciō, -ere, -iēcī, -iectum - *to reject, refuse*

relinquō, -ere, -līquī, -lictum - *to leave behind, abandon*

reliquus, -a, -um - *the rest* (of the remaining)

remaneō, -ēre, -mānsī, -mānsum - *to remain, stay*

remittō, -ere, -mīsī, -missum - *to send back*

removeō, -ēre, -mōvī, -mōtum - *to remove, take off*

repellō, -ere, reppulī, -pulsum - *to push back, thrust back*

repōnō, -ere, -posuī, -positum - *to replace, put back*

reportō (1) - *to bring back, carry back*

reprehendō, -ere, -dī, -hēnsum - *to reproach, blame, rebuke, censure*

rēs, reī, f. - *thing, matter, business*

resistō, -ere, -stitī (+ dat.) - *to resist, oppose*

respondeō, -ēre, -spondī, -spōnsum - *to respond, answer*

respōnsum, -ī, n. - *response, answer*

restituō, -ere, -tuī, -tūtum - *to restore, give back, return*

retrō (adv.) - *backwards, back*

reveniō, -īre, -vēnī, -ventum - *to return*

rēx, rēgis, m. - *king*

rīdeō, -ēre, rīsī, rīsum - *to laugh, smile*

rīte (adv.) - *with correct religious procedure, properly*

rogō (1) - *to ask*

ruō, -ere, ruī, rutum - *to rush, hasten*

rursum (adv.) - *back*

S

sacerdōs, -ōtis, m. - *priest*

sacrificium, -iī, n. - *sacrifice*

sacrificō (1) - *to offer sacrifice*

saepe (adv.) - *often*

saevus, -a, -um - *savage, cruel, harsh*

sagitta, -ae, f. - *arrow*

sāl, salis, m. - *salt*

saliō, -īre, saluī, saltum - *to jump, leap*

salūs, -ūtis, f. - *health, welfare, safety*

saltem (adv.) - *at least*

salūtō (1) - *to greet*

salvus, -a, -um - *sound, healthy, safe*

sanguis, -inis, m. - *blood*

sānitās, -tātis, f. - *sanity, good sense*

sānō (1) - *to heal*

sānus, -a, -um - *sound, healthy, sane*

sapiēns, -ntis - *wise*

sapientia, -ae, f. - *wisdom*

Sarpēdōn, -onis, m. - *Sarpedon*; king of the Lycians, son of Zeus

satis (indecl. adj.) - *enough, sufficient*

satisfaciō, -ere, -fēcī, -factum - *to give satisfaction, make amends for*

saturō (1) - *to fill, satiate, satisfy*

saucius, -a, -um - *wounded*

saxum, -ī, n. - *rock, stone*

scindō, -ere, scindī, scissum - *to tear, rend*

sciō, -īre, -īvī, -ītum - *to know*

scrībō, -ere, scrīpsī, scrīptum - *to write*

scūtum, -ī, n. - *shield*

Scȳrus, -ī, f. - *Scyros*; an island in the Aegean where young Achilles had been in hiding and Neoptolemus/ Pyrrhus was born

sē: see suī

sēcrētō (adv.) - *apart, in private*

secundus, -a, -um - *second*

sed (conj.) - *but*

sedeō, -ēre, sēdī, sessum - *to sit*

sēdēs, -is, f. - *seat, abode*

sēdō (1) - *to calm*

sella, -ae, f. - *seat, chair*

semel (adv.) - *once* (only)

semper (adv.) - *always*

senectūs, -tūtis, f. - *old age*

senex, senis (adj. + m. noun) - *old, old man*

sentiō, -īre, sēnsī, sēnsum - *to feel, perceive, think, experience*

sepeliō, -īre, -īvī, -ultum - *to dispose of a corpse in the proper fashion; to burn, bury*

septem (indecl. adj.) - *seven*

sequor, sequī, secūtus sum - *to follow*

sērō (adv.) - *late, too late*

serpēns, -entis, m. - *snake, serpent*

servitūs, -tūtis, f. - *servitude, slavery*

servō (1) - *to save, preserve*

servus, -ī, m., serva, -ae, f. - *slave*

sevērus, -a, -um - *severe, strict, serious*

sī (conj.) - *if*

sīc (adv.) - *so, thus*

sīcut (adv.) - *just as*

significō (1) - *to indicate, refer to, mean*

silva, -ae, f. - *forest, wood*

similis, -e (+ dat.) - *similar to, like*

simulō (1) - *to imitate, pretend, feign; to liken to, make like, put on the appearance of*

sīn (conj.) - *but if, if however*

sine (prep. + abl.) - *without*

sinō, -ere, sīvī, sītum (+ acc. + inf.) - *to allow*

sistō, -ere, stitī or **stetī, statum** - *to cause to stand, to stop*

socius, -iī, m. - *companion, ally*

sōl, sōlis, m. - *sun*

sōlācium, -iī, n. - *solace, comfort*

soleō, -ēre, sollicitus sum (+ inf.) - *to be accustomed to*

sollicitus, -a, -um - *troubled, anxious*

solum, -ī, n. - *ground, earth*

sōlus, -a, -um - *alone, only*

somnium, -iī, n. - *dream*

somnus, -ī, m. - *sleep*

soror, -ōris, f. - *sister*

sors, sortis, f. - *lot, fate*

Sparta, -ae, f. - *Sparta;* city ruled by Menelaus in the Greek Peloponnesus

spectō (1) - *to look at, see, observe, watch*

spērō (1) - *to hope*

spēs, speī, f. - *hope*

spīritus, -ūs, m. - *breath; spirit, soul*

splendidus, -a, -um - *bright, splendid*

spoliō (1) - *to strip, strip off, plunder*

spolium, -iī, n. - *arms, equipment, plunder, booty*

statim (adv.) - *immediately, at once*

stō, stāre, stetī, statum - *to stand, stand still; set up, establish*

strangulō (1) - *to strangle*

stultus, -a, -um - *foolish*

sub (prep. + abl.) - *under*

subitō (adv.) - *suddenly, at once*

suī, sibi, sē, sē (third person reflexive pronoun) - *himself, herself, itself; themselves*

sum, esse, fuī, futūrus (irreg.) - *to be*
    es (s. imp.), **este** (pl. imp.)

sūmō, -ere, sūmpsī, sūmptum - *to take*

super (prep. + acc.) - *over, above*

superior, -ius - *more powerful, superior*

superō (1) - *to surpass, overcome, conquer*

superstō, -stāre, -stetī - *to stand over*

supplicō (+ dat.) - *to supplicate, beg*

surgō, -ere, surrēxī, surrēctum - *to get up, arise, swell*

suspiciō, -ōnis, f. - *suspicion*

suus, -a, -um - *his own, her own, its own; their own*

T

tabernāculum, -ī, n. - *tent, encampment*

tālis, -e - *such, such a*

tam (adv.) - *so*

tamen (adv.) - *nevertheless, still, however*

tandem (adv.) - *at last, finally*

tangō, -ere, tetigī, tactum - *to touch*

tantopere (adv.) - *so greatly*

tantum (adv.) - *only; so much*

tantus, -a, -um - *so large, so great, so much*

tegō, -ere, tēxī, tēctum - *to cover, protect*

Tēlemachus, -ī, m. - *Telemachus;* son of Ulysses and Penelope

templum, -ī, n. - *sacred area, temple*

temptō (1) - *to try, attempt*

tempus, -oris, n. - *time*

tendō, -ere, tetendī, tentum - *to stretch, extend*

tenebrae, -ārum, f. - *shadows, darkness*

teneō, -ēre, tenuī, tentum - *to hold, keep, possess; restrain*

ter (adv.) - *three times*

tergum, -ī, n. - *back*

terra, -ae, f. - *land, earth, country*

terreō, -ēre, -uī, -itum - *to terrify, frighten, deter*

terribilis, -e - *terrifying, terrible*

terror, -ōris, m. - *terror*

tertius, -a, -um - *third*

Thetis, -idis, f. - *Thetis;* a sea nymph, daughter of Nereus, mother of Achilles

timeō, -ēre, timuī - *to fear, be afraid of*

timor, -ōris, m. - *fear*

tingō, -ere, tinxī, tinctum - *to wet, color, stain*

titubō (1) - *to totter, stagger*

tollō, -ere, sustulī, sublātum - *to lift up, raise; remove, destroy*

tot (indecl. adj.) - *so many*

tōtus, -a, -um - *whole, entire, all*

tradō, -ere, -didī, -ditum - *to give over, surrender*

trahō, -ere, trāxī, tractum - *to draw, drag*

tranquillus, -a, -um - *tranquil, quiet, calm*

trāns (prep. + acc.) - *across, over*

tremō, -ere, tremuī - *to tremble*

tremor, -ōris, m. - *shaking, trembling, tremor*

trēs, tria - *three*

tribuō, -ere, -uī, -ūtum - *to grant, bestow, give, attribute*

trīstis, -e - *sad, sorrowful*

Trōia, -ae, f. - *Troy,* city in western Turkey

Trōiānus, -a, -um - *Trojan*

   Trōiānī, -ōrum, m. pl. - *the Trojans*

   Trōiānae, -ārum, f. pl. - *the Trojan women*

triumphō (1) - *to act triumphantly, exult*

tropaeum, -ī, n. - *trophy* (made by hanging the enemy's armor from a tree or cross-like post)

tū, tuī, tibi, tē, tē - *you* (s.)

tueor, -ērī, tūtus sum - *to protect, look at, regard*

tulī: see *ferō, ferre*

tum (adv.) - *then*

tumultus, -ūs, m. - *uproar, confusion*

tumulus, -ī, m. - *burial mound, grave*

tunc (adv.) - *then*

tunica, -ae, f. - *tunic*

turpis, -e - *shameful, disgraceful*

turris, -is, f. - *tower*

tuus, -a, -um - *your* (s.)

tum (adv.) - *then, at that time, thereupon*

tūtus, -a, -um - *safe*

U

ubi (adv. + conj.) - where, where?; when

ubique (adv.) - *everywhere*

ulcīscor, -ī, ultus sum - *to avenge, punish*

Ulixēs, -is, m. - *Ulysses;* the Greek Odysseus, king of Ithaca

ūllus, -a, -um - *any*

ultimus, -a, -um - *last, furthest*

ululō (1) - *to scream, howl*

umquam (adv.) - *ever, at any time*

ūnā (adv.) - *together*

undique (adv.) - *from all parts, from everywhere*

unguō, -ere, ūnxī, ūnctum - *to smear, anoint with oil, rub*

ūnus, -a, -um - *one*

urbs, urbis, f. - *city*

urna, -ae, f. - *urn, pitcher*

ūsus, -ūs, m. - *use*

ut (conj. + indicative) - *as, when, like;* (+ subj.) - *in order to, so that, that*

uter, utra, utrum (interrog. adj. + pronoun) - *who? which (of two)?*

utinam (adv. + subj.) - *would that, if only*

ūtor, ūtī, ūsus sum (+ abl.) - *to use, employ*

utrum (conj.) - *whether*

utrum . . . an (conjs. introducing disjunctive questions) - *whether . . . or*

uxor, -ōris, f. - *wife*

V

vacuus, -a, -um - *empty*

valdē (adv.) - *very, exceedingly*

valeō, -ēre, -uī, -itūrus - *to be strong, have power; farewell*

validus, -a, -um - *strong, mighty, powerful*

vānus, -a, -um - *useless, foolish, vain*

vātēs, -is, m. - *prophet*

-ve (conj. added to the second of two words to be joined) - *or*

vehementer (adv.) - *strongly, vehemently*

vehō, -ere, vexī, vectum - *to carry, convey*

vel (conj.) - *or* (as an optional alternative)

    vel . . . vel - *either . . . or*

velut (adv.) - *just as*

venēnātus, -a, -um - *poisoned*

venēnum, -ī, n. - *poison*

venia, -ae, f. - *pardon, forgiveness*

veniō, -īre, vēnī, ventum - *to come, go*

Venus, -eris, f. - *Venus;* goddess of love; the Greek Aphrodite; mother of Aeneas

verbum, -ī, n. - *word*

vereor, -ērī, veritus sum - *to fear, respect*

vēritās, -tātis, f. - *truth*

vērō - *in truth, indeed, truly, really*

vertō, -ere, vertī, versum - *to turn, change*

vērus, -a, -um - *true, real, proper*

vescor, -ī (+ abl.) - *to feed on, eat*

vester, -tra, -trum - *yours* (pl.), *your*

vestis, -is, f. - *clothing, attire*

via, -ae, f. - *road, path, way*

vibrō (1) - *to brandish, shake*

vīcēsimus, -a, -um - *twentieth*

victor, -ōris, m. - *victor, winner*

victōria, -ae, f. - *victory*

videō, -ēre, vīdī, vīsum - *to see, understand*

    videor, -ērī, vīsus sum - *to be seen; to seem, appear*

vincō, -ere, vīcī, victum - *to conquer, overcome*

vīnum, -ī, n. - *wine*

vir, virī, m. - *man, husband*

virgō, -inis, f. - *maiden, virgin*

virtūs, -tūtis, f. - *manliness, courage; virtue, character*

vīs, vīs, f. - *force, power, violence;* pl. **vīrēs, -ium** - *strength*

vīta, -ae, f. - *life, mode of life*

vītō (1) - *to avoid*

vituperō (1) - *to find fault with, criticize, vituperate*

vīvō, -ere, vīxī, vīctum - *to live*

vīvus, -a, -um - *alive, living*

vix (adv.) - *hardly*

vocō (1) - *to call*

volō (1) - *to fly*

volō, velle, voluī - *to wish, want, be willing (to)*

volvō, -ere, volvī, volūtum - *to turn round*

vōs, vestrum, vōbīs, vōs, vōbīs - *you* (pl.)

vōx, vōcis, f. - *voice*

vulnerō (1) - *to wound*

vulnus, -eris, n. - *wound*

vultus, -ūs, m. - *face, expression*

ℬℭ LATIN Readers

Series Editor: Ronnie Ancona, Hunter College and CUNY Graduate Center

These readers, written by experts in the field, provide well-annotated Latin selections to be used as authoritative introductions to Latin authors, genres, or topics. Designed for intermediate/advanced college Latin students, they each contain approximately 600 lines of Latin, making them ideal to use in combination or as a "shake-it-up" addition to a time-tested syllabus.

See reviews of BC Latin Readers from *Bryn Mawr Classical Review*, *Classical Outlook*, and more at http://www.bolchazy.com/readers/

An Apuleius Reader
Selections from the METAMORPHOSES
Ellen D. Finkelpearl
xxxviii + 160 pp., 4 illustrations & 1 map (2012)
5" x 7 ¾" Paperback, ISBN 978-0-86516-714-8

A Caesar Reader
Selections from BELLUM GALLICUM and BELLUM CIVILE, and from Caesar's Letters, Speeches, and Poetry
W. Jeffrey Tatum
xl + 206 pp., 3 illustrations & 3 maps (2012)
5" x 7 ¾" Paperback, ISBN 978-0-86516-696-7

A Cicero Reader
Selections from Five Essays and Four Speeches, with Five Letters
James M. May
xxxviii + 136 pp., 1 illustration & 2 maps (2012)
5" x 7 ¾" Paperback, ISBN 978-0-86516-713-1

A Latin Epic Reader
Selections from Ten Epics
Alison Keith
xxvii + 187 pp., 3 maps (2012)
5" x 7 ¾" Paperback, ISBN 978-0-86516-686-8

A Livy Reader
Selections from AB URBE CONDITA
Mary Jaeger
xxiii + 127 pp., 1 photo & 2 maps (2010)
5" x 7 ¾" Paperback, ISBN 978-0-86516-680-6

A Lucan Reader
Selections from CIVIL WAR
Susanna Braund
xxxiv + 134 pp., 1 map (2009)
5" x 7 ¾" Paperback, ISBN 978-0-86516-661-5

A Martial Reader
Selections from the Epigrams
Craig Williams
xxx + 185 pp., 5 illustrations & 2 maps (2011)
5" x 7 ¾" Paperback, ISBN 978-0-86516-704-9

BOLCHAZY-CARDUCCI PUBLISHERS, INC.
WWW.BOLCHAZY.COM

An Ovid Reader
Selections from Seven Works
Carole E. Newlands
xxvi + 196 pp., 5 illustrations (2014)
5" x 7 ¾" Paperback, ISBN 978-0-86516-722-3

A Plautus Reader
Selections from Eleven Plays
John Henderson
xviii + 182 pp., 1 map & 5 illustrations (2009)
5" x 7 ¾" Paperback, ISBN 978-0-86516-694-3

A Propertius Reader
Eleven Selected Elegies
P. Lowell Bowditch
xliv + 186 pp., 5 illustrations & 2 maps (2014)
5" x 7 ¾" Paperback, ISBN 978-0-86516-723-0

A Roman Army Reader
Twenty-One Selections from Literary, Epigraphic, and Other Documents
Dexter Hoyos
xlviii + 214 pp., 7 illustrations & 2 maps (2013)
5" x 7 ¾" Paperback, ISBN 978-0-86516-715-5

A Roman Verse Satire Reader
Selections from Lucilius, Horace, Persius, and Juvenal
Catherine C. Keane
xxvi + 142 pp., 1 map & 4 illustrations (2010)
5" x 7 ¾" Paperback, ISBN 978-0-86516-685-1

A Roman Women Reader
Selections from the Second Century BCE through the Second Century CE
Sheila K. Dickison and Judith P. Hallett
xxii + 225 pp., 3 illustrations (2015)
5" x 7 ¾" Paperback, ISBN 978-0-86516-662-2

A Sallust Reader
Selections from BELLUM CATILINAE, BELLUM IUGURTHINUM, and HISTORIAE
Victoria E. Pagán
xlv + 159 pp., 2 maps & 4 illustrations (2009)
5" x 7 ¾" Paperback, ISBN 978-0-86516-687-5

A Seneca Reader
Selections from Prose and Tragedy
James Ker
lvi + 166 pp., 6 illustrations & 1 map (2011)
5" x 7 ¾" Paperback, ISBN 978-0-86516-758-2

A Suetonius Reader
Selections from the LIVES OF THE CAESARS and the LIFE OF HORACE
Josiah Osgood
xxxix + 159 pp., 1 map & 7 illustrations (2010)
5" x 7 ¾" Paperback, ISBN 978-0-86516-716-2

A Tacitus Reader
Selections from ANNALES, HISTORIAE, GERMANIA, AGRICOLA, and DIALOGUS
Steven H. Rutledge
xlvii + 198 pp., 5 illustrations, 2 maps, & 3 charts (2014) 5" x 7 ¾" Paperback
ISBN 978-0-86516-697-4

A Terence Reader
Selections from Six Plays
William S. Anderson
xvii + 110 pp. (2009) 5" x 7 ¾" Paperback,
ISBN 978-0-86516-678-3

A Tibullus Reader
Seven Selected Elegies
Paul Allen Miller
xx + 132 pp., 2 illustrations (2013) 5" x 7 ¾"
Paperback, ISBN 978-0-86516-724-7

BOLCHAZY-CARDUCCI PUBLISHERS, INC.
WWW.BOLCHAZY.COM

ANNOTATED LATIN COLLECTION

Read Catullus, Cicero, Horace, and Ovid with these well-annotated texts designed for intermediate to advanced students. With same-page notes and vocabulary, introductory essays on each author and work, full glossaries, and helpful appendices, reading unadapted Latin has never been more rewarding.

Cicero: PRO ARCHIA POETA ORATIO 3rd Edition

Steven M. Cerutti

xxxi + 157 pp. (2014) 6" x 9" Paperback, ISBN 978-0-86516-805-3

This text contains the entire oration (**397 lines**). This revised edition includes input from Linda A. Fabrizio, author of the Teacher's Guide, and a new appendix featuring eight selections from Quintilian.

Horace: Selected ODES and SATIRE 1.9 2nd Edition, Revised

Ronnie Ancona

xxxiii + 171 pp., 4 maps (2014, 2nd edition revised) 6" x 9" Paperback, ISBN 978-0-86516-608-0

Contains (**533 lines**) *Odes* 1.1, 5, 9, 11, 13, 22, 23, 24, 25, 37, 38; 2.3, 7, 10, 14; 3.1, 9, 13, 30; *Satire* 1.9. The revised second edition features an updated bibliography and more visually appealing maps.

Ovid: AMORES, METAMORPHOSES Selections, 3rd Edition

Charbra Adams Jestin and Phyllis B. Katz

xxx + 212 pp. (2013) 6" x 9" Paperback, ISBN 978-0-86516-784-1

Amores I.1, I.3, I.9, I.11, I.12, III.12, III.15; *Metamorphoses* I.1–88 (Creation), I.452–567 (Apollo and Daphne), IV.55–166 (Pyramus and Thisbe), VIII.183–235 (Daedalus and Icarus), VIII.616–723 (Philemon and Baucis), X.1–85 (Orpheus); and X.238–297 (Pygmalion). **907 lines**.

BOLCHAZY-CARDUCCI PUBLISHERS, INC.
WWW.BOLCHAZY.COM

Writing Passion: *A Catullus Reader* 2nd Edition
Ronnie Ancona

xl + 264 pp. (2013) 6" x 9" Paperback, ISBN 978-0-86516-786-5

Four additional poems expand the elegiac selections about Lesbia. This text includes (**827 lines**) Catullus 1–5, 7–8, 10–14a, 22, 30–31, 35–36, 40, 43–46, 49–51, 60, 64 (lines 50–253), 65, 68 (lines 1–40), 69–70, 72, 75–77, 83–87, 92, 96, 101, 107, 109, 116.

Writing Passion Plus
A Catullus Reader Supplement
Ronnie Ancona

ix + 22 pp. (2013) 6" x 9" Paperback, ISBN 978-0-86516-788-9

For those who want a little more spice in their Catullus, this text provides poems 6, 16, 32, and 57 (**52 lines**).

Watch for New Editions of These Popular Texts

Cicero: *Pro Caelio, 3rd Edition*
Stephen Ciraolo

xxxi + 239 pp. (2010) 6" x 9" Paperback, ISBN 978-0-86516-559-5

This user-friendly text features the entire oration (**991 lines**) with vocabulary and commentary on grammar, style, history, and Roman institutions; introductory essays on the lives of Cicero and Caelius and on Roman oratory; and several appendices.

Cicero: *De Amicitia Selections*
Patsy Rodden Ricks and Sheila K. Dickison

x + 73 pp. (2006) 6" x 9" Paperback, ISBN 978-0-86516-639-4

This text, which contains *De Amicitia* V.17–VII.23 (**199 lines**), makes for a great introduction to Cicero. Vocabulary, notes, English overviews of the missing sections of the *De Amicitia*, and a Glossary of Figures of Speech complete this text.

BOLCHAZY-CARDUCCI PUBLISHERS, INC.
WWW.BOLCHAZY.COM

Catullus: *Expanded Edition*
Phyllis Young Forsyth and Henry V. Bender

xii + 140 pp. (2005) 8½" x 11" Paperback, ISBN 978-0-86516-603-5

This student-friendly text offers (**805 lines**) Catullus 1–5, 7, 8, 10–14a, 22, 30, 31, 35, 36, 40, 43–46, 49–51, 60, 64 (lines 50–253), 65, 68–70, 72, 76, 77, 84–87, 96, 101, 109, and 116.

Lucretius: *Selections from DE RERUM NATURA*
Bonnie A. Catto

xxx + 272 pp. (1998) 8½" x 11" Paperback, ISBN 978-0-86516-399-7

This text provides 53 passages (**1,291 lines**) spanning the entire epic. Each section features a short introduction, discussion questions, vocabulary and line-by-line notes on facing pages, and a variety of illustrative quotations from ancient and modern authors.

The *Thebaid* of Statius: *The Women of Lemnos*
Patrick Yaggy

xxvii + 242 pp. (2014) 6" x 9" Paperback, ISBN 978-0-86516-819-0

The high-interest story of Hypsipyle and the women of Lemnos (*Thebaid* 5.1–637) makes the perfect introduction to Statius's *Thebaid* for intermediate readers of Latin (**637 lines**).

Vergil's *Aeneid*: *Expanded Collection*
Barbara Weiden Boyd

xl + 449 pp. (2013) 6" x 9" Paperback, ISBN 978-0-86516-789-6

This well-annotated Latin text (**2,596 lines**) makes the perfect introduction to Vergil's *Aeneid*. Passages include 1.1–756 • 2.1–56; 199–297; 469–620; 735–805 • 4.1–449; 642–705 • 6.1–211; 295–332; 384–425; 450–476; 847–901 • 8.608–731 • 10.420–509 • 11.498–596; 664–835 • 12.791–842; 887–952.

BOLCHAZY-CARDUCCI PUBLISHERS, INC.
WWW.BOLCHAZY.COM

Caesar: *Selections from his* COMMENTARII DE BELLO GALLICO

Hans-Friedrich Mueller

xlii + 372 pp. (2012) 6" x 9"
Paperback, ISBN 978-0-86516-752-0 • Hardbound, ISBN 978-0-86516-778-0

This text provides (**827 lines**) *De Bello Gallico* 1.1–7; 4.24–35 and the first sentence of chapter 36; 5.24–48; 6.13–20 with same-page vocabulary and notes. Annotated English passages from Books 1, 6, and 7 provide additional context for the Latin passages.

Cicero's First Catilinarian Oration

Karl Frerichs

xviii + 62 pp. (1997, reprint 2000, 2004) 8½" x 11" Paperback
ISBN 978-0-86516-341-6

This edition provides the entire speech (**317 lines**) with the essential vocabulary and assistance students need. A historical narrative introduces the oration.

Res Gestae Divi Augusti

Rex E. Wallace

xxii + 80 pp. (2000, on demand 2007) 6" x 9" Paperback
ISBN 978-0-86516-455-0

The *Res Gestae* (**327 lines**) reveals as much about Augustus through what it omits as what it contains. This edition allows students rare access to nonliterary historical Latin.

Seneca's Moral Epistles

Anna Lydia Motto

xxxi + 213 pp. (2001, on demand 2007) 6" x 9" Paperback
ISBN 978-0-86516-487-1

An intriguing selection of 40 letters (**2,724 lines**) of Seneca in Latin on philosophical and practical topics provides a fascinating glimpse into daily life in Rome. Selections are Epistles 1–3, 5–7, 11, 12, 15, 16, 18, 21, 23, 27, 28, 34, 37, 38, 41–44, 47, 50, 52–54, 56, 60–63, 72, 80, 84, 90, 96, 112, 114.

BOLCHAZY-CARDUCCI PUBLISHERS, INC.
WWW.BOLCHAZY.COM

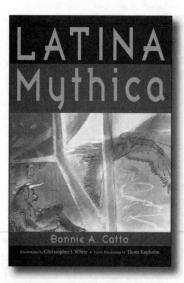

Latina
Mythica

Bonnie A. Catto

Illustrations by
Christopher J. White

xiv + 202 pp. (2006)
6" x 9" Paperback
ISBN 978-0-86516-599-1

This graded Latin reader has twenty lively and discussion-rich stories from Greek and Roman mythology—from the rise of the gods to the prelude to the Trojan War. It is designed for use after one year of high school Latin or one semester of college Latin. Facing-page grammatical/vocabulary notes boost reading speed and reader confidence.

Each story has an introduction in English and citation for the ancient sources of the myths. All stories are patterned after ancient authors, making this reader a perfect way to review and reinforce grammar and basic vocabulary, explore classical mythology, and ease into advanced author reading.

Special Features
- Grammar and comprehension questions
- Discussion questions
- Cultural influences of the myth in art, music, ballet, and literature
- 41 black and white illustrations, including 10 originals by Christopher J. White
- Map of place-names mentioned
- 5 genealogical charts
- List of ancient sources cited
- Bibliography
- End vocabulary

BOLCHAZY-CARDUCCI PUBLISHERS, INC.
WWW.BOLCHAZY.COM